Hegel's
Philosophy
of
Spirit

Hegel's Philosophy of Spirit

edited by
Peter G. Stillman

State University of New York Press

Published by
State University of New York Press, Albany

For information, address State University of New York
Press, State University Plaza, Albany, N.Y., 12246

Library of Congress Cataloging in Publication Date

Hegel's philosophy of spirit.

   (SUNY series in Hegelian studies)
   Includes bibliographical references and index.
   1. Hegel, Georg Wilhelm Friedrich, 1770-1831.
Philosophie des Geistes.   2. Mind and body.   I. Stillman,
Peter G.   II. Series.
B2919.H43   1987   193   86-23030
ISBN 0-88706-476-0
ISBN 0-88706-477-9 (pbk.)

10 9 8 7 6 5 4 3 2

Contents

Editor's Introduction

Hegel's philosophy of spirit (*Geist*) is the third and final major part of his mature systematic philosophy. It follows logic—the development of the laws and forms of thought—and the philosophy of nature—the hierarchical ordering of natural phenomena from the most atomistic, separated, and inert to the most organic, unified, and alive. To the philosophy of spirit, then, remains vast scope: the development and achievements of human subjectivity and social and political life as well as the spheres where human beings participate in the eternal. The first division of the philosophy of spirit is subjective spirit, which includes what Hegel calls anthropology, phenomenology (or the development of consciousness), and psychology; in subjective spirit, subjectivity develops from nature and natural life into psychologically complex, active, and expressive unities of self-consciousness. The second division is objective spirit, where free human subjects live in an objective world of legal forms, moral commands, and *Sittlichkeit*, the ethical community whose patterned social interactions both express individual subjectivity and exist as objective substance. The final division is absolute spirit, where the finitude and limits of subjectivity and objectivity are transcended in the infinity and unity of artistic creation, religious sentiment, and philosophical thought.

Hegel presents his philosophy of spirit in the *Enzyklopädie der philosophischen Wissenschaften im Grundrisse* (*Encyclopædia of the Philosophical Sciences in Outline*). Printed first in 1817 and revised extensively in 1827 and again in 1830,[1] the *Encyclopædia* contains the skeletal statement of his mature philosophical system. As with the *Philosophy of Right*,[2] the form of the *Encyclopædia* derives from its purpose: to publish Hegel's philosophy to the public as a system and at the same time to produce a text for his lectures to university students. So Hegel, in presenting his comprehensive systematic science, "has no room for a detailed exposition of particulars, and must be limited to setting forth the commencement of the special sciences and the notions of cardinal importance to them" (*Enz.*, §16); consequently, as he wrote Victor Cousin, the *Encyclopædia* is "nothing but a succession of theses."[3]

Such constraints in public presentation exactly suited the demands of Hegel's professorial responsibilities. Following common German practice, Hegel taught by writing a paragraph of text on the board and developing its meaning and implications in his lecture. So the numbered paragraphs present the unadorned essentials of Hegel's system; as his late nineteenth century translator, William Wallace, lamented, "paragraphs concise in form and saturated with meaning postulate and presuppose the presiding spirit of the lecturer to fuse them into continuity and raise them to higher lucidity."[4] As an aid to the reader, Hegel wrote *Anmerkungen* (remarks) to elucidate some arguments in numbered paragraphs; after Hegel's death, editors added *Zusätze* (additions) culled from Hegel's own lecture notes and students' notes of Hegel's lectures to provide readers with additional explications, implications, and examples.

In the 1830 version of the *Encyclopædia*, which is the one commonly republished and translated, the text runs to 577 numbered paragraphs: after an introduction (*Enz.*, §§1–18), part I on logic (*Enz.*, §§19–244), and part II on the philosophy of nature (*Enz.*, §§245–376), part III (*Enz.*, §§377–577) treats the philosophy of spirit. The riches that lie in these 201 paragraphs are further elaborated in other works by Hegel that expand specific aspects of the philosophy of spirit. Ever since 1801, Hegel had been working on systematic philosophy, and his "early writings" (most of which he himself did not publish) examine many of the same topics that eventually constituted the *Encyclopædia* philosophy of spirit.[5] Some of the section of subjective spirit on phenomenology receives extensive treatment in Hegel's *Phenomenology of Spirit*,[6] which he published in 1807, before the *Encyclopædia*. The philosophy of objective spirit is unfolded in larger compass in the *Philosophy of Right*, which Hegel published in 1821. Using the techniques by which they wrote the *Zusätze*, Hegel's students assembled four multi-volume posthumous works: on history, the last section of objective spirit,[7] and on aesthetics, religion, and philosophy,[8] the three sections of absolute spirit.

Hegel's philosophy of spirit as a whole is difficult to study. Since it includes essentially all of his systematic philosophy except for logic and nature, its scope extends over many areas which in the modern university have become distinct disciplines compartmentalized from each other. Whether as presented only in the brief 201 paragraphs in the *Encyclopædia* or including also the relevant other books Hegel published, his early writings, and the lecture cycles, the philosophy of spirit is extraordinarily rich—in particular aperçus, incisive discussions of recurring issues of thought, and systematic comprehension. Finally, Hegel's style is notoriously complex. In the *Encyclopædia* Hegel presents his mature system in a condensed, terse, and occasionally laconic—and almost always demanding—manner.

The chapters in this book directly address the difficulties raised by the scope, richness, and terseness of Hegel's philosophy of spirit. The authors—professors from different disciplines and different concentrations within disciplines—have written chapters and accompanying commentaries that unravel and expose Hegel's meaning on central or exemplary aspects of the philosophy of spirit. Because of Hegel's importance in the history of philosophy and his continuing influence, the authors also locate his positions in the history of thought, including twentieth century thought.

The first two chapters focus on *Geist* or spirit. Robert Williams provides an introduction and overview to Hegel's philosophy of spirit by examining and evaluating three major influential interpretations of "Hegel's Concept of *Geist*." Eric von der Luft approaches spirit from the perspective of its emergence in Hegel's system out of the shortcomings of some medical theories and the failures of reductionist science. The next two chapters concentrate on subjective spirit. Murray Greene discusses the central issue of the development of subjectivity out of natural life. Showing how Hegel treats an important specific issue in subjective spirit, John Sallis scrutinizes a few paragraphs from the *Encyclopædia* to elucidate "Imagination and Presentation." In the fifth chapter, Leo Rauch analyzes Hegel's views of recognition, a concept central for both subjective and objective spirit; in the sixth, Harry Brod studies specific institutions of objective spirit, the legislature and public opinion, to discern "The 'Spirit' of Hegelian Politics." The complex relation between objective and absolute spirit—in terms of the relation between politics and religion in Hegel's day and at present—is the subject of Merold Westphal's chapter. The final two chapters clarify absolute spirit in the process of examining its constituent elements: William Desmond explores "Art as 'Aesthetic' and as 'Religious'" and Martin De Nys investigates "Speculation and Theonomy at the Close of Hegel's System." These closing discussions impel the reader to a renewed consideration of the meaning of Hegel's concept of *Geist* and to a recapitulation of Hegel's full philosophy of spirit.

These chapters and commentaries were originally delivered as papers and comments at the Eighth Biennial Meeting of the Hegel Society of America, held on 4–6 October 1984 at Russell Sage College in Albany, New York. As is the case with all Hegel Society meetings, the Society determined the meeting's theme and issued a general Call for Papers; authors submitted prospective papers to the Program Chair; the Chair and an (anonymous) Program Committee evaluated them and chose the best for presentation at the meeting and, after revision, publication in the proceedings.[9] The Program Chair then chose the commentators, with expertise a prime requisite. So these chapters represent the polished results of a process of evaluation, selection, and public presentation.

As Program Chair for the 1984 meeting, I should like to thank especially the (still-anonymous) members of the Program Committee who refereed the papers submitted; Russell Sage College and Professor Rolf Ahlers, who served as hosts for the meeting and provided a congenial intellectual atmosphere; and the members of the Society, who contributed incisive questions at the presentations of the papers and the commentators' remarks. As editor of these proceedings, I should like to thank especially Carolyn Priest-Dorman, whose extensive skills at copy-editing, typing, communicating with a computer and its software, and maintaining her good humor made the process of moving from manuscripts to finished book a relatively easy and even enjoyable undertaking for me. Specific thanks should also go to Charlie Steinhorn of the Department of Mathematics at Vassar College, who provided crucial assistance in convincing the typesetting computer to inflect Greek, to Mitchell Miller of the Department of Philosophy at Vassar, who reconstituted several of the transliterated Greek words, and to Tyson R. Henry, Mark A. Resmer, and Karen J. Lukas of the Academic Computer Center at Vassar, who helped solve several programming and printing quandaries. I should also like to thank William Eastman at the Press for his support and Vassar College for providing the encouragement that has facilitated my own work on Hegel and the funding that has underwritten this book.

Peter G. Stillman
March, 1986

Notes

1. The standard German edition is G. W. F. Hegel, *Enzyklopädie der philosophischen Wissenschaften im Grundrisse* (1830), hrsg. Friedhelm Nicolin und Otto Pöggeler (Hamburg: Felix Meiner, 1959). It does not contain the *Zusätze* (or additions) that Ludwig Boumann wove together after Hegel's death from Hegel's and students' lecture notes; they are included in G. W. F. Hegel, *Werke*, Band 10 (Berlin: Duncker und Humblot, 1845), and in his *Sämtliche Werke: Jubiläumsausgabe*, Banden 8–10, hrsg. Hermann Glockner (Stuttgart: Frommann, 1927–1940). The third part of the *Encyclopædia*, containing the philosophy of spirit, is translated into English as *Hegel's Philosophy of Mind*, trans. William Wallace and A. V. Miller (Oxford: Clarendon Press, 1971); Wallace translated the numbered paragraphs and remarks, which he published (Oxford: Clarendon Press, 1894), and A. V. Miller retained Wallace's translations and added his translations of Boumann's *Zusätze* to complete the 1971 edition. M. J. Petry has translated, with extensive critical apparatus, the first division of the philosophy of spirit as *Philosophy of Subjective Spirit*, 3 vols. (Dordrecht and Boston: D. Reidel, 1978); he has also translated *The Berlin Phenomenology* (Dordrecht and Boston: D. Reidel, 1981). The first part of the *Encyclopædia* is translated as *The Logic of Hegel*, trans. William Wallace (Oxford: Oxford University Press, 1975 [first edition 1873, second edition 1892]). The second part has recently been accorded two separate translations, published in the same year with identical titles: *Hegel's Philosophy of Nature*, trans. A. V. Miller (Oxford: Clarendon Press, 1970); and *Hegel's Philosophy of Nature*, 3 vols., trans. M. J. Petry (London: George Allen and Unwin, 1970). Further references to the *Enzyklopädie* are found in parentheses in the text; preceded by "*Enz.*," citations are to the paragraph number, common to all editions, and not to page number.

2. The fine standard translation is *Hegel's Philosophy of Right*, trans. T. M. Knox (Oxford: Clarendon Press, 1942).

3. As quoted in the *Enzyklopädie*, hrsg. Nicolin and Pöggeler, p. *xxix*.

4. *The Logic of Hegel*, trans. Wallace, p. *x*.

5. For a detailed investigation of Hegel's early years as well as a complete bibliography, see the two volumes by H. S. Harris: *Hegel's Development: Toward the Sunlight,* 1770–1801 (Oxford: Clarendon Press, 1972) and *Hegel's Development: Night Thoughts,* 1801–1806 (Oxford: Clarendon Press, 1982).

6. The fine standard translation is now *Hegel's Phenomenology of Spirit,* trans. A. V. Miller (Oxford: Clarendon Press, 1977); an earlier one is *Hegel's Phenomenology of Mind,* trans. J. B. Baillie (New York: Harper and Row, 1967 [second edition Macmillan, 1931]).

7. Two current but inadequate translations that derive from a truncated German edition are G. W. F. Hegel, *The Philosophy of History,* trans. J. Sibree (New York: Dover Books, 1955 [1858]), and G. W. F. Hegel, *Reason in History,* trans. Robert S. Hartman (Indianapolis, Ind.: Library of Liberal Arts, Bobbs-Merrill, 1953). The introductory lectures have been well translated: G. W. F. Hegel, *Lectures on the Philosophy of World History: Introduction,* trans. H. B. Nisbet (Cambridge: Cambridge University Press, 1975). Nisbet's translation is based on an excellent German edition: G. W. F Hegel, *Die Vernunft in der Geschichte,* hrsg. Johannes Hoffmeister (Hamburg: Felix Meiner, 1955). For most of the lectures, the best text remains G. W. F. Hegel, *Vorlesungen über die Philosophie der Weltgeschichte,* Banden II, III, und IV, hrsg. Georg Lasson (Hamburg: Felix Meiner, 1968 [second edition 1923]).

8. For Hegel's philosophy of art, the fine standard translation is *Hegel's Aesthetics,* trans. T. M. Knox (Oxford: Clarendon Press, 1975). For his philosophy of religion, a new translation is underway: G. W. F. Hegel, *Lectures on the Philosophy of Religion,* ed. Peter C. Hodgson (Berkeley: University of California Press, 1984–). For his history of philosophy, the current and somewhat unsatisfactory translation is *Hegel's Lectures on the History of Philosophy,* trans. E. S. Haldane and F. H. Simson (London: Routledge and Kegan Paul, 1892–96); there now exist two fine translations of introductory lectures in Quentin Lauer, *Hegel's Idea of Philosophy* (New York: Fordham University Press, 1971), and, more extensive, G. W. F. Hegel, *Introduction to the Lectures on the History of Philosophy,* trans. T. M. Knox and A. V. Miller (Oxford: Oxford University Press, 1985).

9. As a courtesy, traditional in many professional societies, the Presidential Address receives dispensation from these rigors.

Hegel's Concept of *Geist*

Robert R. Williams

Few would deny the importance of *Geist* in the philosophy of Hegel. If *Geist* is the systematic concept which unifies Hegelian philosophy, then the interpretation of *Geist* is crucial to the proper understanding and appreciation of that philosophy. The interpretation of *Geist* raises many of the major problems of Hegel-interpretation. Unfortunately, a successful, comprehensive interpretation of *Geist* and, with it, Hegelianism, has thus far eluded interpreters. Our situation is not unlike that portrayed in the Hindu fable of the blind men and the elephant. About the only safe comment is that in our case the "elephant" is very big and surpasses our ability to take it all in. The more cynical may harbor the suspicion that not even Hegel knew what he really meant. I do not pretend to possess the key which unlocks all doors, or to have somehow succeeded where all others have failed. However, I do want to provoke and advance the interpretive discussion by presenting what I take to be an important but hitherto ignored or suppressed interpretation of *Geist*, at least in English-speaking circles. My perspective is informed by a recent study of the *Phenomenology* and by recent scholarship on the concept of recognition (*Anerkennung*) in Fichte and Hegel.

At least three different concepts or interpretive models of *Geist* appear in Hegel interpretation. One interpretation sees *Geist* as a more or less direct descendant of Kant's transcendental ego (Findlay, Solomon). Accordingly, Hegel's philosophy is regarded as an instance of transcendental philosophy (Taylor, Westphal). However, this view overlooks or ignores Hegel's severe criticism of transcendental philosophy. To paraphrase Jacobi's remark concerning the thing-in-itself, it is impossible to enter the Kantian philosophy without taking a transcendental turn, but it is equally impossible to remain in the Kantian philosophy after taking the transcendental turn. For Kant raised but did not resolve the problem of the *ontological interpretation* of the transcendental ego, and, with it, transcendental philosophy. Hence, as Hegel repeatedly pointed out, Kant is trapped in the impossible predicament of attempting to know before he knows. The problem of the ontological interpretation of transcendental philosophy can be postponed, but not avoided, save at the price of a merely methodological idealism, which Kant is not willing to accept. This brings us to the second interpretive model.

What is the ontological interpretation of the transcendental ego? Several problems rear their ugly heads when this question is addressed. If the transcendental ego is retained, it seems to require a referent or "carrier." If the referent is identified with "human being," the result is a "left-Hegelian" interpretation. However, this interpretation calls into question the foundational status of the transcendental subject as the ultimate condition of possible experience, and calls forth the charges of psychologism and relativism. In order to avoid relativism and anthropologism, the "right-Hegelian" interpretation rejects the identification of the transcendental subject with the human subject, and works out instead an onto-theological interpretation of *Geist*. Then Hegel is regarded as a transcendent metaphysical theologian in the Aristotelian-Neo-Platonic sense: the self-othering of *Geist* in nature is understood as a version of the Neo-Platonic emanation theory which has been transformed by a concept of subjectivity as negatively dialectical. The problem with this interpretation is that the transcendental method is ruined by the apparently dogmatic postulate of onto-theology. Hegel would recognize and reject both of these alternatives, for the former is basically a warmed-over version of the subjective idealism of Fichte, and the latter a version of the dogmatic *Naturphilosophie* of the early Schelling. Common to both is the acceptance and/or retention of the transcendental ego. I think that Hegel rejects this concept, or transforms it. He does not take up the ontological question in this form.

Third, there is the social-intersubjective interpretation of *Geist*. This interpretation of *Geist* has recently been set forth in an interesting study by Ludwig Siep[1] and has begun to receive attention by other German scholars.[2] I wish to explore this model. The question is, if *Geist* is fundamentally social-intersubjective, then what does Hegel's so-called "idealism" mean? For in its common acceptation, "idealism" seems to contradict and exclude intersubjectivity because it eliminates the ontological transcendence of the other, and is haunted by the problem of solipsism, as both Husserl and Sartre have pointed out.[3] Moreover, Sartre claims that Hegel's ontological idealism founders on the problem of intersubjectivity: the *Geist* that is certain of being all reality has displaced the other ontologically. But it might with greater accuracy be replied that what is interesting about Hegel's concept of *Geist* is that it is the result of, and consequently *presupposes*, the very intersubjective meditation which Sartre (wrongly) thinks it eliminates!

In what follows our strategy will be to show, first, that the transcendental interpretation of *Geist* does founder on the problem of intersubjectivity. That is one reason why Hegel rejects transcendental philosophy, and why *Geist* can be properly understood only as a departure from treanscendentalism and foundationalism. Second, we shall examine Hegel's philosophy of absolute *Geist* to determine whether and how far the social-intersubjective interpretation may be sustainable on this level.

1. Destruction of the Transcendental-Foundational Model

Some interpreters see Hegel's concept of *Geist* simply as a version of Kant's transcendental ego and program.[4] This is not entirely incorrect, since Hegel himself acknowledges Kant's influence and points out that the transcendental unity of apperception lies behind the *Begriff*.[5] Nevertheless, it is more misleading than helpful to stress the similarities between *Geist* and Kant's transcendental ego. On the contrary, it is Hegel's conscious departure from Kant's transcendentalism that requires the terminological shift from transcendental ego to *Geist*. For when Hegel introduces the concept of *Geist* in the *Phenomenology*, he shows that *Geist* is not a transcendental structure *a priori*, an "I think" that must accompany all representations, but rather a result, an intersubjective accomplishment. The transition from consciousness to self-consciousness is not simply a reflective accomplishment that the self can give to itself; rather, this transition is accomplished through the intersubjective process of recognition. Instead of a transcendental ego, Hegel speaks of an I that is also a We, and a We that is also an I.[6] The significance of this departure from transcendental idealism (Kant) can best be appreciated by reference to Fichte and Hegel's critique of Fichte.

Fichte introduced the term *Anerkennung* and with it first thematized the problem of intersubjectivity within German Idealism. Specifically, he conceived *Anerkennung* as a transcendental condition of right, and offered the following transcendental deduction of intersubjectivity: "The finite rational being cannot ascribe to itself a freedom efficacious in the external world, without also ascribing such freedom to others, and without assuming therefore the existence of other rational finite beings besides itself."[7] Note that this is a transcendental argument concerning freedom, not unlike Strawson's arguments concerning persons and "P-predicates." A condition of ascribing freedom to oneself, or "seeing oneself as free," is some prior consciousness of what freedom means in the case of others. The other is not inductively inferred, but rather co-implicated in the first-person consciousness of freedom as its transcendental condition. However, Fichte goes further than Strawson's "merely transcendental" argument, which seems finally to culminate in a possible other. Fichte's step is suggested in the above passage, namely, if the other is more than a transcendental condition of the consciousness of freedom, the other must exist. This point is further developed in Fichte's discussion of *Anerkennung*, which raises and pursues the problem of intersubjectivity within the framework of transcendental philosophy. Recall that Fichte relies on the Kantian moral philosophy, in which the existence and knowledge of freedom is problematic. Is freedom a postulate? Or is it a fact of reason? In either case, how is it possible to "see oneself as free" or discover one's freedom? Kant apparently sticks to his general thesis of a denial of knowledge in order to make room for moral faith and freedom. Hence freedom is a belief, a postulate about the self which is inseparably bound up with the moral law. For Fichte, the self's consciousness of itself as free is synonymous with the problem of how the self can be an object for itself.

Fichte proposes that the self discovers itself as free only through be-

4

ing recognized by and recognizing others. Consequently, freedom is inter-subjectively mediated. The self-consciousness of freedom is not attained simply through a reflective act.[8] Since the self cannot objectify itself entirely, it cannot "give" itself the full consciousness of itself as free. The self-consciousness of freedom requires something different than a reflective act; it requires that the self re-cognize itself through the mediation of an other. Fichte points out that the other is the source of requests and demands (*Aufforderungen*) that the self encounters. The other functions as a kind of ethical *Anstoß*, a summons to free self-activity. Through its response to requests, the self discovers its own freedom. But this consciousness of freedom is not reducible to having concepts *a priori*, or to having empirical intuitions. Neither the self nor its other are concepts or percepts in the sense of these terms established in the *Critique of Pure Reason*. Nevertheless, Fichte's whole discussion of *Anerkennung* occurs within, and probably explodes, his transcendental philosophical program.

The question is, what is the significance of *Anerkennung* for Fichte's larger project of *Wissenschaftslehre* and practical philosophy? Fichte says that *Anerkennung* is a transcendental condition of natural law (*Naturrecht*). But now is this transcendental condition related to the ultimate transcendental condition, the absolute ego (*das Ich*) which is the first principle of the entire system? Clearly it is subordinate to the absolute ego, for Fichte regards *Anerkennung* as a *Bewußtseinshandlung*, and *Bewußtsein* is a constituted, derivative level of Fichte's transcendental program. Thus *Anerkennung* is only relatively, but not absolutely, *a priori*; it must be regarded as relative to and constituted by the transcendental ego. It is far from clear what such relativity and constitution might mean, partly because the status of the absolute ego is itself problematic. In the *Wissenschaftslehre* of 1794, Fichte apparently regarded the transcendental ego as a postulate, and thus held a metholdological rather than an ontological idealism. Later, under the impact of the *Atheismusstreit* and the need to integrate *Anerkennung* into his system, Fichte sought to address and clarify the issue of the ontological status of the absolute ego, which he came to identify not with the human ego, but with God. However, it is an open question whether this interpretation can incorporate, much less clarify, his concept of recognition.

In his *Differenzschrift* Hegel attacks Fichte, focusing on the apparent separation between the transcendental and the empirical egos.[9] Hegel points out that Fichte's basic speculative stance requires that he identify the transcendental with the empirical, thereby overcoming all contrast and deriving knowledge from a single unifying principle, the absolute identity—I am I. But Hegel complains that Fichte fails to unify the transcendental and the empirical, with the consequence that the reflective form of the system contradicts its speculative foundation or *Grundsatz*. Hegel identifies a fundamental problem in transcendental philosophy. On the one hand, it is necessary to distinguish the transcendental from the empirical ego in order to account for the possibility of actual knowledge and to ground its objective validity. The transcendental thus grounds the empirical, and is foundational for the empirical. Therefore the transcendental must not be identified or confused with the empirical. However, when the ontological implications of such a distinction are sought, then the question arises, who or what is the transcendental ego? If the transcendental ego is other than the human ego, the methodological dualism appears to turn into an onto-logical dualism. Is the transcendental ego then God? If so, does this not run the risk of lapsing into dogmatic metaphysics? Is the transcendence of God identifiable with the transcendence of the transcendental ego? Yet, if this step is not taken, what are the ontological foundations and grounds of the universality and necessity of knowledge? On the other hand, if the transcendental ego is identified with the human ego, then it is bound up and identified with finitude, existence and historicity. How then can the transcendental serve as a foundation? To identify the transcendental ego with the human subject is to give up the transcendental in the founda-tionalist sense. Either way, transcendental philosophy appears to be self-subverting—whether into dogmatic theological metaphysics (which ruins the transcendental method) or into an historical-cultural relativism (which retains the method but surrenders objective validity and universality).

What is Hegel's response to this dilemma? He does not remain in the halfway house of transcendental methodological idealism. But neither does he lapse into metaphysics (cf. the first attitude of thought towards objectivity in the *Encyclopædia*). Rather, he abandons transcendental phi-losophy in the foundationalist *a priori* sense. Hegel retains transcendental moves, to be sure. But this is not a transcendental in the Kantian sense of a world-founding structure or world-constituting act. The exact sense of transcendental philosphy as it is retained in Hegel's version of identity-theory is obscure, and one reason for the obscurity is that the transcendental is no longer ontologically separate from the world. Whatever else may be meant, the transcendental has ceased to be an *a priori* condition or foundation of the phenomenal world, and has instead become a medium of access to the life-world. Transcendental deduction has been displaced by transcendental phenomenology, which describes and discovers the meaning of the experience made by ordinary consciousness. The argument of Hegel's *Phenomenology* proceeds on the presupposition of the collapse of foundationalism: there are no absolute, unproblematic foundations or first principles with which to philosophize; the search for such first philosophy lies behind the Cartesian and Kantian transcendental turn, and it culminates in the *cul-de-sac* of knowing before you know. The only way out is not to enter in the first place, and so Hegelian phenomenology begins where Husserl eventually ended, namely, the turn to the life-world. The problem of foundations is not simply abandoned, but is rather displaced from the beginning of philosophy (the so-called first philosophy) to its end, i.e., to the results of philosophical labor. Critical subjectivity is not a given, but must be accomplished, brought about. The result of philosophical labor is not a transcendental ego purified of all empirical content, but rather something which is historically and culturally shaped, a developing foundation. What holds this notion of a non-foundational transcendental together with the equally strange notion of a developing foundation is *Geist*.

Thus Hegel takes over Fichte's account of *Anerkennung*, deepens it, and jettisons the transcendental philosophy. Purged of foundationalism, *Anerkennung* serves as the phenomenological account of the existential genesis of *Geist*.

Hegel on *Anerkennung*

A full account of Hegel's discussion of *Anerkennung* is not possible here. I am hoping to complete a book on this topic; the following summary will have to suffice. First I shall sketch the departure from transcendentalism which is required in order to understand *Anerkennung*. In transcendental philosophy, the transcendental subject is invoked as the *a priori* inclusive condition of possible experience. It prescribes and imposes conditions of appearance, carries and embeds universal structures, and performs acts of constitution which formally make experience possible. In order to do this the transcendental subject must be complete *a priori*, independent of experience. In it there can be no passivity or receptivity; as Fichte reiterates, nothing can be in or for the ego which is not posited by the ego. Hence there can be no reciprocity between that which founds and that which is founded.

With the introduction of *Anerkennung*, we migrate from transcendental deductions to descriptive phenomenology and social ontology. The starting point of the various Hegelian accounts of recognition is not the disembodied transcendental ego of Cartesian heritage, but rather the embodied subject as desire (*Begierde*). Desire finds itself already in the world: the desiring subject is not complete and self-possessed in advance of experience; rather, it is empty and lacking. It needs to be filled by, and so is dependent on, its object (e.g., food). However, desire is not satisfied when such natural needs and wants are satisfied. It is willing to risk its entire natural existence for something yet more important, namely, the recognition of its freedom. Hegel's break from Cartesian transcendentalism is the discovery that the self is dependent on other for recognition, specifically, the recognition of its freedom. Recognition is thus a condition of the discovery of freedom. If we may speak here of recognition as an *a priori* condition of freedom, this is a concrete life-world *a priori* and not an abstract *a priori*.

To be sure, Fichte had anticipated this in his account of recognition as a transcendental condition of natural law. Hegel proceeds further: human self-consciousness is accomplished in and through community, and is intersubjectively mediated. Hence self-consciousness is essentially an intersubjective accomplishment. This accomplishment requires that the self wrench itself away from its merely natural existence, for freedom is decisively manifest only in the transcendence of natural existence. But precisely for this reason recognition is not a simple given, nor is it automatic. Recognition is jointly brought about only by overcoming prior moments of refusal and rejection. Hence recognition essentially involves and presupposes alienation, conflict, and struggle, even where such elements are not present on the empirical level.

There are several different accounts of the struggle for recognition. The struggle assumes several different shapes and points of contention, e.g., honor, property, and recognition (as τέλος [*telos*]) itself, as the fundamental possibilities are considered in different empirical-cultural contexts. We follow Siep in distinguishing two levels (*Stufen*) of recognition, namely, a dyadic or I-I (or I-Thou) relation, and a triadic or I-We relation. The initial situation in the *Phenomenology* account is confrontation. Each self is naïvely and provincially self-certain, but absolutely uncertain about the other. This objective uncertainty is intolerable, and the self sees itself threatened with the loss of its own self-certainty. It seeks to elevate its private self-certainty to public truth by compelling the other to recognize. But, for reasons too subtle and complex to develop here, to struggle against the other is to struggle against oneself (the self is already dependent on the other, and it learns this in the course of the struggle). Hence, if the other is simply annihilated, the quest for recognition has ended in failure. The first phase (*Stufe*) of the process of recognition stops short of annihilation, but also short of full recognition. One side gives up its demand for recognition in exchange for survival. Thereby it shows its inability to transcend the merely natural level of existence. It recognizes the other as master, while the master recognizes it not as co-equal, but only as thing, as slave. Here we have the unequal one-sided form of recognition, the dyadic model of master and slave. Since the unequal form of recognition contradicts the fundamentally social, interdependent nature of the self, it is an imperfect, unstable relationship. The ideal goal of recognition, its $\tau\acute{\epsilon}\lambda o\varsigma$, is mutual reciprocal recognition: "A one-sided action is useless, because what is supposed to ocur can come about only through the reciprocal and mutual action of both .... They recognize themselves as mutually recognizing and recognized."[10]

In such reciprocal recognition a new social reality is brought about which is more than the sum of its parts. Since the new reality cannot be accomplished by the single action of any one of its members, or controlled by any one of its members, it transcends while including the original self-consciousness. Conversely, the original self-consciousness undergoes not a loss of being but rather an expansion: the I becomes a We, and is propelled forward into an open future as a member of the community. Hegel terms this new social reality *Geist*:

> Since a self-consciousness is here the object, it is both I-subject and at the same time I-object. With this the concept of *Geist* presents itself to us for the first time. Con-

> sciousness will subsequently experience what this *Geist* is, this absolute ethical substance which in perfect freedom and independence of its opposites—namely different independently existing self-consciousnesses—is the unity of such opposites: the I that is We and the We that is I.[11]

With the accomplishment of the second level of recognition, consciousness undergoes expansion: self-consciousness is not merely a simple form of consciousness which the self can reflectively give to itself; rather, self-consciousness equally and essentially depends upon the mediation of others. Hence self-consciousness and the full self-identity are not to be confused or identified with products of reflection or intellectual constructs *a priori*; rather, they are intersubjectively mediated. To be sure, they cannot come about if the self is not a conscousness, or otherwise lacks an existence for itself. But neither is self-conscousness in Hegel's sense possible if the self is *only* a being-for-itself. Being for self is thus a necessary condition of intersubjective recognition, but it is not the sole or sufficient condition.

Further, it is important to note that the social self or We moves beyond the dyadic or I-I relation of master/slave. Instead of a dyadic structure the We has a triadic structure of twofold or double mediation. In the joint two-sided process of recognition, each side is both an extreme standing in opposition and contrast to its other, and at the same time it is the mediator through which the other self is recognized (or fails to find recognition). It is important to see this twofold mediation; for unless the intersubjective mediation is twofold we have only the dyadic unequal form of recognition. When the twofold mediation occurs, there emerges a third over above the original two selves, namely, the We, or social self. The We is the result of this process of twofold mediation, and for this reason the We must be distinguished from a transcendental consciousness or structure. As the concrete universal which is inclusive of and the result of the joint action of its members, the We is a social infinite. This is perhaps Hegel's major contribution to philosophy: the social infinite or community principle is a distinctive kind of being, which is irreducible to the standard subject-object epistemology and its categories, or to the standard "first person" and "third person" approaches to the philosophy of mind.[12]

To conclude this section, the claim is that Hegel is not doing transcendental philosophy in the traditional Kantian foundationalist sense—that *Geist* is not a transcendental ego, but rather an intersubjective-social self resulting from reciprocal recognition. The introduction of the concept of recognition (*Anerkennung*) compels the displacement or drastic modification of transcendental philosophy by depriving transcendental subjectivity of its foundational status. The transcendental is retained, if at all, in a more modest sense of being a medium of access to other-being. Further, other-being is not merely a negation; it is a co-partner in bringing about the We. The question remains whether intersubjectivity is merely one phase in the development of *Geist* which is passed through and left behind, or whether *Geist* on all its levels is essentially an intersubjective social infinite. How is the *Phenomenology* related to the *Encyclopædia*? The later philosophy of *Geist* appears to de-emphasize the term *Anerkennung*. This invites the question, whether there could be a *Geist* which is not social, which is not a social infinite? Is that how the distinction between objective and absolute *Geist* is to be understood? I think not.

2. Hegel's Concept of Absolute *Geist*

Obviously, justice cannot be done to the topic in the limited space remaining. I shall sketch with broad strokes and present my case in a highly vulnerable but I hope suggestive form. The problem is first to determine how Hegel conceives absolute spirit in light of our earlier analysis of *Geist* as intersubjective. Second, what is the ontological interpretation of *Geist*? Does Hegel develop his understanding of absolute *Geist* as intersubjective? In the *Phenomenology* there is no question but that the answer is affirmative. For when Hegel introduces the concept of *Geist* he introduces it as the accomplishment of mutual reciprocal recognition: "The word of reconciliation is the concrete existing *Geist*, which intuits the pure knowledge of itself as universal being in its counterpart, namely the pure knowing of itself as absolute particular. *This is a mutual (gegenseitiges) Anerkennen which is the absolute Geist.*"[13]

However, with Hegel matters are seldom so clear-cut that one text alone settles an issue. Jürgen Habermas in an important essay[14] observes that Hegel has perhaps two different modes of *Geist*. One is an intersubjective model, in which *Geist* serves not as a foundation but as a communication medium, i.e., an intersubjective medium of access. The other model is identified by Habermas as the idealist model, in which the infinite is an infinite accomplished in reflection, not a social infinite. In this case absolute *Geist* is conceived as a transcendental subject which unconsciously produces nature, and then re-discovers itself in its investigation of nature, and thereby returns to itself (i.e., becomes self-conscious) out of nature as its other. But nature as the other of the absolute turns out to be an other which is not-other; for nature is the absolute itself in alienated or estranged form. That is why Hegel can speak of a return to self out of other and treat this as a logical double negation, or negation of negation. Habermas thinks that the latter idealist model of *Geist* cannot do justice to the intersubjective dimension, because the absolute *Geist*, like Kant's transcendental ego, is solitary (*einsamer*). This vision of unity and infinity is haunted by solipsism because its other is not a *Gegenspieler* but merely an epistemological *Gegenbild*.[15] Habermas' thesis that Hegel has two different, if not incompatible, models of *Geist* deserves serious attention and scrutiny.

Granting Habermas' distinction, from each model of *Geist* a different sense of the concept and its self-identity emerges. In the idealist model the self-identical unity of *Geist* is reflectively achieved in pure self-transparency, I am I.[16] This self-identical unity is pure knowledge, and no intersubjective mediation is necessary. Conversely, the intersubjective model of *Geist* requires intersubjective mediation; this is not simply an I am I, but rather an I that is a We, a social infinite. These different models may not in the final analysis be mutually exclusive, as Habermas seems to think, but they are surely distinct, and they are both present in Hegel's writings from early to late.

Michael Theunissen shows that both concepts of *Geist* are present in the late philosophy of *Geist*. In his study, *Hegels Lehre vom absoluten Geist als theologisch-politischer Traktat*,[17] Theunissen takes account of Habermas' distinction, sharpens it, and brings out what is apparently a confusion on Hegel's part. For if we take the intersubjective model of *Geist* as fundamental, then transcendental subjectivity plays no foundational role; it is a medium of access to being, or a communication medium. Reflection is derivative from this concrete context. But in the later system Hegel apparently inverted this relationship and constructed the doctrine of absolute *Geist* not as social but rather on the idealist model. The absolute subject, in relating itself to others, is in fact only relating to itself.[18] Theunissen thus finds Hegel inconsistently holding two different concepts of absolute *Geist*:

> ...Hegel is never able to clarify satisfactorily the relation between the *Geist* which functions as medium, and the *Geist* which is the self-consciousness which comprehends the intersubjective medium. And a satisfactory explanation is excluded in principle because a series of explanations which refers us from God to *Geist*, from *Geist* to self-consciousness, from self-consciousness to a self-identity which is constituted by finding oneself in another, and then a final expanation which sums up the whole series as comprehended and unified by a single self-consciousness, is incapable of explaining the [intersubjective] medium.[19]

Given this analysis, the confusion is serious: Hegel may have no coherent doctrine of *Geist*. Theunissen's excursus on Bruno Bauer makes it evident that the Left-Hegelians divided from Hegel precisely on the issues raised by this apparent confusion. Hegel's theology in this interpretation—ultimately a version of Spinoza and Aristotle—ruins his intersubjectivity theory and lapses into substance metaphysics. Given the choice between a theory of absolute spirit in which substance becomes subject, and an intersubjective theory of spirit which points towards the formation of a community of freedom, Bauer opted for the latter over against the former. Theunissen shows that Hegel is hardly defenseless against the left-wing interpretation, but that issue does not concern us here. Instead, let us examine the two different concepts of *Geist* which will occur side by side in the late philosophy of spirit, for this will show that perhaps there is ambiguity in Hegel's thought on this topic.

One text which manifests the ambiguity in the late philosophy is the following paragraph from the *Encyclopædia* which introduces the concept of absolute *Geist*:

> The absolute *Geist* is both an identity which is ever returning and ever returned into itself. It is the one and universal substance which as spiritual (*geistige*) exists as a judgement in itself and a knowing for which it is as such. Religion, as this highest sphere may in gen-

> eral be characterized, is to be considered also from two perspectives. First, as proceeding from the subject, and as it exists in the subject. Second, as objectively proceeding from the absolute *Geist*, which is *Geist* in its community.[20]

It appears that in the first sentence *Geist* is conceived on the idealist model. On the other hand, the last sentence appears to conceive *Geist* on the intersubjective model as *Geist in seiner Gemeinde*. The English translation confirms this ambiguity by translating *Geist* as "mind" in the first sentence, and as "spirit" in the last sentence. All the basic Hegelian terminology—being-for-other, return-to-self-out-of-other, to be at-home-with-the-self-in-other, the other as *aufgehoben*—depends for its significance on which sense of *Geist* is meant and which sense is fundamental. Until such determination can be conclusively made, we do not know whether we have to do with an absolute *Geist* which is to be understood as the a-cosmic pantheism of Spinoza, or a social-intersubjective ontology of community which may displace the traditional concept of God but is not reducible to anthropology (Feuerbach). Hence the interpretive problem: is absolute *Geist* a substantial infinite which comes to expression in pure self-transparency (*Ich bin Ich*)? Hegel's repeated citation of Aristotle may point in this direction, in which case Hegel rejoins and sums up the Western intellectualist tradition. Or is absolute *Geist* rather a social infinite? If the "other" means an intersubjective other, then the manifestation and expression of absolute *Geist* is equivalent to the creation of an intersubjective community. The We is a new social self or community which is not simply a rendering explicit of what *Geist an sich* already (implicitly) is. Obviously this reading has implications for the significance and place of history in Hegel's system. In this reading, the *Aufhebung* of the other is not an elimination of the other by reduction to the primordial identity of I am I; rather, it is the elevation of the self and its other into community. In the final analysis Hegel's absolute *Geist* is not a pure I am I, but rather *Geist in seiner Gemeinde*.

I should like to conclude with three observations concerning Theunissen's commentary on absolute *Geist*. First, Theunissen suggests (perhaps following Habermas) that Hegel's two concepts of *Geist* are incompatible. Hence one must pick and choose. Picking and choosing means deciding which is primary and which is derivative. Habermas claims that if the idealist model of *Geist* is primary, it is impossible to derive a plausible concept of *Geist* in the social-intersubjective sense. Hence it would appear that Habermas and possibly Theunissen would defend the proposition that idealist subjectivity must be taken as derivative from intersubjectivity, and not the other way around. I think that this proposition is false. Rather, it would seem that subjectivity and intersubjectivity are correlative, reciprocal notions. It is not as if self-consciousness is "created" by intersubjectivity or is merely a small slice of intersubjectivity, for a condition of being-for-other is being-for-self. So all the cognitive apparatus which Hegel analyzes in the sections devoted to consciousness (*Bewußtsein*) must be functioning if the self is to perceive and respond to the other. Hence intersubjective apprehension presupposes subjectivity (reason, imagination, sensibility, etc.). On the other hand, given Hegel's critique of foundationalism, the archaeology of the subject which he sets forth in the *Phenomenology* and *Encyclopædia* must not be mistaken for a new foundation from which intersubjectivity is to be "transcendentally deduced." Hegel's original contribution to this discussion is to show that a condition of being-for-self is being-for-other, that the self depends on its very being on the other. Hence it is crucial to distinguish the naïve, immediate self-identity of being for self from the full self-identity which is mediated by and won through the intersubjective struggle for recognition. The former sense of subjectivity is Cartesian; in the latter Hegelian conception of self-identity, subjectivity and intersubjectivity are equi-primordial, reciprocal conceptions.

Second, Theunissen's discussion prescinds from the whole topic of *Anerkennung* as the existential origin of *Geist*. This undoubtedly makes it easier to drive a wedge between the idealist model of *Geist* and the intersubjective model. For in the later writings not only does *Geist* play a lesser role than in the 1807 *Phenomenology*, but *Anerkennung* seems to be restricted to accounting for the genesis of objective *Geist*. This creates the impression that Hegel abandons the intersubjective model of *Geist* to anthropology, and that his concept of absolute *Geist* is out-and-out idealism. The ultimate significance of absolute *Geist* according to this interpretation is to be found in Neo-Platonism. However, there is another interpretation which is possible. Although *Anerkennung* is downplayed somewhat in the later writings, it does not disappear entirely. The earlier suggestions in the *Phenomenology* that Hegel conceived the divine-human relationship to be one of recognition are still present in the *Encyclopædia* and later *Lectures on the Philosophy of Religion*. For *Anerkennung* implies intersubjective reciprocity and mutuality, and these features are very much present in the so-called "late" accounts. Consider, for example, the aphorisms of C. F. Goschel which Hegel cites with obvious approval:

> To understand what God as *Geist* is—to apprehend this accurately and distinctly in thoughts—requires careful and thorough speculation. It includes in its forefront the following propositions: God is God only insofar as he knows himself; his self-knowing is further a self-consciousness in man and man's knowledge of God, which proceeds to the self-knowing of man in God.[21]

Whatever else this passage might mean, it seems to require a conception of the divine-human relation as intersubjective, and this suggests that *Anerkennung* is presupposed even if the term itself is not used. The same conception of absolute *Geist* as fundamentally social is to be found in the lectures on the proofs for the existence of God:

> If in fact religion is to be understood only as relation from us to God, this conception would not permit a being of God independent of human consciousness; God would exist only in religion as something posited and produced by us .... but a one-sided relation is no relation at all .... In the religious relation it is implied not merely that we stand in relation to God, but also that God stands in relation to us.[22]

Hegel would land in flat self-contradiction if the two-sided reciprocal relation of *Anerkennung* were to collapse into the pure identity of the *Ich bin Ich*. That would mean that the *Aufhebung* of the other is tantamount to its elimination. I believe that Hegel intends to say that the *Aufhebung* of the other means the elevation of the self and other into community; the *Aufhebung* of the other means the constitution of the We, or the divine *Geist in seiner Gemeinde*. Hence *Anerkennung* leads not to a restoration of a primordial identity, but to a totality. For only a totality can maintain the other as not-other (i.e., as non-alien) without eliminating the other *per se*.

Third, not only does Theunissen fail to take up the topic of *Anerken-*

nung, but he operates with a deficient conception of intersubjectivity. He appears to have a dialogue or I-Thou conception of intersubjectivity, which has a dyadic structure. This is not entirely incorrect, but it corresponds only to the first level (*Stufe*) of recognition. I believe that Theunissen has some such dialogue model of intersubjectivity in mind when he criticizes Hegel for not explaining satisfactorily how *Geist* can be both medium of access to the other and the comprehension of the whole, the We, i.e., how can it be both the medium of apprehension and the medium as comprehended?[23] This is to ask how intersubjectivity relates to or bears upon traditional epistemology. If one remains with the dialogue model of intersubjectivity, one is virtually imprisoned within a first-person account of other minds. By its very nature this account is restricted, one-sided. On such assumptions it is difficult to see any solution to the so-called "problem of other minds." But it should be noted that Hegel's conception of intersubjectivity as *Geist* is much richer than the dialogue model. For although *Anerkennung* begins with the I-I relationship, this is not its goal. The goal is mutual reciprocal recognition in which the I becomes a We, which implies the formation of an enduring social self or totality. This point comes out in Hegel's discussion of the social institution of marriage, which begins at the standpoint of a contract between two independent individuals, but whose τέλος is to transcend the merely individualistic standpoint of contract. That is what *Geist* and *Sittlichkeit* are all about.

Hegel thus has resources for meeting Theunissen's objection. For the I that is a We is *both* a particular extreme of the I-I intersubjective relation which excludes the other extreme *and* the We which arises out of the entire mutual-reciprocal relation. The τέλος of recognition is precisely the mutual reciprocity between selves which comprises the new universal-social consciousness. It is precisely the formation of the We, the social self and community, which takes Hegel's discussion of *Geist* beyond a merely impersonal dialogue and beyond the nominalistic conception of persons as atomic individuals. The dyadic structure of the dialogue model is inadequate to conceive or portray the meaning of *Geist*. Since *Geist* is constituted through a process of mutual-reciprocal recognition in which each is both extreme and mediator, *Geist* must be conceived as a social infinite with a triadic structure. Hegel's retention of the language of trinity (but not the classical Christian doctrine of trinity) is not simply a nostalgia for the past, or a convenient illustration of an abstract idea; rather, it is a phenomenologically oriented social ontology. Hegel's so-called absolute idealism may not finally exclude the intersubjective model of *Geist*; rather, it is the theoretical expression of Hegel's theory of *Sittlichkeit*, with its central conception of *Geist* as social infinite. Perhaps no one has understood this better than Josiah Royce in his book *The Problem of Christianity*.[24]

Notes

1. Ludwig Siep, *Anerkennung als Prinzip der praktischen Philosophie: Untersuchungen zu Hegels Jenaer Philosophie des Geistes* (Freiburg/München: Verlag Karl Alber, 1979).

2. Michael Theunissen, *Hegels Lehre vom absoluten Geist als theologisch-politischer Traktat* (Berlin: Walter De Gruyter, 1970); Andreas Wildt, *Autonomie und Anerkennung: Hegels Moralitätskritik im Lichte seiner Fichte-Rezeption* (Stuttgart: Klett-Cotta, 1982).

3. See Edmund Husserl, *Formal and Transcendental Logic*, trans. by D. Cairns (The Hague: Nijhoff, 1972); *Cartesian Mediations*, trans. by D. Cairns (The Hague: Nijhoff, 1960); Jean-Paul Sartre, *Being and Nothingness*, trans. by Hazel Barnes (New York: The Philosophical Library, 1956).

4. See J. N. Findlay's Forward to *Hegel's Philosophy of Mind*, the English translation of part III of Hegel's *Encyclopædia*, trans. W. Wallace and A. V. Miller (Oxford: Clarendon Press, 1971). See also R. C. Solomon, "Hegel's Concept of 'Geist'," in *Hegel: A Collection of Critical Essays*, ed. A. MacIntyre (New York: Doubleday Anchor, 1972). Solomon's essay is a condescending caricature which fails to deal with Hegel's fundamental notions and intentions. It is typical of the difficulties Hegel's thought has had in finding understanding, critical or sympathetic, in English-speaking countries.

5. G. W. F. Hegel, *Wissenschaft der Logik, Werke: Theorie Werkausgabe* (Frankfort: Suhrkamp Verlag, 1969), Vol. 6, p. 254. Hereafter cited as *Werke*, Sk.6:254.

6. G. W. F. Hegel, *Phänomenologie des Geistes*, Sk.3: 144ff, Hoffmeister *Ausgabe* (Hamburg: Felix Meiner, 1952), p. 140; English translation, *Hegel's Phenomenology of Spirit*, trans. A. V. Miller (Oxford: Oxford University Press, 1977), p. 110.

7. J. G. Fichte, *Grundlage des Naturrechts nach Principien der Wis-*

senschaftslehre, Werke, hrsg. I. H. Fichte, *Band* III (Berlin: Walter de Gruyter, 1971), p. 30.

8. For Fichte's critique of reflection theory and the Cartesian tradition, see Dieter Henrich, "Fichte's Original Insight," trans. D. Lachterman, in *Contemporary German Philosophy*, Vol. I, ed. D. Christensen (University Park: Pennsylvania State University Press, 1982).

9. G. W. F. Hegel, *Differenz des Fichteschen und Schellingschen Systems der Philosophie, Werke,* 2:52ff; English translation, *The Difference between Fichte's and Schelling's System of Philosophy,* trans. H. S. Harris (Albany: State University of New York Press, 1977).

10. Hegel, *Phänomenologie,* Sk.3:146ff; Hoffmeister 142–3; English translation 112.

11. *Ibid.,* Sk.3:144; Hoffmeister 140; English translation 112.

12. For example, Jerome Shafer in his *Philosophy of Mind* (Prentice-Hall Foundations in Philosophy Series) writes as if the so-called first person and third person approaches to mind exhaust all possible forms of inquiry. Behind this view lies a crucial presupposition, namely, that mind is to be interpreted nominalistically, i.e., the presupposition that persons are atomic individuals existing in independent isolation. However, as a I that is also a We, *Geist* transcends the first person and third person alternatives. The nominalistic assumption is challenged by all philosophers in German Idealism, and decisively rejected by Hegel. But this assumption pervades much contemporary philosophy. In addition to Shafer's discussion noted above, cf. Husserl's transcendental phenomenology. This is widely regarded as a first-person orientation on both the empirical and transcendental levels. This in turn creates the impression that the performer of transcendental intentionality is an individual. No wonder Husserl is worried about solipsism as a transcendental problem! In my view it is more misleading than helpful to retain the terminology of the transcendental subject in thinking about *Geist,* as does Merold Westphal in his recent book *History and Truth in Hegel's Phenomenology* (Atlantic Highlands, N.J.: Humanities Press, 1980). For *Geist* is not so much an answer to Westphal's question of "who is the transcendental subject?" as it is a dissolution of the presuppositions of that question.

13. G. W. F. Hegel, *Phänomenologie,* Sk.3:493; Hoffmeister 471; English translation 408.

14. Jürgen Habermas, *"Arbeit und Interaktion: Bemarken zu Hegels Jenenser Philosophie des Geistes,"* in G. W. F. Hegel, *Frühe politische Systeme,* hrsg. Gerhard Gohler (Frankfurt: Ullstein, 1974), pp. 786ff.

15. *Ibid.,* p. 808.

16. This is the "standard interpretation" of idealism. However, in view

of Henrich's challenging but obscure article ("Fichte's Original Insight"—see n. 8, above), the standard interpretation needs revision. On the other hand, Habermas himself seems to adopt the standard interpretation in reference to Hegel's concept of absolute *Geist*.

17. Theunissen, *op. cit.*

18. *Ibid.*, p. 57.

19. *Ibid.*, p. 58.

20. G. W. F. Hegel, *Enzyklopädie der philosophischen Wissenschaften*, *hrsg*. Nicolin *und* Pöggeler (Hamburg: Meiner, 1959), p. 440; Sk.10:336; English translation 292. The English translation is here virtually unsuitable for critical work, for Wallace translates *Geist* as "mind" in the first sentence, and as "spirit" in the last. This shows how difficult it is to translate Hegel; not only does the English language lack a suitable term to translate *Geist*, but it probably lacks the concept as well. In this particular case the translator has deprived the reader of an important interpretive decision by concealing the fact that Hegel uses the same word in the two case. Wallace's different translations of *Geist* first as "mind" and then as "spirit" tend to confirm the ambiguity in the concept of *Geist* even as this ambiguity is concealed from the English reader.

21. *Ibid.*, p. 447; Sk.10:317f; English translation 298.

22. G. W. F. Hegel, *Vorlesungen über die Beweise vom Dasein Gottes*, Sk.17:382f. This text is a further commentary and elaboration on the Goschel aphorisms cited in the preceding quotation. This strengthens my case that Hegel has *Anerkennung* or something like it in mind, even though the term is absent from this passage.

23. See above, n. 19.

24. Josiah Royce, *The Problem of Christianity* (New York: Macmillan, 1913).

Commentary on
"Hegel's Concept of *Geist*"

Richard Dien Winfield

If the widening repudiation of past philosophy has borne any fruit of late, it is the growing attention given to intersubjectivity. While Kant and Husserl come under fire for treating consciousness both as a privileged foundation and as a pure unworldly structure, and as ever more alternative positions have their assumptions unmasked, the clamor has risen for philosophy to abandon its traditional claim to an eternally valid, autonomous reason. Increasingly, philosophers are urged to heed the concrete situation of philosophical inquiry, where thought allegedly lies bound to given terms and conceptual schemes embedded in the very fabric of discourse.

These developments have all precipitated a turn towards intersubjectivity. For many, this turn has meant conceiving intersubjectivity as the ground of consciousness, supplanting the unity of apperception as the foundation of knowledge. Some, like Habermas and Apel, have considered intersubjectivity to provide an ideal, universal structure of non-distorting communication within which truth and justice can still be known once and for all. Others, drawing their inspiration as much from Heidegger and Wittgenstein as from Marx, have understood intersubjectivity to be an historically developing reality, conditioning discourse and stamping knowing with historicity. However differently these positions conceive intersubjectivity, whether rooting it in language, culture, or economic relations, they all agree that intersubjectivity is the fundamental structure from which subjectivity is derived, and that it is an epistemological foundation, juridically conditioning all knowledge.

Williams' chapter is important for bringing Hegel's discussion of spirit to bear upon the current debate on intersubjectivity. In arguing that intersubjectivity is the fundamental structure of spirit, Williams interprets Hegel as the progenitor of the modern turn to intersubjectivity. With apparent approval, Williams suggests that Hegel subscribes to the two theses defining that turn: that subjectivity is derivative of intersubjectivity, and that intersubjectivity is the ultimate ground of knowledge, comprising the medium of access to being. Yet can these theses be true, and does Hegel's analysis of spirit really lend support to either one?

It makes sense to first examine whether intersubjectivity can be the ground of knowledge. This question does not figure within Hegel's *Philosophy of Spirit*, for Hegel already treats it in his *Phenomenology of Spirit*. There he provides no doctrine of spirit, but rather seeks to show how all attempts to ground knowing in any structure, egological or intersubjective, are doomed to failure. If one were to give intersubjectivity the foundational privilege of being the ground of knowledge, one would commit the familiar transcendental fallacy of seeking to know before knowing. Namely, one would make immediate knowledge claims concerning the character and epistemological primacy of intersubjectivity, even though the whole turn to intersubjectivity is motivated by the need to bracket out all truth claims until the conditions for knowing have been determined. Taken to its logical conclusion, this difficulty implies that philosophy cannot begin with any foundation, but must rather undertake an investigation whose categories derive from no given content and whose development follows no given method. Only after that investigation, historically initiated by Hegel in his *Science of Logic*, can one proceed to conceive real structures, such as consciousness and intersubjectivity, not as epistemological foundations but as topics in the philosophy of reality.

Hegel's *Philosophy of Spirit* does directly bear upon whether subjectivity is derivative of intersubjectivity because this is a question for the philosophy of reality and not an epistemological issue. Certainly, Hegel understands consciousness to be a very concrete structure that can only be conceived as the embodied awareness of a living individual inhabiting a world of nature common to others. Further, he does link various features of mind to intersubjective relations. Most notably, he argues that thinking requires language for its expression and that certain forms of self-consciousness depend upon practical involvements with other subjects. In addition, when he turns to justice he argues that all roles in which individuals bear rights and duties are dependent upon the interactions in which those roles are constituted. Nevertheless, Hegel makes it quite clear that many of the most important features of subjectivity are not dependent upon intersubjective relations, and that, on the contrary, intersubjectivity is inconceivable without independently given subjective endowments.

Language may make conceptual thought possible, but linguistic acts are themselves impossible without a prior representative intelligence (*Philosophy of Mind*, §§458–462). It must already be at hand, endowed with both a productive verbal imagination to create signs and a reproductive verbal imagination to retain the connection between representations in which the established semiotic meaning consists. Similarly, a struggle for recognition may be required to generate the type of self-awareness that is reflected in the acts and understanding of another. Yet Hegel is clearly aware that such a struggle presupposes individual selves already possessing the self-consciousness of desire, as well as the theoretical and practical capabilities needed to perceive and act towards others (*Philosophy of Mind*, §§424–430). The same holds true of all relations of justice. Individuals may be able to exercise the artificial agencies of property owner, moral subject, family member, civilian, and citizen only by participating in the interactions in which each role is at home. But no exercise of rights and duties can occur unless one enjoys the body, mind, and choosing will needed to recognize the acts of others, performs one's obligations, and take the acts of freedom to which one is entitled.

These examples, all prominently supported by Hegel's text, indicate how the self has important faculties that are presupposed by, rather than derived from, intersubjective relations. It also shows that Hegel does not identify spirit with intersubjectivity, but instead conceives intersubjective relations as features figuring in only some forms of spirit. Further, since Hegel understands intersubjectivity to comprise such non-social realities as language, property relations, morality, the family, and politics, it would be a category mistake to equate intersubjectivity with social community.

To conceive intersubjectivity in its proper place is not to deny that philosophy is necessarily practiced by living individuals with bodies and minds, employing language in a community whose institutions and culture are products of history. There is no harm in granting that all these factors are conditions of discourse. It just must not be forgotten that, as such, they are conditions of true as well as false discourses. Therefore, none can play the role of an epistemological principle determining what makes knowledge valid rather than invalid. Similarly, the non-derivative features of subjectivity do not entail solipsism because they are no more foundations of knowledge than are any other factors. Hegel is well aware of this, and we would do well to follow him in regarding intersubjectivity for the limited reality it is, instead of fetishizing it as a social divinity.

The Birth of Spirit for Hegel out of the Travesty of Medicine

Eric von der Luft

Spirit (*Geist*), although it always underlies and informs Hegel's dialectic, is not present as such in the dialectic *ab initio*, as are, for example, logic, being, and indeterminacy. Rather, spirit emerges at a certain point— a fairly advanced point—within the dialectic, and only then is it able to dominate the dialectic and be the goal of further development. We can learn much about the character and function of spirit in Hegel's philosophy by examining the immediate transition to this certain dialectical point.

It is no accident that Hegel's first sustained discussion of spirit in the *Phenomenology*, outside of the preface, occurs in the context of the oft-slighted section on phrenology.[1] The prevailing or traditional view is that this section is just a digression from the mainstream of argument, at best a concession to the topical concerns of 1806, and at worst completely out of place in a systematic philosophical work. This view finds support in the generally low opinion in which Hegel's whole philosophy of nature has usually been held, an opinion which, until recently challenged,[2] had always taught the readers of the *Encyclopædia* to read only Parts One and Three, and the readers of the *Phenomenology* to skip directly from stoicism, skepticism, and the unhappy consciousness to the actualization of rational self-consciousness. What this opinion fails to notice is that these moments are essentially transitional and therefore indispensable to a full understanding of the unified dialectical progress of both the *Encyclopædia* and the *Phenomenology*. The advent of spirit in the *Encyclopædia* cannot be understood properly unless seen as a logical "rebirth" or growth out of natural life (*Naturleben*)[3]—for spirit does not spring full-blown from the culmination of logic alone, but must also be a product of nature. Similarly, in the *Phenomenology*, the actualization of rational self-consciousness—and thus of spirit—cannot be understood properly without an appreciation of observing reason and all that this reason entails, for the self-consciousness which emerged from the dialectic of the self-certain I and its other cannot become rational—or spiritual—until it has immersed itself in empirical studies and learned the limitations of empirical methods. Let us, therefore, closely examine the transition to spirit in each of these two works, first in the *Phenomenology*.

Having penultimately failed to find itself in the rather simple world of itself and its objects, consciousness proceeds (*Phän.*, pp. 133–150; *Phen.*, pp. 104–119) to the world of more than one consciousness, i.e., the world of self-consciousness, the social world. Not satisfied by the results of the dialectic which creates masters and slaves within the social world, the passionate desire (*Begierde* or $\check{\epsilon}\varrho\omega\varsigma$) of self-consciousness forces self-consciousness to retreat, through stoicism, skepticism, and unhappy religion (*Phän.*, pp. 151–171; *Phen.*, pp. 119–138), from the social world into the refuge which it believes is afforded by reason (*Phän.*, pp. 175–182; *Phen.*, pp. 139–145). Reason is characteristically private and individual, not social, insofar as it reduces everything outside of the individual, including other individuals, to categories. As it employs these categories in its development, its first, and most extreme, station is Fichtean idealism, which proceeds through Berkeleyan and Kantian idealism to the realization that reason *qua* idealism cannot either comprehend or be all reality for the I because it stands against the I. Idealism fails because it wishes to reduce all perception and understanding to a single perfected or "ideal" subjectivity. But because the I is, for the time being, outside of the reality which can be grasped by reason, reason cannot be all reality. Self-consciousness has not yet found or accounted for itself. This situation, where self-consciousness realizes that reason has not yet brought it to find either itself or its world (§239; *Phän.*, pp. 181–182; *Phen.*, p. 145), is very much akin to the situation described by Wittgenstein in the *Tractatus*, 5.632: "*Das Subjekt gehört nicht zur Welt, sondern es ist eine Grenze der Welt*"—"The subject does not belong to the world, but is a limit of the world."

The failure of reason *qua* idealism leads self-consciousness to reject not reason *in toto*, but only idealism. It had begun with raw empiricism, has travelled through decidedly non-empiricist phases, but now it returns to empiricism (*Phän.*, pp. 183–254; *Phen.*, pp. 145–210), not its original, pre-rational empiricism of sense-certainty, etc., but a sophisticated, systematic, exploring empiricism. Since it has failed to grasp itself from within, through reason alone, it will now try from without (or as if from without) by observing itself as an element of nature as if it were just a thing. Hegel's model for this investigative science is a unified biology in which the actual living organism has primacy.

Whereas matter and its shapes are, in their essential nature, determinate (or determinable), the organism is, in its essential nature, indeterminate. The flaw which will eventually lead to the failure of observing reason (*beobachtende Vernunft*) is therefore apparent early: the observing subject, trying to observe and discover itself, is of an essential nature different from that which is observed. The observing subject looking at itself is not looking at a subject, but at an object, and thus in fact is not really looking at itself. The dialectical idealism which had grown out of the failure of the three traditional idealisms now resolves itself into the dialectic of the "inner" and the "outer," played out on the empirical field of *Naturwissenschaft*.

Speaking just of natural science, not of philosophy, there is reductionist science and there is hierarchic science. (Of course, much subcategorizing is possible within these two broad categories, as is some degree of overlapping between them, but, at least for the heuristic purposes of this paper, the following oversimplified presentation of them is permissible and should suffice.) Reductionist science, championed by, for example, B. F. Skinner,[4] holds that all observable phenomena can be exhaustively explained in terms of a continuous chain of cause/effect relations grounded in a perfected physics.[5] Hierarchic science, championed by, for example, Paul A. Weiss,[6] holds instead that observable phenomena exhibit quite distinct levels of organization, and thus can only be studied and explained *each on its own specific level* in terms of cause/effect relationships.[7]

On the view of reductionist science, the same set of laws governs molecules, organelles, cells, organs, and organisms; but on the view of hierarchic science, each of these levels works only under its own proper set of laws.[8] Again on the reductionist view, the most complex organic phenomena, including life itself, are exhaustively describable in terms of the most basic physical phenomena, i.e., in terms of the nature and behavior of atoms and even subatomic particles; but on the hierarchic view, although the various levels certainly influence and "help" each other, they do not dictate the actions of the next level, either upward or downward. On the reductionist view, the complete explanation of the molecule necessarily includes within it the explanation of all of which that molecule is a part, the organelle, the cell, etc.; but on the hierarchic view, the complete explanation of the molecule only shows forth the preconditions under which the organelle may come into being and do its work, and in no way does the molecule necessitate the organelle. On the reductionist view, the explanation of the molecule becomes an integral part of the explanation of the organelle; but on the hierarchic view, the explanation of the organelle is completely unified on its own level, and the explanation of the molecule becomes the explanation for the infrastructure of the organelle, just as the explanation of the organelle becomes the explanation of the infrastructure of the cell, and so on.

Reductionist science has, and can have, no possible conception of "infrastructure," the myriad of tiny physical events which necessarily accompany any more complex originative action, e.g., the neural impulses of which I am strictly unconscious but must perforce take place whenever I type a sentence. I am not thinking of how to move my muscles to hit the keys—I am thinking about the content of the sentence—but the movement of the muscles occurs within the more complex context of the thought about this sentence. Reductionist science is fully and irretrievably materialistic, and, unless we admit that the smallest sub-atomic particles "think," it can never account for the most complex observable phenomena, such as the results of conscious thought. Hierarchic science, on the other hand, because it divides observable phenomena into carefully categorized levels of organization, allows new and higher degrees of complexity on every successive level, and thus can account for the introduction of life, originative action, thought, etc., each on its own proper level.[9] Its greatest single advance over reductionist science is that it does not see the more basic levels as causally connected to the more complex levels, but instead sees these basic phenomena just as the necessary, but not sufficient, conditions for the existence of the higher levels.[10] Some, Edward Pols for example, have

argued that hierarchic science can account for the origin of human consciousness, i.e., by showing that the fact of human consciousness makes
sense in the light of the latest biological data.[11]

The biologist who is familiar with distinct, though intimately related,
levels of organization within a single organism is *eo ipso* familiar with a concept directly analogous to Hegel's most basic insight. Indeed, the Hegelian
system is one of the chief speculative roots of modern biological hierarchy
theory. In both hierarchic biology and the Hegelian dialectic alike, each
higher, more complex (and in many cases, more nearly self-determining)
level of organization is the principle which unifies the next lower, more basic
level. Each higher level prevents each lower level from being merely episodic
and meaningless. In scientific language, molecules are unified by the organelle, organelles are unified by the cell, cells by the organ, and organs by
the organism; translated into Hegelian language, molecules are *aufgehoben*
in the organelle, organelles are *aufgehoben* in the cell, etc. For both the
hierarchic biologist and the Hegelian philosopher, the ultimate level which
unifies and gives meaning to the whole human organism is the level of conscious individuality, the rational level which alone can pronounce the word
"I." Thus, we may say that the organism is unified by—or *aufgehoben*
in—the individual.

At the phase of observing reason, the individual, or spirit proper, has
not yet developed. The current dialectical function of reason is to prepare
the way for spirit, to create a situation in which "reason is spirit when its
certainty of being all reality has been raised to truth, and it is conscious of
itself as its own world, and of the world as itself" (*Phän.*, p. 313; *Phen.*,
p. 263). Before this development can be achieved, the sharp dualism of
the indeterminate "inner" and the determinate "outer" which is inherent
in scientific observation must be fully explored, explained, and overcome.
Obviously, spirit cannot be its own world, nor its own world be it, if there
actually exist two worlds, the conscious world of the observer and the
unconscious world of the observed. The purpose, then, of this section of
the *Phenomenology*, on the philosophy of natural science, is, in the larger
context of the book, exactly to beat this dualism to death. Hegel's weapon
for this purpose is the *reductio ad absurdum*. Phrenology is the final
absurdity which allows Hegel to lay this dualism to rest, with a definitive
"hier liegt nur eine bloße Vorstellung" — "Here lies nothing but a mental

image"—on its tombstone.[12]

When the concept (*Begriff*) sinks to the level of mental imagery (*Vorstellung*), observation sees the "outer" as the expression of the "inner." In this formula, first occurring in §262 (*Phän.*, p. 199; *Phen.*, p. 160) and often repeated by Hegel, the "outer" and the "inner" can be interpreted either as two ontologically distinct entities, mysteriously thrown together, as in the case of Ryle's famous caricature of Descartes' "ghost in the machine"—or as limiting concepts, as opposite poles of an essentially unified organic continuum, poles which are only distinct when that which connects them is unjustifiably ignored. The most primitive natural science chooses the former; Hegel chooses the latter, and the dialectic of this section moves through the former toward an appreciation of this latter position. Hegel is no reductionist, either on the materialistic or the spiritualistic side; he is, if anything, a "unicist," not a crass monist, but a syncretist with ultimate unity as his goal. Just as St. Augustine in Book Two of *De Trinitate* uses the metaphor of one substance in different forms—now ice, now water, now ice again—to explain the substantial unity in the persons of the Trinity, so Hegel might explain the substantial unity of the "inner" and the "outer." His entire philosophy of natural science, and especially the section on phrenology, may safely be regarded as the progressive clarification of the proposition "*daß das Äussere der Ausdruck des Innern ist*"—"*that the outer is the expression of the inner*" (*Phän.*, p. 199, Hegel's emphasis; cf. *Phen.*, p. 160).

The "inner" is essentially process, or the origination of process, while the "outer" is essentially the completion of process. The "inner" is, like spirit later, what it *does*, while the "outer," the dead thing, is simply what it *is*. We cannot fix or grasp the concept of "process" in an inert, determinate, observable thing; and yet we know that there is process because, among other things, observation itself is a species of process (cf. *Phän.*, pp. 205–206; *Phen.*, p. 166). Over against the definition of the "inner" as "process" or as "what it does," the "outer" is defined as "the *structured shape* (*Gestaltung*) in general, the system of life articulating itself in the *element* of being, and at the same time essentially the being *for an other* of the organism—objective being in its *being-for-self* (*Fürsichsein*)" (*Phän.*, p. 211, Hegel's italics; *Phen.*, p. 170). The "outer," therefore, though indeed a thing, is not its own thing, but just an extension of the "inner."

Against the particularity of the "outer," the "inner" is purely and simply universal (*Phän.*, pp. 211–212; *Phen.*, pp. 170–171). Both the "inner" and the "outer" then are but abstractions of the organic whole being, which, after all, is the unity with which Hegel is primarily concerned. The main point of §§286–297 (*Phän.*, pp. 212–221; *Phen.*, pp. 171–180) is that the tension of "inner" versus "outer" is only unsuccessfully referred to the inorganic or determinate realm which natural science may observe, but that it can be referred somewhat more successfully to life, freedom, or the organism *qua* unity. However, since the former reference is too particular, and since the latter is too universal, neither a reference to specific data nor a reference to general life principles is adequate to account for the complexities of the relationship between the indeterminate universal "inner" and the determinate particular "outer." A further excursion into each side is necessary before the dualism can finally be overcome.

The first excursion (§§298–308; *Phän.*, pp. 221–227; *Phen.*, pp. 180–185) concerns psychological observation, in which the observing subject turns upon itself, attempting to approach itself even nearer, and thereby to achieve the simple synthetic unity of self-reflection, but falling short, achieving only a codification of the laws of thought. Reason is left with the idea that it must more clearly and completely characterize its individuality.

The second excursion (§§309–346; *Phän.*, pp. 227–254; *Phen.*, pp. 185–210) returns to the realm of determinate actuality in order to seek, this time more desperately, some means to fix or "determine" the nature of the individual. Hegel begins this section by harking back to conclusions he had reached in §254 (*Phän.*, pp. 193ff.; *Phen.*, pp. 154ff), namely, that "the individual is in and for itself: it is *for itself*, or is a free doing (*freies Tun*); but it is also *in itself*, or it has a *primeval* (*ursprünglich*) determinate being of its own—a determinacy which, according to the concept, is that which psychology sought to find outside of the individual" (*Phän.*, p. 227, Hegel's emphasis; cf. *Phen.*, p. 185). The thesis of natural science at this stage is that if the "inner" is what it does, and if the "outer" is the expression of the "inner," then the observation of the "outer" in itself will reveal the "inner." According to this thesis, with regard to the whole individual, "*jede Seite seines Gegensatzes ist selbst dies Ganze*" — "each aspect of the opposition is in itself the whole" (*Phän.*, p. 228; cf. *Phen.*, p. 186). The trouble with such sciences as physiognomy and phrenology is that they overlook the fact that the "outer" really has two aspects: (1) its aspect as the expression of the "inner," in which it is "living"; and (2) its aspect as a mere thing, in which it is "dead." The "outer" can express the action of the "inner" only while the "inner" is actually acting—after the act is complete the "outer" expresses nothing at all. In the case of physiognomy, the so-called "expression" of the "inner" by the "outer" is conditioned by culture, by discretion, and even by the deliberate concealing motions of the "inner" itself. We each, of course, have the power to control the expression of our own "inners" by our own "outers," and thus have the power, by willful *fiat*, insofar as we may be talented "actors," to become fully inscrutable.

Franz Josef Gall (1758–1828), the founder of phrenology, held that the skull forms itself as a reflection of the greater or lesser development of certain areas and functions of the brain. In other words, something less complex becomes the signifier of something more complex. But how could anything fully express something more complex than it itself? Shakespeare could express a clown, but could a clown express Shakespeare? The brain could express the skull (as, indeed, it was an intelligent creature who drew the phrenological map), but could the skull express the brain—and further, could even the brain express the whole individual? Hegel often indicates (e.g., *Phän.*, pp. 236, 249, etc.; *Phen.*, pp. 193, 205) that those who have been accused by the phrenologist of having characters which are discoverable in their skulls have the right to repay their accuser violently for the insulting insinuation that they are so utterly simple that their most complex human traits and emotions are reducible to a mere bone.

Gall's most fundamental error was to assume that the brain, i.e., in his view, a person's character, and the skull, i.e., the outward expression of that character, were connected in a strictly causal way. True to reductionist science, he sought to explain complex phenomena exhaustively in terms of simpler phenomena. Needless to say, his theory did not permit the purely originative expression of character, or of a spontaneous new development of character, but held instead that future outbursts of character were determined by the manifest expressions of past outbursts. The skull, therefore, influenced the brain as much as the brain influenced the skull. Everything was accounted for except human freedom.

All materialism, from Anaxagoras through Gall to Skinner, has insulted human dignity by denying the real existence of individual freedom and consciousness, by claiming to be able to provide full accounts of these "fantasies" in terms of merely physical events. The insult is especially annoying since there is clear scientific evidence to support the contention that these very complex states of life and biological organization actually do exist. I am not speaking of the "occult" or of any airy spook. I am only speaking of the incontrovertible fact that each of us can, at any time we wish, immediately think or pronounce the word "I" with meaning, and that we can just as immediately know that meaning to be true.

In the phrenology section Hegel is, above all, combating a grotesque reduction of the "inner" to the "outer." He realizes, as Gall apparently did not, that all such reductionism presupposes a dualism of the observer and the observed, of the indeterminate and the determinate, a dualism which, in psychology and biology, manifests itself, pictorially speaking, as "inner" and "outer."[13] It is this dualism which must be *aufgehoben* as a precondition for the advent of spirit.

The discussion of spirit which pervades the rest of the book officially begins in §327, where Hegel defines it as "not abstractly simple, but a system of movements (*ein System von Bewegungen*) in which it differentiates itself into phases" (*Phän.*, p. 240; cf. *Phen.*, p. 197). Are we to believe that this connection of phrenology with spirit is just an accident? Or are we to believe instead that Hegel means, in the most illustrative way possible, to show that spirit is certainly not akin to a one-sided entity like the Cartesian *res cogitans*, but rather is the whole unity of the individual, working in the world through organs which, in turn, are surrounded by a dead outer shell—the *caput mortuum* of spirit (*Phän.*, p. 241; *Phen.*, p. 198)? Neither the "inner" nor the "outer" is spirit; but spirit involves them both, unifies them, and makes them poles of a continuum of life rather than mutually exclusive entities. We cannot learn about either by studying just the other, but only by studying the whole being while remembering the basic polar character of the "inner" and the "outer" with respect to the whole.

Holism, whereby the various higher forms of biological unity and organization are studied as emergent or teleologically conditioned developments out of the lower forms of organization, was a theory summarily embraced by Hegel, though it remained unnamed for a century after him.[14] All of Hegel's systematic transitions represent new emergences, new, yet in many ways "predictable" developments in the progressive movement of spirit, which arise in response to dead ends in previous paths of development. Both Hegel and twentieth century holism agree that growth always results in new unities, new types of unity, and new degrees and complexities of unity. Specific developments cannot be predicted in their particulars—indeed, such predictability would belong to materialism—but growth is predictable in the sense that the dialectic of holism demands that some higher, more adequate, more fully mediated, better organized structure will always be produced.

Hegel, the first modern holist, involved not only biology in his quest for unity, but all knowledge. In this greater schema, biology is only an aspect of natural science, which in turn is only an aspect of a more complete knowledge. But each and every aspect of knowledge, and therefore of spirit, is interrelated and necessary to the whole. Nothing can or should be studied *in vacuo*—this is the epistemological conclusion of the *Phenomenology*. Realizing this, Hegel built his system as a continuous philosophical history of thought. A "philosophical history" is one which avoids and outmaneuvers tendencies toward episodic or parochial views of concepts, and which tries instead to set a broader conceptual context for every aspect of knowledge. The philosophical history of science, then, is the history of science which urges science to be holistic, to consider the whole along with the part (without committing the fallacy of composition), to see unity rather than division, and to use the knowledge of the part only as a means toward understanding (and healing) the whole. In this light we consider phrenology.

Just as the phrenological skull is the *caput mortuum* of the progress of the embryonic spirit, so phrenology itself is the *caput mortuum* of the progress to that point of both natural and philosophical science. It is important to recall that in its own time phrenology was regarded as a species and branch of *medicine*, rather than of psychology, biology, or some other science. Hegel, as we clearly see in the *Encyclopædia*, regarded medicine as the highest form of natural science, insofar as its concern is to preserve and protect the life and health, i.e., the greatest immediate value, of the highest form of the animal, which is the highest form of the organism, which is the highest phase of nature. Hegel would, therefore, quickly regard the debâcle or antinomy of medicine as the effective end of all natural science, and thus as the herald of the transition to a new phase. The self-consciousness which, in the *Phenomenology*, had been led to seek itself in the realm of observing reason now finds that the empirical method has reached its logical terminus, and this self-consciousness thus goes over to the phase of the actualization of rational self-consciousness, the direct antecedent of the emergence of spirit as a systematic vital force. Unless it had first passed through the stage of phrenology, this self-consciousness would not have been able to achieve any deep appreciation of the essentially holistic character of spirit, and thus would not have been able to become either rational self-consciousness or spirit. In the *Encyclopædia* the transition is *directly* from the end of medicine to the growth of spirit.

The place of nature in the *Encyclopædia*, as the dialectical midpoint between logic and spirit, and the place of medicine, as the culmination of this investigation of nature, just at the point of the important transition of the human being from a mere animal to a spiritual being (*geistiges Wesen*), together indicate that for Hegel medicine plays a special role in the development of spirit. The human body is, after all, the highest development of physical nature, and the healthy human body is higher still. The completeness, fullness, or "ripeness" of physical nature must occur before this nature can go over into the higher form characterized by spirit. Only medicine can ensure this completeness. Yet, medicine itself is always foiled by that same physical nature which it alone comprehends: the organism dies.[15] Hence, the transition to spirit and the philosophy of spirit may be instigated by a quixotic search for eternal life—but I would not want to push this point too far,[16] even though the *Zusatz* to §376 of the *Encyclopædia* asserts that "superseding this death of nature, *proceeding* from this dead husk, there rises the finer nature of *spirit*" (*Nature*, III, 211, Hegel's emphasis).

Yet death is indeed the absolute terminus of nature, both speculatively and actually. The immediate awareness of death, or the dread of death, rather than death itself, could therefore be that which for Hegel propels the human being from existing as a merely natural being towards existing on a higher plane as a spiritual being. According to Hegel himself in §376, the natural death of an organism is the demise of only one side of the whole being, i.e., the abstract side, while the other side, i.e., the concrete side, emerges as the idea of life. This interpretation harmonizes well with what Hegel has said specifically about phrenology in the *Phenomenology*, where the dead thing, the *caput mortuum* of life, is seen as the absurd or abstract terminus from which nothing but a higher, more adequate form of self-conscious life could arise. In any case, whether we choose to regard the death of which Hegel speaks in §376 of the *Encyclopædia* either as real physical death or as just the deep consciousness of death, Hegel still claims that through death nature goes over into its truth, namely, the subjectivity of the concept. The concept (*Begriff*) now at this stage, through the tough experience of death, is itself, in its objective form, its own reality. The conceptual unity of this subjectivity of the individual with the bleak objectivity of the death of the individual creates a new form of existence (*Dasein*) for the concept, namely, the concrete universal which Hegel explicitly calls spirit (*Enz.*, p. 309; *Nature*, III, 210–211).

Hegel's conclusions regarding medicine and phrenology may be extended to apply in general to problems of the physical versus the spiritual (*geistig*). The brain has a function, and the skull has a function, but they are not the same function; different laws govern each. Similarly, "I" myself have a function, and my body has a function, but "I" and my body are not the same thing and do not have the same function; different laws govern each. The laws which govern the physical body are subsumed under the laws which govern the individual self, but not vice versa. The hierarchic structure of the human organism is primally evident here, at this complex level of the connection between originative action and the physical conditions which limit this action. Hegel, especially in his philosophy of nature, has introduced hierarchic conceptions of physical or material organization in order to show the logical development from these levels into spiritual organization, with which he is mainly concerned. His fight against materialism has borne fruit in our scientifically oriented age. He knew that each level is a system in its own right, that each system must slowly grow into the next, that the body is a system which is an aspect of the person but is not equivalent to the person, and that the physician can do no more than to care for the body while the patient is doing the real work to get well. Above all, he knew that if the order of systems were disregarded, then all knowledge would collapse for lack of a sound basis. New types of natural science can only proceed beyond mere empiricism if they become integrated rather than episodic, grounded in logic and in accurate observational data, and acutely aware of both the findings and the limitations of earlier forms of systematic science. False sciences which are able to achieve temporary prominence will be undercut eventually both by the demands of spirit and by the the unrelenting necessity of Hegel's dialectic, which claims that accidental developments cannot survive because they have not properly "grown" into their place:

> On the animal side the human configuration *Gestalt* is the highest form in which spirit appears. But on the spiritual side this configuration is only the *first* appearance of spirit, and *language* is at once spirit's more nearly perfect expression. This configuration is indeed the existence closest to spirit, but at the same time, in its physiognomic and pathognomic determinacy, it is something *accidental* for spirit. To have wanted to raise physiognomy, and moreover, cranioscopy, to the status of *systematic sciences* (*Wissenschaften*) was one of the most inane ideas, even more inane than the theory of *signatura rerum*, according to which the healing power of plants was supposedly able to be discerned from their shape (*Gestalt*).[17]

If a philosopher ever bothers to judge an issue of current popular interest, such as phrenology, he usually does so in a forum somewhat less esoteric than one of his technical, professional treatises. Surely nobody understood better than Hegel that the acceptance of phrenology was just a passing phase of world history; and yet, he considered it a serious enough threat against *Wissenschaft* to assail it, not only in the *Phenomenology* and the *Encyclopædia*, but also in the posthumously published *Lectures on Aesthetics*. Each of these three attacks drives home one central point: if we are doomed to go to Calvary, then let us not linger there any longer than necessary, but let us proceed on toward the renewal of life. Hegel was never above punning, nor, as in the *Aesthetics*, was he always above personal abuse:

> For us physiognomy can only be of importance in that pathognomy is just concerned with how determinate feelings and passions occur corporeally in certain organs. Thus it is said, for example, that anger is seated in the bile (*Galle*), and courage in the blood. This, incidentally, is a patently false saying. For even if the activity of particular organs matches particular passions, then indeed anger is not *seated* in the bile, but rather, to the extent

that anger becomes corporeal, it is principally the bile
in which the appearance of the efficacy of anger takes
place .... Every organ must, in this respect, generally
be considered from two points of view, from the merely
physical, and from the side of the expression of the spiritual. To be sure, we may not proceed in this as does
Gall, who makes spirit into a mere Calvary, a place of the
skull.[18]

Notes

1. G. W. F. Hegel, *Phänomenologie des Geistes*, 6th ed. (Hamburg:
Felix Meiner, 1952), pp. 237–254 [hereafter cited as *"Phän."*]. G. W. F.
Hegel, *Phenomenology of Spirit*, trans. by A. V. Miller (Oxford: Clarendon
Press, 1977), pp. 195–210 [hereafter cited as *"Phen."*]. Where helpful, the
paragraph number begins the citation, all of which are in parentheses in the
text. All translations are mine, but references to English versions of this
and other works are given to facilitate whatever comparisons the reader may
wish to make. I am grateful to both Quentin Lauer and George L. Kline for
their good suggestions to improve my translations.

2. The movement toward a re-evaluation of Hegel's philosophy of nature
is being led by Errol E. Harris, and involves many, such as George R. Lucas,
who see Hegel from a Whiteheadian perspective. Cf. Harris, "The Philosophy of Nature in Hegel's System," *The Review of Metaphysics* 3 (1949):
213–228; "Hegel and the Natural Sciences," *Beyond Epistemology: New
Studies in Hegel's Philosophy*, ed. by F. G. Weiss (Hague: Nijhoff, 1974),
pp. 129–153; "The *Naturphilosophie* Updated," *The Owl of Minerva* 10,2
(Dec. 1978): 2–7; and Lucas, *Two Views of Freedom in Process Thought:
A Study of Hegel and Whitehead* (Missoula, Mont.: Scholars Press, 1979).
Although several cogent attempts have been made—e.g., Lawrence S. Stepelevich, "The Hegelian Conception of Space," *Nature and System* 1 (1979):
111–126—to show the connections between the principles of Hegel's logic
and his philosophy of nature, there still exists, in general, a great need to
discover and to explain clearly whatever links Hegel may have established
between his philosophy of nature and his philosophy of spirit.

3. On the necessity of spirit emerging from the merely natural life of
spirit, Hegel writes in his Foreword to Hermann F. W. Hinrichs' *Die Religion
im inneren Verhältnisse zur Wissenschaft* (Heidelberg: Groos, 1822; reprint,
Brussels: Culture et Civilisation, 1970), on p. *iii*, that spirit must be free, i.e.,

must be reborn out of natural life into spiritual wholeness: *"...eben weil es der freie Geist, nicht ein Naturleben ist, was erzeugt werden soll, weil der freie Geist nur als ein Weidergeborner ist,"* and again, on p. *xviii*, after quoting I Cor. 2:14 to show that the natural human being (*der natürliche Mensch*) is not able either to detect or to comprehend what pertains to spirit: *"...und der Geist ist dies ...nicht ein Naturleben, sondern ein Weidergeborner zu sein."*

4. Especially in *Beyond Freedom and Dignity* (New York: Knopf, 1971).

5. With respect to the alleged "physics envy" of biology and other life sciences, see J. E. Cohen, "Mathematics as Metaphor," *Science* 172 (1971): 674–675, cited by T. F. H. Allen and Thomas B. Starr on pp. 65 and 255 of *Hierarchy: Perspectives for Ecological Complexity* (Chicago & London: University of Chicago Press, 1982). I am grateful to Willem de Vries and others at the lunch table at Russell Sage College on October 5, 1984, for pointing me in the direction of Allen and Starr.

6. Especially in "The Living System: Determinism Stratified," in *Beyond Reductionism: New Perspectives in the Life Sciences*, ed. by Arthur Koestler and J. R. Smythies (London: Hutchinson, 1969), pp. 3–55.

7. Allen and Starr, in their glossary (pp. 269–70, 276), define reductionism as "a descriptive and investigative strategy which gives account of phenomena in terms of a series of isolated parts, coupled together by direct causal linkages. Ambiguity in relationships between parts is met with further sub-division until the ambiguity disappears." They define holism (which they identify with hierarchy theory) as "a descriptive and investigative strategy which seeks to find the smallest number of explanatory principles by paying careful attention to the emergent properties of the whole as opposed to the behaviors of the isolated parts chosen by the observer in a reductionist strategy. Both holism and reductionism seek to explain emergent behavior by invoking a lower level of organization." They define the holon (the basic conceptual unit of holism) as "the representation of an entity as a two-way window through which the environment influences the parts, through which the parts communicate as a unit to the rest of the universe. Holons have characteristic rates for their behavior, and this places particular holons at certain levels in a hierarchy of holons. What a holon shall contain is determined by the observer." After Allen and Starr take note of the various advantages and disadvantages of each of these two strategies, as epitomized in their assertion (p. 130) that "reductionism sacrifices philosophical integrity in order to obtain those critical data that holism might miss," they pronounce their verdict (p. 130): "clearly a dual reductionist-holist strategy is optimal."

8. Two separate collections of papers—*Hierarchical Structures: Pro-*

ceeding of the Symposium held November 18–19, 1968 at Douglas Advanced Research Laboratories, Huntington Beach, California, ed. by Lancelot Law Whyte, Albert G. Wilson, and Donna Wilson (New York: American Elsevier, 1969); and *Hierarchy Theory: The Challenge of Complex Systems*, ed by Howard H. Pattee (New York: Braziller, 1973)—each include several papers which discuss the types of laws and interactions which affect molecules and organisms. Generally the problem breaks down into accounting for distinctions between structure and function, so that at least two sorts of hierarchies may be posited, structural and functional. For definitions, descriptions, and distinctions, see especially the papers of Lancelot Law Whyte (pp. 3–16), Mario Bunge (pp. 17–28), Robert Rosen (pp. 52–53), Marjorie Grene (pp. 56–58), Howard Pattee (pp. 161–177), and Ronald G. Jones (pp. 284–285) in the former collection; and those of Herbert A. Simon (pp. 1–27), Clifford Grobstein (pp. 29–47), and H. H. Pattee (pp. 71–108) in the latter.

9. Michael Polanyi makes a similar point in several locations. For example, in *Personal Knowledge: Towards a Post-Critical Philosophy* (Chicago: University of Chicago Press, 1958), on pp. 382ff, he argues "that the observed evolution of human consciousness plainly exemplified . . . active emergence." But this is primarily an epistemological claim, not an ontological one, for on pp. 393–394 he writes "that, strictly speaking, it is not the emerged higher form of being, but our knowledge of it, that is unspecifiable in terms of its lower level particulars. We cannot speak of emergence, therefore, except in conjunction with a corresponding progression from a lower to a higher *conceptual* level. And we realize then that conceptual progression may not always be existential, but that it becomes so by degrees" (Polanyi's emphasis). See also his two essays reprinted in *Knowing and Being*, ed. by Marjorie Grene (Chicago: University of Chicago Press, 1969), pp. 211–224, 225–239: "The Structure of Consciousness," *Brain* 88 (1965): 799–810; and "Life's Irreducible Structure," *Science* 160 (1968): 1308–1312. I am grateful to Harry and Michael Prosch for telling me about *Knowing and Being*.

10. Of course, given the many types of hierarchy theory, some of which being quite distinct from the oversimplified version I have sketched here, there are a number of vigorous debates within the community of hierarchic scientists, such as—and I am grateful to Howard P. Kainz for bringing this to my attention—the debate, told in Evelyn Fox Keller's "Feminism, Science, and Democracy" (*democracy* 3, 2 [Spring 1983]: 50–58), of Barbara McClintock's interactionist hierarchy theory, in which the DNA's coded message is influenced by the cell's environment, versus the formerly dominant theory of a linear hierarchy in which the DNA is considered to be a "master molecule" which autonomously determines cellular development. But this and other ongoing debates, however divisive they may be, are yet only "in-

house" debates among hierarchists, who are still in general united with their attendant philosophers against the behaviorism of Skinner, the identity theory of J. J. C. Smart, the materialism of D. M. Armstrong, the reductionism of Herbert Feigl, the "embodiment of mind" philosophy of Warren S. McCulloch, or the pure physicalism of those who would, as Edward Pols writes in *Meditation on a Prisoner: Towards Understanding Action and Mind* ([Carbondale: Southern Illinois University Press, 1975] p. 23), "claim that, whatever experiments originally entered into the discovery of a law of biology, the law could have been deduced without experiment if we had had the laws of a perfected physics available to us."

11. Pols' *Meditation on a Prisoner* is an eloquent systematic exposition of biological hierarchy theory. In arguments influenced by Plato, Hegel, Whitehead, Heidegger, and Bergson, he does thorough justice to philosophy and empirical science alike in a respectful attempt to reconcile the two. His purpose is not to define consciousness, will, or originative action as philosophical terms to set over against the data of observed behavior, but instead to define a metaphysical *structure*, in accord with empirical science, into which consciousness, will, and originative action may logically fit, be seen to make sense, and to be explained without being compromised. Cf. especially pp. 38–68. Cf. also his *The Acts of our Being: A Reflection on Agency and Responsibility* (Amherst: University of Massachusetts Press, 1982).

12. Although much has been written about phrenology, precious little has been written about Hegel's relation to phrenology. But notably, Alasdair MacIntyre's "Hegel on Faces and Skulls" in his *Hegel: A Collection of Critical Essays* (Garden City, N.Y.: Anchor Books, 1972) considers Hegel's critiques of physiognomy and phrenology, not with regard to the rest of the *Phenomenology*, but with regard to comparable twentieth century issues in psychology; and pp. 132–136 of George Lanteri-Laura's *Histoire de la phrenologie: L'homme et son cerveau selon F. J. Gall* (Paris: Presses Universitaires de France, 1970) presents a more balanced appraisal, but still concludes that Dr. Gall is *"une ultime figure de la conscience malheureuse"* because phrenology represents *"ce qui advient à la conscience de soi quand elle se cherche un être du type des realités naturelles anatomiques"* (p. 136). It may be a bit dramatic to identify the founder of phrenology with the consciousness which stands *"erwartend und drängend um die Geburtsstätte des als Selbstbewußtsein werdenden Geistes"* (*Phän.*, p. 525; *Phen.*, p. 456); although, indeed, *"das Grab seines Lebens"* (*Phän.*, p. 164; *Phen.*, p. 132) which confronts consciousness in the Crusades may also confront it at the stage of phrenological inquiry.

13. Cf. MacIntyre, p. 266, who notices that most non-medical contemporary arguments against Gall, e.g., those of Jeffrey and Brougham, were based on a very naïve, simplistic form of the Cartesian or Christian dualism.

Hegel was the first to argue against Gall using another sort of dualism, a penultimate dualism which led to the systematic hierarchic unity of body and spirit.

14. The term is generally admitted to have been invented by Jan Christiaan Smuts in *Holism and Evolution* (1926).

15. G. W. F. Hegel, *Enzyklopädie der philosophischen Wissenschaften im Grundrisse* (1830), 7th ed. (Hamburg: Felix Meiner, 1969), §§375–376 [hereafter cited as "*Enz.*"]. G. W. F. Hegel, *Philosophy of Nature*, 3 vols., ed. and trans. by M. J. Petry (London: George Allen & Unwin; New York: Humanities, 1970), III, 209–213 [hereafter cited as "*Nature*"].

16. For a paradigm of just how far the idea of personal immortality can be legitimately pushed with Hegel, cf. A. V. Miller, "Absolute Knowing and the Destiny of the Individual," *The Owl of Minerva*, 15, 1 (Fall 1983): 45–50.

17. *Enz.*, §411, Hegel's emphasis. Cf. G. W. F. Hegel, *Philosophy of Subjective Spirit*, 3 vols., ed. and trans. by M. J. Petry (Dordrecht, Germany & Boston, Mass.: D. Reidel, 1978), II, pp. 410–411, and note, pp. 627–628.

18. G. W. F. Hegel, *Vorlesungen über die Ästhetik* (Berlin: Duncker und Humblot, 1835–37), II, pp. 372–373, Hegel's emphasis. Cf. similar passages in *Phän.*, pp. 239, 564; *Phen.*, pp. 196, 493.

Commentary on "The Birth of Spirit for Hegel
out of the Travesty of Medicine"

Quentin Lauer

More than one commentator has puzzled over the amount of space Hegel allots, in the *Phenomenology of Spirit*, to the pseudo-sciences of physiognomy and (particularly) phrenology, despite the mileage these peculiar forms of empirical observation were getting in Hegel's day. It is clear that Hegel considers these branches—of "medicine," no less—as spurious "sciences," and it is clear to us today that Hegel was right. Why, then, does he waste so much time on them? It is not without significance that they do not show their ugly heads (no pun intended) in the abbreviated version of "Phenomenology" contained in the *Encyclopædia*. On the other hand, Jakob Loewenberg has argued quite plausibly that, if these "sciences" had not existed, Hegel would have had to invent them, in order to render the dialectical passage from mere nature to free spirit complete. Physiognomy and phrenology represent, so to speak, the last ditch stand of empirical observation to reduce *all* knowledge worthy of the name to empirical knowledge. It is not, then, an otiose digression.

Eric von der Luft has seen this quite clearly and has argued most cogently, particularly in regard to phrenology, that Hegel was quite justified in employing a prolonged—and, in fact, rather boring—*reductio ad absurdum* in order to lay to rest once and for all reductionist "science" of the human, which sees in the emergence of spirit—if indeed it sees spirit as a reality at all—no more than a complex concatenation of natural causes and effects. The fact that B. F. Skinner has raised pseudo-science from the dead (not, of course, in the naïve form impugned by Hegel) is no argument against Hegel's success; it merely shows that empiricism continues to exercise a fascination, particularly in the area of human behavior and among those who contend that science is not science, knowledge is not knowledge, unless it is empirical. There remains, it would seem, an option: either reason can see itself as "all reality"—which it is concretely only as spirit—thus justifying the search for reason in nature, or reason can convince itself, in spite of itself, that nature is all reality, thus doing away with the troublesome concept of spirit, which concept makes questionable the absolute universality of deterministic causal explanation.

None of this, of course, says that Hegel finds fault with empirical method or empirical science; he, in fact, quite consistently employs empirical method to "verify" (one might better say illustrate) the ideal truth which has not been discovered empirically. It does say that Hegel sees the empirical method reaching its "logical terminus" (p. 35), where it is no longer adequate to the knowledge which thought seeks. Plato had seen two millenia before Hegel that the material components of reality offer no adequate explanation of the whole of reality, particularly its complexification, and Hegel agrees with Plato. It is refreshing to find that Luft recognizes and expresses concisely the compatability of a biology of increasing complexification, which does not claim to explain the whole of organic reality as no more than the sum total of its parts—not even of interacting parts—with the Hegelian dialectic of emerging spirit, which sees the whole of reality as an "essentially unified organic continuum" (p. 30).

Luft is, I am sure, not the first to have noted that in the *Phenomenology*—except in its prologue-epilogue preface, and the anticipatory introduction—the term *Geist* does not receive sustained treatment until the death knell of physiognomy-phrenology has been sounded (a sort of condition for the emergence of self-consciousness as spirit). But we can be grateful to Luft for reminding us of this. It is precisely because the task of tracing the pathway of consciousness from appearing to be merely a natural function (*natürliches Bewußtsein*) to its truth as free (self-determining) spiritual activity has to go down all the dead-end streets of "certainty" to arrive at the "truth" of its certainties that the quasi-necessity of the *reductio ad absurdum* becomes patent. The turn from a *Wissenschaft der Erfahrung des Bewußtseins* to a *Phänomenologie des Geistes* was not merely accidental.

Hegel himself has made it clear that, if we are to follow in the direction he points, we must go as far as each dead-end street will take us, because each one points the direction we cannot but go. As a consequence, the dead-end street of phrenology takes us to the logical limits of empiricism. From this point on the pathway will be that of "the self-actualization of rational self-consciousness," which will have its own dead-end streets, each pointing beyond itself, until the whole culminates in a "knowing" which is "absolute." In the movement which follows, one important realization from the present section will be retained, namely, that what appears outwardly will be an expression of what is inward, not, however, as an "outer" which expresses an "inner" that *was*—such an "outer" is simply dead, a *caput mortuum*—but an "outer" which expresses an "inner" now operative, an ongoing process. There is no need to see the relation of "inner" and "outer" in terms either of a "ghost in the machine" or of a "machine" that needs no "ghost" at all. Rather, one can see the "outer" as the merely partial expression of the "inner," and one can see the "inner" as both actualizing itself in the "outer" and totalizing "inner" and "outer" in an integral whole which is real precisely because it is integral and continuous. It is because this is so that self-consciousness can be said to find both itself and its world in the concreteness of spirit, that is neither the "inner" nor the "outer" but the unified integration of both which, by themselves, "are but abstractions of the organic whole being" (p. 31).

Luft has, then, in my opinion, scored well in highlighting the contrast between "reductionist" and "hierarchic" science, a contrast which permits him to link contemporary biological theories of "complexification"—reminiscent of Teilhard de Chardin, whom he does not mention—and Hegelian dialectical reasoning in a knowing which is "holistic." "Hegel, the first modern holist," he says, "involved not only biology in his quest for unity, but all knowledge. In this greater schema, biology is only an aspect of natural science, which in turn is only an aspect of a more complete knowledge" (p. 34). Having grasped this, we can also come to grips with what turns out to be the principal contention of Luft's paper, i. e., that "the current dialectical function of reason is to prepare the way for spirit, to create a situation in which 'reason is spirit when its certainty of being all reality [meaning, I take it, the locus where it must look to find reality] has been raised to truth, and it is conscious of itself as its own world, and of the world as itself'" (p. 29, citing *Phän.*, p. 313).

Having said this much, I should be very content to stop, but it would seem that the rules of the game would insist that a discussant, if he is to play the game, must engage in some negative criticism. Since I have none of substantive nature, I shall confine myself to what I might call infelicities of expression, and there are only a few of these.

There is a tendency, it seems to me, to equate "determinate" and "deterministic," which can lead to confusion, as it does early in the chapter, where Luft says: "Whereas matter and its shapes are, in their essential nature, determinate (or determinable), the organism is, in its essential nature, indeterminate" (p. 27). For Hegel it is indispensable to the real that it be determinate (absolute Spirit, for example, is wholly determinate). But there is a world of difference between the determinate which is self-determined and the determinate which is other-determined. In organisms there are varying degrees of self-determination, culminating in the absolute self-determination of wholeness.

I detect (on p. 33) an oversimplification of the degrees of awareness of the "I" in simply saying "I"—all the way from the "motionless tautology" of "I is I" to the full self-awareness of "absolute Spirit." I suspect it can be confusing to speak of "the incontrovertible fact that each of us can, at any time we wish, immediately think or pronounce the word 'I' with meaning, and that we can just as immediately know that meaning to be true." I tend to question whether "each of us" is likely to do this "at any time"—only *special* times.

He gives all of us too much credit when he says: "All of Hegel's systematic transitions represent new emergences, new, yet in many ways 'predictable' developments in the progressive movement of spirit, which arise in response to dead ends in previous paths of development" (pp. 33–34). I might, after thirty-five years of struggling with Hegel, be willing to call them "predictable," but one has to struggle to make them predictable.

From Jena to Heidelberg:
Two Views of "Recognition"

Leo Rauch

There are any number of good reasons why we might compare the Jena *Geistesphilosophie* of 1806 with the Heidelberg *Geistesphilosophie* of 1817 (and after), but it seems to me that the most tantalizing reason is this: each of the texts is part of a system—and this commits Hegel to certain consequences, of a reciprocal nature, for the two. The two systems share authorship, general subject matter, and point of view. It would therefore be reasonable to expect the latter system to be in large measure an amplification of the former. But if this is not the case, then it is precisely their claim to systematicity (separately and in conjunction) that we must question. Thus, if something is present in one system but absent from the other, we might ask ourselves this: must we conclude that the latter system, as a totality, is systematically incomplete (or, contrariwise, that the former is excessively "replete")? In any event, is the respective incompleteness/repleteness in any way damaging to the one or the other? Along similar lines, if one system gives a strong and central treatment to a certain concept, while the other system de-emphasizes it or has it serving a very different function in the whole, then that difference, too, ought to make us question the claims to completeness of the systems.

Accordingly, the Jena/Heidelberg comparison ought to be made, if only as an indication of the "systematicity" (or lack thereof) of Hegel's view of spirit. This is obviously too wide-ranging a project to be accomplished here. I shall therefore limit my scope by focusing upon the topic of objective mind; in this I shall be considering one concept, that of "recognition" (which is prominent in the 1806 philosophy but is given a weak and contrary

47

interpretation in 1817). I shall be asking these questions: first, what is the meaning of the concept, in general, as Hegel sees it? Second, what is its role in the 1806 text? Third, what might its role have been in the 1817 text? Fourth, how is the 1817 text affected by the treatment given to the concept there?

1. It could be said that "being recognized" is, for Hegel, the most basic category of the human social ontology. Hegel speaks of man as the being who bestows recognition and is recognized. We might be led to say, therefore, that for Hegel the social existence of man is conceptually derivable from "being recognized"—but this would be altogether misleading, as we shall see.

We know how the concept of recognition works in the *Phenomenology*: the struggle for recognition is what produces the master/slave relation. In effect, that relation is supposed to function, in theoretical terms, as a primordial society in miniature, involving as it does the elements of freedom and constraint, superiority and inferiority, independence and dependence. But in my view the most important characteristic of the master/slave discussion in the *Phenomenology* is that it is intended to demonstrate that this primordial recognition is the basic ingredient in self-consciousness—which, in turn, becomes the armature of social existence.

The Adam story and Hobbes's saga are schematizations of the same idea. The result for Hegel we know: man emerges from his immediacy and bestows recognition on another or eventually grants recognition to himself by internalizing it (after his defeat and enslavement). In the *Phenomenology* the function served by the concept of recognition is that it supposedly enables Hegel to go from subjective mind to social mind. Individual self-consciousness is fulfilled in social self-consciousness: the I becomes We. Yet the point to keep in view is that "recognition" is still within the scope of the subjective, as a mere aspect of self-consciousness, i.e., within self-consciousness as emergent *toward* its fulfillment. Thus, Hegel's apparent ease in going from subjective mind to objective mind in the *Phenomenology* ought not to blur that division in other contexts, such as the *Encyclopædia*, where the division is not so easily overcome.

Essentially, the ego, in its self-assertion, will turn outward and will thus become objective mind. But this comes by way of the struggle which is as vital as life itself. In the *Phenomenology*, then, recognition comes only through conflict (*der Kampf des Anerkennens*). It is a struggle to the death; but recognition is worth risking everything for, since we thereby become individuals, entering a new ontological status. To be is to be recognized—a truth which I shall encapsulate in a Berkeleyan-sounding phrase as *esse est agnosci*. I might also coin a Kantian-sounding statement: selfhood without recognition is empty, recognition without the element of superiority is blind, and superiority not gained at the risk of life is meaningless.

In the *Phenomenology*, each protagonist in the conflict is aware that his self-assertion must exclude the other's selfhood. This conflict is polarized to its ultimate point, where the personhood of each negates the other's in its totality. Yet each wants to be regarded as total person in the other's eyes—although the other, whose respect he wants, is negated by him. If the entire episode were meaningful only in terms of its goal, it would negate itself; but what gives it its significance is the process itself. I do not first attain individuality and then assert it; rather, I attain it through its assertion and in the struggle for it—and the more I risk for it, the more important it becomes. The struggle is not merely *problematic*, in that I risk my life for what I may not live to enjoy; rather, it is entirely *paradoxical*, in that, taken to its ultimate extreme, I must die *in order* to be recognized! This can even be seen if the struggle includes something as mundane as property as an element of recognition. In the first set of Jena Lectures (1803–4), Hegel presents this added dimension: in possession there lies the contradiction that something external, a thing, a universal [tract] of earth, should be under the control of a single [will, i.e., family]," and my struggle to maintain possession leads me to "perpetrate the contradiction of wanting to affirm the singularity of my being and my property; and this affirmation passes over into its contrary, that I offer up everything that I possess, and the very possibility of all possession and all enjoyment, my life itself."[1]

Is Hegel saying that the life-and-death struggle for recognition is an absolute element, a necessary condition for establishing social existence? Certainly not. But the fact that it is a step in the phenomenological trajectory of self-consciousness would indicate that we cannot understand social personhood in any other way but as an adversary relation.

It is because we might wish to accept the main thrust of Hegel's exposition that we might wish to see the master/slave relation as a society in miniature. But that would be stretching the idea, since the outcome of the master/slave scenario is not the social existence we might expect from the tales of Genesis or *Leviathan*. Rather, the result is the internalization of various world-outlooks (scepticism, stoicism, the unhappy consciousness). As phenomenology, this sequence is quite in order; but as a picture of social development it hardly works: these outlooks presuppose society, they do not produce it. Thus the struggle for recognition, taken in itself, remains at the subjective level, and cannot (in the *Phenomenology*) truly serve as a bridge of transition to objective mind.

2. In the 1806 Jena Lectures, the matter is entirely different: first, there is no life-and-death struggle for recognition; and second, recognition is no longer placed in the sphere of subjective mind alone, but as subjective it is already in the sphere of objective mind, underlying as it does the all-pervasive mutuality of our social existence. The recognition-struggle is no longer used conceptually to "form" society; instead, the 1806 Jena Lectures show how mutual recognition is already embedded in the very fabric of ongoing social interchange.

It is as though Hegel had gone from the proto-Hobbesian model in the *Phenomenology* to a proto-Lockean model here (but I shall argue that the analogy does not hold). The transition is methodological: we are out of phenomenological analysis and into an ontological analysis of social existence. Hegel speaks of *Anerkanntseyn*, or "being recognized," as the "immediate" reality of objective mind.[2] This is also the most fundamental element in personhood, for to be recognized as person is to exist as person.[3] "...*das Anerkanntseyn ist das Daseyn*."[4] That recognition is already social. There is no need to go from struggling selves, fighting for recognition, to social selves fully possessing it. Rather, the individual's will already incorporates within itself all its outer determinations. Thus, the subjective mind is already operative in the sphere of objective mind, so that there is no need of a theoretical bridge between them. Moreover, the will, in its external expression, is reflected back into itself as indeterminate; and this internalization is in turn reflected outward in actual consciousness,[5] "*eigentliches Bewußtsein*,"[6] which is directed to an external object. The self need not struggle against other selves to arrive at its fulfillment; rather, it achieves it through labor, which is self-objectification, through my working on nature and thereby imposing my will on it, and through possession of something which is the extension of my selfhood. Thus, the will, inevitably pointed outward, is implicitly social, inherently recognized.

In the 1806 Jena Lectures, moreover, the interrelation of selves is not struggle but love,[7] wherein recognition occurs not in a reciprocal and conscious bestowal of selfhood, but in the fact that each party knows itself immediately in the other (i.e., without consciously affirming it), and makes this real in the interrelation. Thus, one negates one's being-for-oneself in one's being-for-another—and this is where recognition occurs: in implicit mutuality, not in conflict. The two individuals, sharing recognition and their lives, turn outward to share labor, form a family and acquire property—in what we might call an *embourgeoisement* of the psyche!

Thus, just as Locke might say that the individual in the state of nature has a full battery of rights, so Hegel now speaks of the individual in the subjective sphere as possessing a full array of external connections: to others, to society, to property—and all these rest on recognition, so that one's very being is a recognized being (*anerkanntes Seyn*). Man, instead of groping toward selfhood by way of recognition, already has this, *qua* human: "Man is necessarily recognized and necessarily gives recognition."[8] The word "necessarily" (*nothwendig*) is of great significance here, and Hegel goes on to point out that necessity is man's own, not something we impose upon what we see of man. If there is a struggle at all, it is over property, a struggle involving exclusion and insult to one's self-image, perhaps, but the entire thing is carried on within a social setting, and between free selves acknowledged as such.[9]

The model of social formation presented by John Locke regards the individual as primary, and his labor is the extension of his individuality. *Per contra*, Hegel sees primordial labor as already implicitly social and shared (desire, like recognition, having a universal, spiritual subsistence), and individuality is then itself the product of social existence.[10] Labor is a mode of self-recognition; it is consciousness making itself into a thing: "*das sich zum Dinge machen des Bewußtseyns.*"[11] But in this self-objectification there is the ever-present possibility of a corruption of selfhood, a dehumanization. What has been of great interest to writers such as Lukács,

Marcuse, and Avineri is the way Hegel adumbrates the notion of alienated labor, here in the Jena Lectures, by seeing it as a breakdown of the recognition process.

Labor becomes abstract when it is seen to satisfy the needs not of the person working but of society at large, and when the needs of the individual worker require the labor of many others. The result is a complex network in which the concrete *reference* of work is lost. The abstractness of work has the effect, in turn, of reducing the self to abstractness, so that the working individual is no longer "an all-encompassing spirit, rich in content, ruling a broad range and being master of it."[12] but rather a psychologically fragmented creature whose work is fragmented as well. (The extraordinary similarity of Hegel's analysis to that of Marx's essay, "Alienated Labor," has been remarked upon at length, but it is worth noting again.)

Eventually, as the result of the process of abstraction, labor itself becomes mechanical and subject to a many-sided determinacy; for his free and creative side, man substitutes the machine. Another telling characteristic of this abstract stance is that the system of production is itself understood abstractly—i.e., in analytic terms, "dissecting the concrete world into its many abstract aspects"[13]—and what this says to me is that, in Hegel's view, the "rationalization" of industry is anything but that, since the operative rationality of the individuals concerned has lost all concreteness. Men are then regarded quantitatively, as "labor force," resulting in a depersonalization of them (in their own sight and as well at the hands of those who "manage" them) which is tantamount to the collapse of the network of recognition. (This critique of the industrial system, in terms of its dehumanization of man, must have been little more than prophetic or conjecturable in 1806; but the impact of that critique must have been terrifying by 1931, when the Jena Lectures were published for the first time, an impact intensified with the first publication of Marx's Paris Manuscripts in 1932!)

When needs and their reciprocal satisfactions proliferate, they are seen abstractly in terms of a generalized value, expressed in money (its most abstract equivalent). The exchange of an article involves the mutual recognition of the two parties to the exchange: the possessor negates the existence of the article as his, thereby voluntarily negating his recognized hold, and in the exchange mediating his self-negation through the negation of the other; the value of the thing is in the possessor's evaluation, but its exchange value is decided by what the other person will give for it, in exchange for which the possessor will release possession and recognition. Further recognition converts the possession into property. This is where the element of universality enters in, as the dimension of social meaning and acceptance. Property can also be transferred through inheritance, thus adding yet another aspect of universality.

Like Locke, Hegel says that the origin of property is labor, involving the recognition of my activity whereby I put myself into the thing. My existence is thereby externalized, yet preserved in the thing. So my existence is materialized (in the thing), yet spiritual (in the recognition of it as mine, and of my will as counting for something). Things and their meanings, the material and the spiritual, are two sides of the individual's ontology—and in the process of exchange, the being-recognized has itself become object.[14]

To enter into a contract I must be a person. Therefore, I cannot warrantably make a contract that would negate my personhood,[15] e.g., a contract that would mean my enslavement, suicide, etc. A contract is more intangible than an exchange, since the parties give nothing more than their word, in an externalization or alienation (*Entäußerung*) of their respective wills. The will of each is mediated through that of the other, so that the negating of the one is the positing of the other. Yet this involves the possibility of a separation of the individual will (of one of the parties) from the shared or universal will. This separation (on the part of the criminal) is the basis of crime, and it too involves recognition, i.e., of the individuality of the victim, his will being taken as universal. The basis of a contract, then, is that my will exists only in its being recognized. If I go back on my word I lose my recognition-base, and with this some part of my personhood as seen in its social perspective. What Hegel can say about the contract, therefore, is that "I become compelled to be a person,"[16] "*ich werde gezwungen, Person zu seyn.*"[17]

We can read this as emblematic of Hegel's views regarding the social humanization of the individual—with an echo of Rousseau's phrase, "*on le forcera d'être libre.*" Recognition has its coercive side, although Hegel insists that it does not constrict personhood.[18] It is *as* person, in the legal and social sense, that the contract compels me to perform an action— and the same is true with regard to society's compulsion of me as an I.

Hegel links this compulsion to society's absorption of the individual, as the basis of his recognition as person. "Not merely my possession and my property are posited here, but also my personhood—i.e., this insofar as my existence includes my all, my honor and life."[19] About these there can be no contract. The contract allows my word to stand for the deed, and society does this for me as well, because I am recognized as person. Compulsion is therefore justified, we could say, only if it "forces" us to be free, to be persons.

3. What role might the concept of recognition have played in the *Encyclopædia*? Hegel here abandons the line he took in the 1806 Jena Lectures, in which we saw how the social structure could be viewed as a fabric of recognition. Rather, he falls back on a compressed version of the line taken in the *Phenomenology*, where the struggle for recognition precedes social existence, and the intermediate master/slave relation can be seen as a society in embryonic form. The entire discussion occurs in §§430 to 435, in the sub-section of subjective mind devoted to phenomenology, i.e., the few pages devoted to "recognitive self-consciousness." (I shall also refer to the 1830 *Zusätze*.)

Once again, we have the stand-off wherein each individual is an object for the other, yet wishes to be granted the status of subject and free, and to be recognized as such by the other. Each is an ego, yet each is entirely immersed in the immediacy of its own subjectivity. At stake is nothing less than the conceptual demonstration whereby men could emerge from that subjectivity and, for *its* reasons, enter into social relations. The proximate result is conflict: I must try to suppress your self-sufficiency in order to assert my own. If you are independent of me, then you are superior to me, and then (by implication) I am your inferior and your dependent. To myself I am a free subject, to you I am a corporeal thing. We could, in principle, acknowledge one another's autonomy—but we cannot do this in actuality, because we are imprisoned in our own immediacy, our natural/corporeal being.[20] Each is for the other a phenomenon; for himself, each wishes to demonstrate his noumenal selfhood by getting the other to see it. The mere assertion of freedom will not suffice; it must be won through *risking* the life of that very natural/corporeal existence we are striving to overcome. Yet the risk of life is "only quite abstract," Hegel says, since the death of either one would mean no recognition for the survivor. (This makes it a mere problem—and a far cry from the vital paradox we saw in connection with the 1803–4 Jena Lectures, i.e., that I must die in order to gain recognition.)

In the *Zusatz* to §432, Hegel says that this struggle occurs only in the state of nature, not in society, where the structure of recognition is already established. To me, this shows that the *Encyclopædia* discussion of the struggle and the subsequent master/slave relation are otiose; they cannot take us into objective mind and communal life. Yet Hegel does go on to say that in the master/slave relation we see "the emergence of man's social life and the commencement of political union."[21] But the "emergence" is not described here, and so we have no general means of transition from subjective to objective mind. Hegel himself admits that we are left with the self-consciousness of the slave, and that this is not yet the universal, rational will that is the basis of political society.[22] The slave may incorporate the elements of civilization *in nuce* (by learning to subdue egotism and self-will), so that he can appreciate freedom *when* he gets it—but this is a long way from the social existence embodied in objective mind.

The Universal Self-Consciousness discussed in §§436 and 437 entails a quantum leap from the master/slave relation, not an emergent continuum with it: quite abruptly, we are now in a society of *reciprocal* recognition, "the affirmative awareness of self in an other self"[23]—but with no idea of how we got here. In §435Z, Hegel says that the master will, so to speak, see the light, realizing that the suppression of the slave applies to himself as well, in that he (the master) must submit to the will of the community. How is it possible, at all, for the master to achieve this stroke of empathy, after what the *Phenomenology* has said about him, is not revealed. Nor are we shown how this change of heart *must* come about, phenomenologically, as a matter of the inevitable dialectic of the situation itself and of how it is conceived by the parties. Obviously, the master has not gone through what the slave has gone through, and it is thus incorrect to expect the master to undergo the same self-suppression, or that this would serve as the basis for social conformity in the same way for the two, or to the same extent. We are merely *told*[24] self-consciousness is the result of the struggle; what we miss is seeing how it came about as a result of the wills and desires of the principal parties. Nor are we shown, in the *Encyclopædia*, how recognition gives actual shape to social interrelations and structures. That is the main role the concept of recognition might have played here.

4. What we have, in the *Encyclopædia*, is the conceptual priority of recognition to social formation. And yet, if it is also true that society provides the established foundation for the fabric of social recognition, then it also makes sense to speak of the converse: the conceptual priority of social formation. The 1806 Jena Lectures, as we saw, avoided this confusion entirely by showing how society is co-extensive with its fabric of recognition, so that the problem of conceptual priority does not arise.

I suggested earlier that Hegel seemed to have gone from a Hobbesian to a Lockean model, and then I added, parenthetically, that this analogy does not hold (for the 1806 Jena Lectures). I see both these models as sharing the questionable notion of a rational process in which society is deliberately set up. This involves a number of conjecturable notions regarding conscious intent, and so on (which we cannot discuss here). Now, it seems that the master/slave relation (however sound it may be as phenomenological description) is, when used in a formational or "social contract" sense, altogether out of place—since, on methodological grounds, we ought to abstain from any reference to such causal sequences in order to preserve the descriptive integrity of our phenomenological analysis. So long as Hegel speaks of the master/slave relation as eventuating in man's social life, he is confusing conceptual priority with temporal priority, where an implicit element of causality enters in. Thus Hegel suggests that the master/slave relation, once established, can serve as an "instrumentality" for the satisfaction of wants, etc.[25] Again, the struggle precedes social life, and that is the reverse of reality. The only way to correct this confusion is to abstain from talking in terms of "instrumentalities" altogether.

In the *Encyclopædia*, the phenomenological discussion is in the wrong place, surrounded by psychological discussions of mind, thought, emotion, etc. By virtue of its placement, therefore, it is prevented from serving as the means of transition to objective mind. But in addition, by virtue of its content (i.e., its inadequate discussion of recognition), it fails to illuminate the role of recognition in the workings of "property," "contract," "right and wrong," etc., or any other of the elements of *Sittlichkeit*.

Returning to my opening remarks, therefore, we might ask whether the opposed senses of "recognition" render their respective systems incompatible with one another. I do not think so. Rather, the fact that the concept of "recognition" can be put to such widely different uses by Hegel, and that each such use is compatible with its own system, gives us a further mark of the richness and variety of his thinking.

Notes

1. G. W. F. Hegel, *System of Ethical Life and First Philosophy of Spirit*, H. S. Harris and T. M. Knox, eds. and trans. (Albany: State University of New York Press, 1979), pp. 238–239.

2. Leo Rauch, *Hegel and the Human Spirit* (Detroit, Mich.: Wayne State University Press, 1983), p. 120. This is a translation, with commentary, of the Jena Lectures on the Philosophy of Spirit (1805–6).

3. *Ibid.*, p. 122.

4. G. W. F. Hegel, *Jenaer Systementwürfe III*, Rolf-Peter Horstmann, ed., *Gesammelte Werke Band* 8, Rheinisch-Westfälische Akademie der Wissenschaften (Hamburg: Felix Meiner Verlag, 1976), p. 226.

5. Rauch, p. 100.

6. Hegel, *Jenaer Systementwürfe III*, p. 203.

7. Rauch, p. 107.

8. *Ibid.*, p. 111.

9. *Ibid.*, p. 117.

10. *Ibid.*, p. 120.

11. Hegel, *Jenaer Systementwürfe III*, p. 224.

12. Rauch, p. 121.

13. *Ibid.*, p. 121.

14. *Ibid.*, p. 124.

15. *Ibid.*, p. 124n.

16. *Ibid.*, p. 126.

17. Hegel, *Jenaer Systementwürfe III*, p. 230.

18. Rauch, p. 127.

19. *Ibid.*, p. 127.

20. G. W. F. Hegel, *Hegel's Philosophy of Mind*, trans. W. Wallace and A. V. Miller (Oxford: Clarendon Press, 1976), §431Z.

21, *Ibid.*, §433.

22. *Ibid.*, §435Z.

23. *Ibid.*, §436.

24. *Ibid.*, §436Z.

25. *Ibid.*, §434.

Commentary on "From Jena to Heidelberg:
Two Views of Recognition"

Samuel Assefa

Professor Rauch has offered us a provocative paper on Hegel's concept, or rather concepts, of recognition. As his title suggests, Rauch sees a significant discrepancy between Hegel's earlier (1806) and later (1817) accounts of *Anerkennung*. While Habermas and Siep, among others, have already drawn our attention to the fact that *Anerkennung* is given a far more extensive field of application in the Jena Lectures than in the "mature" elaboration of the system,[1] Rauch argues for a discontinuity of a more radical sort, a change in the basic typology of *Anerkennung* itself. According to Rauch, the two texts employ different, indeed contrary, paradigms of *Anerkennung*, *Anerkennung* as love and *Anerkennung* as a struggle respectively. Professor Rauch proceeds to draw a striking conclusion from his "two concepts" thesis, namely, that the two versions of *Anerkennung* have contradictory implications for Hegel's relationship to the contract theory of society, that of denial (Jena) and that of affirmation (Heidelberg). In what follows, I shall try to show that, challenging though they are, these claims do not stand up upon closer scrutiny.

The principal difficulty I have with Professor Rauch's rendition of the Jena theory of recognition is rather easy to state: his account consistently suppresses the elements of opposition and struggle in favor of those of unity and harmony. We are told that "the interrelation of selves is not struggle but love," and that recognition occurs "in implicit mutuality, not in conflict."[2] Professor Rauch goes so far as to claim that, in the Jena Lectures, "there is no life and death struggle for recognition."[3] This statement strikes one as especially problematic since Hegel explicitly refers to the confrontation that takes place between two heads of family as "the life and death struggle."[4] However, it seems that Professor Rauch is not contesting the fact that a life and death struggle takes place, but rather that this struggle is a struggle *for recognition*. An indication for this is found in the following remark of his: "If there is a struggle at all, it is over property, a struggle involving exclusion and insult to one's self-image, perhaps, but the entire thing is carried on within a social setting, and between free selves acknowledged as such."[5] In other words, recognition always precedes struggle. This response, however, does not meet the challenge posed by the text. The argument applies to the conflict that ensues *within* the sphere of right (*Rechtszustand*), but not to that struggle to which Hegel is referring in the passage quoted above, namely, the struggle that *leads into* the *Rechtszustand*, struggle triggered by conflicts over possession (*Besitz*) "before" the creation of the institution of property (*Eigentum*). The latter does not take place against the backdrop of a pre-existing structure of mutual recognition but, as Hegel says, "on the contrary, with not knowing oneself in the other, and rather seeing *his*, the other's, being for self in the other."[6] Hegel not only states explicitly that the parties "do not yet [prior to the struggle] recognize each other,"[7] but also singles out recognition as the specific object of struggle: "He [the insulted party] resolves ...to become recognized."[8] Furthermore, recognition is never secured in a once-and-for-all fashion. Thus, even the struggle conducted within the *Rechtszustand* can be viewed as a struggle for recognition insofar as it seeks to restore a structure of mutual recognition which has broken down.

Employing love as a paradigm, Professor Rauch argues that "recognition occurs not in a reciprocal and conscious bestowal of selfhood, but in the fact that each party *knows itself immediately* in the other."[9] Whereas Rauch believes to have found an exhaustive account of the process of recognition in the example of love, I would like to argue that what is realized in love is not *An-erkennung*, properly speaking. I take my clue from a remark that Hegel makes just at the point where the life and death struggle for recognition is set into motion: "the knowing will is to be fulfilled (a) as the will of love, with the knowledge of the immediate unity of both poles, of their unity as selfless; (b) in recognition, with the polar extremes as free selves."[10] Earlier in the text, Hegel uses the term "recognition" in a looser sense, to describe the relationship that obtained between the parties of a family who do not relate to one another as free selves: "This being recognized without the opposition of the will—(i.e., ...wherein they only enter as characters not as free wills)."[11] As if to underscore the fact that he now wishes to assign a stricter meaning to the term, Hegel proceeds to describe the movement from love to struggle as one in which "cognition becomes recognition" (*erkennen wird anerkennen*).[12] I take this to suggest that Hegel is introducing a distinction between the phenomena of "knowing oneself in another," which describes the experience of love, on the one hand, and recognition, narrowly speaking, on the other. Strictly speaking, recognition does not describe the mere unconscious cognition of oneself in another but rather a recognition of oneself by another, in the sense in which we speak of a newly formed state as having gained the recognition of some other state. What the latter recognizes is, of course, the other state's claim to sovereignty and independence, its "right to self-determination," as we say. In sum, recognition is something that takes place between two autonomous parties.

Recognition in this sense no doubt also involves the element of knowing oneself in another, the moment of domestication of otherness. The crucial distinction is that here each party not only sees itself in the other, but sees itself in the other *as free will*. In the family, cognition of oneself in the other signifies a loss of self; the immediate or natural character of the unity they form thwarts the independence (*Selbstständigkeit*) of the individual parties. Hegel refers to this unity as "selfless" (*selbstlos*) in the sense that it is achieved at the cost of having each party assume a self-negating posture. In other words, what is at stake in the movement from *erkennen* to *anerkennen* is the emergence of the "*Ich*," self-conscious individuality.

What is lacking in the experience of love is not only the moment of distantiation but also the self-assertiveness that is required to reach the standpoint of the *Ich*. Hegel's claim for an intimate connection between self-consciousness and self-assertion or self-affirmation finds support in the ambiguity of the German *Selbstbewußtsein*. *Selbstbewußtsein* not only translates as self-awareness, but it also connotes a sort of self-confidence which has as its object not the I but the world. Hegel's point seems to be that there is no self-consciousness in the usual sense of the word without doing what self-confidence requires: regaining oneself by affirming one's place in the world. There is no merely inner truth, only confirmation of truth in dealings with the world.

This self-confirmation is achieved in viewing a world in which one's ontological autonomy is acknowledged. The path to self-confirmation is the life and death struggle. For what one seeks to have recognized, one's quality of being a free will, is not simply there prior to one's attempt to assert or affirm it. Rather, it is in the very attempt to display one's autonomy in the form of readiness to put one's life on the line that one proves oneself, or indeed becomes autonomous and, by implication, worthy of recognition.[13] This, in short, is why recognition and the life and death struggle necessarily belong together.

In the Jena Lectures, no temporal gap separates the life and death struggle and the achievement of mutual recognition. If, as I have argued, recognition cannot precede struggle, neither does it obtain after the struggle. Rather, it is as if the very instant at which each sees the other's willingness to risk his life signals the achievement of recognition. We might say that recognition and struggle are equi-primordial. This is what distinguishes the struggle for recognition as developed in the Jena Lectures from the treatment given in the *Phenomenology* and the *Encyclopædia*. In the latter texts, this equi-primordiality ceases to be in effect. Mutual recognition does not obtain; rather, the struggle eventuates in the famous master-slave dialectic. The difference thus lies in the absence, in the Jena Lectures, not of a struggle for recognition, but of the master-slave scenario. It seems to me that Professor Rauch mistakes the absence of the latter as evidence for the absence of the former.

To conclude, I wish to briefly touch upon an important issue raised by Professor Rauch's paper. If I have understood him correctly, Professor Rauch's declared preference for having love rather than struggle serve as the paradigm for recognition derives from his suspicion that the notion of struggle for recognition contains elements of a contract theory of society. Whereas the model of love presents the structured web of social reality as given, the idea of a struggle seems to commit one to an attempt to derive social reality from some prior source, namely, some quasi-contractual agreement of free subjects to recognize each other's freedom. Incidentally, I should add that, on the face of it, this suspicion would appear to apply far more to the 1806 lectures than to either the *Phenomenology* or the the *Encyclopædia*. In the lectures, the transition is made directly from the struggle for recognition to the *Rechtszustand*, and Hegel explicitly tells us that the struggle takes place in "what is usually referred to as the state of nature, the free and indifferent beings of individuals to one another."[14] In contrast, neither in the *Phenomenology* nor in the *Encyclopædia* does struggle provide anything like a direct transition to objective spirit. Yet I think that Professor Rauch has a point when he claims that, in the Jena Lectures, the sphere of the subjective "is already ... in the sphere of objective mind."[15] After all, the free and indifferent individuals of which Hegel speaks are not pre-social subjects but subjects who have separately gone through the experience of familial love. In contrast, in the *Phenomenology*, the equivalent for the experience of love, life in the πόλις (*polis*), is thematized only after the struggle for recognition.

I nonetheless think that what Professor Rauch has to say about the Jena Lectures in this connection also applies to the *Phenomenology*: the sphere of the subjective is, in an important sense, already in the sphere of objective mind. As Hegel puts it at the outset in the section on spirit:

> all previous modes of consciousness are abstractions
> from it [spirit]; they are constituted by the fact that spirit
> analyzes itself, distinguishes its moments, and halts at
> each individual mode in turn. The isolating of such mo-
> ments presupposes spirit itself and requires spirit for its
> subsistence, in other words, this isolation of modes only
> exists within spirit, which is existence.[16]

In other words, the birth of spirit in Chapter VI of the *Phenomenology* simply repeats an earlier genesis, and this still yet an earlier one. Spirit has a history, but no absolute point of origin. It is the nonoriginating generative field of human life.

It might appear that all this only confirms Professor Rauch's claim for the subordinate place that struggle occupies in relation to love, difference in relation to identity, *für sich sein* in relation to *an sich sein*. Yet this appearance misleads. To say that spirit is "always already," that our actions always occur within the space provided by the pre-positings–practices and institutions, or, better, structures—is not to say that these structures are set over and against the ongoing human activity alone in virtue of which they exist. While there is no doubt a sense in which these structures can be said to be prior to the activity of this or that individual agent, the temptation to translate this priority in ontological terms, i.e., to ascribe to structures a certain self-sufficiency in relation to our willings and doings, is precisely what Hegel believed to be the shortcoming of the attitude of naïve *Sittlichkeit*. "It is eternal," said Antigone of the subterranean principle of the family, "and no one knows whence it came." [17] For Hegel, these words are testimony to the fact that the Greeks were ethical unselfconsciously; the structures of life "wrought and created by the actions of each and all" [18] presented themselves as self-subsistent (*naturwüchsige*) powers steering their activities.

The concept of a struggle for recognition serves as a corrective to this false ontological subordination of *für sich sein* to *an sich sein*. This corrective receives its political expression in Hegel's endorsement of what might be called the Copernican revolution in political philosophy—the attempt to find the true basis of the state, the criterion of political legitimacy, in will rather than in nature. The notion of will is meant to help us determine our place as moderns: we stand where objectivity and substance no longer command our obedience. Unlike Antigone, we (that is, the philosophical "we" of the *Phenomenology*) know that the intersubjective norms which command our obedience do not have a separate and independent ontological status, independent, that is, of our affirmations and reaffirmations of these norms. Their claims are conditioned by what we do and will not do. There is no rock upon which our lives are founded. This, I believe, is the unmistakably modern side of Hegel. The only difficulty is that Hegel is also equally intent upon preserving the language of ethical substance, *sittliche Substanz*, a language which carries with it the promise of return, not a return to naïve *Sittlichkeit* perhaps, but a return nonetheless. The difficulty encountered in thinking this return, this fusion of substance and will, is the difficulty of conceiving of a single perspective which combines the perspectives of both love and struggle.

Notes

1. Jürgen Habermas, "Labor and Interaction," *Theory and Practice*, J. Viertel, trans. (Boston: Beacon Press, 1971). L. Siep, *Anerkennung als Prinzip der Praktischen Philosophie* (Freiburg/München: Verlag Karl Alber,

1979).

2. Leo Rauch, "From Jena to Heidelberg: Two Views of Recognition," p. 51.

3. *Ibid.*, p. 50.

4. Leo Rauch, *Hegel and the Human Spirit* (Detroit, Mich.: Wayne State University Press, 1983), p. 118.

5. Leo Rauch, "From Jena to Heidelberg," p. 51.

6. Rauch, *Hegel and the Human Spirit*, p. 115.

7. *Ibid.*, p. 112.

8. *Ibid.*, p. 116.

9. Rauch, "From Jena to Heidelberg," p. 51 (emphasis added).

10. Rauch, *Hegel and the Human Spirit*, p. 117.

11. *Ibid.*, p. 114.

12. *Ibid.*, p. 117.

13. "In order to count as absolute, however, it must present itself as absolute, as will, i.e., as someone for whom his existence (which he had as property) no longer counts, but rather this: as his known being-for-himself, that has the pure significance of self-knowledge, and in this way comes into existence" (*ibid.*, p. 117). There is one telling inaccuracy in this translation: Rauch renders *Besitz* as "property" instead of "possessions." G. W. F. Hegel, *Gesammelte Werke Band 8: Jenaer Systementwürfe III*, Johann Heinrich Trede and Rolf Peter Horstmann, eds. (Hamburg: Felix Meiner Verlag, 1976), p. 220.

14. Rauch, *Hegel and the Human Spirit*, p. 110.

15. Rauch, "From Jena to Heidelberg," p. 50.

16. G. W. F. Hegel, *Phenomenology of Mind*, trans. J. Baillie (New York: Harper & Row, 1967), p. 459.

17. In the *Philosophy of Right*, Hegel quotes these lines from Antigone's famous speech to Creon (*Antigone*, ll. 405–07) on two separate occasions. In §166 they are used to illustrate the virtue of family piety, "the law of woman, ... the law of the inward life, a life which has not yet attained its full actualization." In the additions to §144, however, Hegel takes Antigone's words to describe more generally the unselfconscious mode of being ethical. *The Philosophy of Right*, T. M. Knox, trans. (Oxford: Oxford University Press, 1952).

18. Hegel, *Phenomenology of Mind*, p. 458.

Imagination and Presentation in Hegel's
Philosophy of Spirit

John Sallis

1. My concern is with the place of imagination in Hegel's philosophy of spirit.[1] More precisely, I want to examine the placing of imagination within presentation, to interrogate the way in which Hegel secures imagination within presentation. In this regard "presentation" is to be taken in at least three senses. These three senses can be discerned in the meanings which the words "*Vorstellung*," "*Darstellung*," and "*Gegenwärtigung*" have in reference to the Hegelian system. The first, expressed in "*Vorstellung*," refers to a kind of activity of theoretical spirit, or rather, more precisely, to a certain range of development of theoretical spirit, a dialectical course stretching from intuition to thought. To ask about the place of imagination within presentation in this sense is to ask, as did Kant, how imagination mediates between intuition and thought. The second sense, expressed in "*Darstellung*," is that according to which one would refer to the presentation of the system, for example, the presentation comprised by the philosophy of spirit.[2] To ask about the place of imagination in presentation in this sense is to broach the question of the agency of imagination in philosophical thought. It is to open an investigation that *could* lead one to conclude, as did Fichte, that imagination is the "faculty which determines whether we philosophize with, or without, spirit."[3] Yet Hegel is not led to such a conclusion. He is not led to it primarily because of the way in which those senses of presentation expressed in "*Vorstellung*" and "*Darstellung*" are rigorously controlled by a third sense, the sense expressed in the word "*Gegenwärtigung*": presentation as making-present, bringing to presence, or, in the most relevant, reflexive form, bringing oneself to self-presence. Here the "one" of "oneself" is, in the end, spirit itself; and it is thus that Hegel thinks this sense of presentation through to its end, all coming to presence being sublated in the self-presentation of spirit, in absolute self-presentation. As such it gathers to itself not only that limited course of development that Hegel terms "*Vorstellung*" but also the very production of science itself, the presentation of the system.[4] If, beyond the Hegelian system, contemporary discussions have succeeded in showing that the position of presence ($\pi\alpha\rho o\nu\sigma\iota\alpha$, *Gegenwärtigkeit*, *Anwesenheit*, etc.) organizes the entire configuration of metaphysical thought, thus governing the entire history of philosophy, this only serves in a sense to confirm that Hegel did indeed think philosophy as such through to its end, that he brought it to its completion.

In focusing on the place of imagination in presentation in its manifold senses, I want to show how Hegel thinks the problem of imagination through to its end. "End" is to be understood, first of all, in an historical sense. In this connection it is a matter of showing how Hegel's presentation of imagination in the philosophy of spirit brings to completion what was prepared from the beginning. Following Hegel's own directive, I shall deal only with Aristotle's theory of imagination, leaving open the question whether, from the standpoint of contemporary discussions, the Aristotelian theory can still be taken as exhaustive. It will be, then, a matter of showing how the essentials of Aristotle's theory of imagination are taken up by Hegel and brought to completion.

But "end" is to have here another sense too. According to this other sense it may be said that Hegel thinks imagination through to the point where, secured in its place within presentation (in all three senses), it is at an end as a problem, is no longer a problem, no longer provocative of questioning nor of the wonder with which, as both Hegel and Aristotle attest,[5] questioning begins. I shall want to raise a question about this appropriation of imagination to presentation, to ask about the securing of imagination within presence thought through to the end, to recall that imagination may have to do also with absence and withdrawal, perhaps in senses that are not merely complementary to presence and presentation.

2. Aristotle's theory of imagination ($\varphi\alpha\nu\tau\alpha\sigma\iota\alpha$) is presented in Book III of his treatise *On the Soul*. Hegel's admiration for what Aristotle accomplished in this treatise is so profound that he regards Aristotle as virtually his only predecessor in the field dealt with in that treatise and the others related to it:

> Thus Aristotle's book on the soul, along with his dissertations on its special aspects and conditions, are still by far the best or even the sole work of speculative interest on this general topic. The essential purpose of a philosophy of spirit can be none other than reintroducing the concept into the cognition of spirit, and so reinterpreting the meaning of these Aristotelian books (*Enz.*, §378).

In the Kehler manuscript, which consists of students' notes on Hegel's lectures of 1825 on the philosophy of spirit, there is a similar testimony: "The best that has been said of spirit has been said by Aristotle, and if one wants to know spirit speculatively one has only to consult him."[6] This statement is followed by a series of quotations in Greek from the treatise *On the Soul*.[7]

Let me, then, following Hegel, turn to the Aristotelian treatise, to the discussion of imagination in Book III, chapter 3 (427a 17–429a 10). For the sake of conciseness—though at the cost of passing over many of the complexities of Aristotle's text—let me attempt to formulate Aristotle's theory of imagination in a series of six theses.

The first thesis expresses something that is determined by Aristotle's very placing of imagination, by his assigning to the investigation of imagination a place within the treatise *On the Soul*. Imagination belongs to the soul, is a part of the soul. More precisely, it is a power or faculty of the soul ($\delta\upsilon\nu\alpha\mu\iota\varsigma\ \tau\tilde{\eta}\varsigma\ \psi\upsilon\chi\tilde{\eta}\varsigma$).

The second thesis assigns to imagination a place within the soul. Aristotle writes: "For imagination is different from both sensation ($\alpha\iota\sigma\theta\eta\sigma\iota\varsigma$) and thought ($\delta\iota\alpha\nu\iota\alpha$); imagination does not occur without sensation, nor judgment ($\upsilon\pi\iota\lambda\eta\psi\iota\varsigma$) without it."[8] The place is thus intermediate. Imagination is an intermediate faculty of the soul.

The third thesis links this intermediate power of the soul to images. Aristotle writes: "Imagination ($\varphi\alpha\nu\tau\alpha\sigma\iota\alpha$) is that by which an image ($\varphi\alpha\nu\tau\alpha\sigma\mu\alpha$) occurs for us." To draw out the subtlety at which Aristotle's statement only hints, imagination is that faculty by which an image not only is born ($\gamma i \gamma \nu \varepsilon \sigma \vartheta \alpha \iota$) but therein comes to be *for us* ($\dot{\eta} \mu \tilde{\iota} \nu$).[9]

But, according to Aristotle, imagination can have to do not only with one image but with many, or rather, with making one out of many. Aristotle writes: "Hence we have the power of making a single image out of a number of images." This is, then, the fourth thesis. It broaches—though not so centrally as it will come to be by Hegel's immediate predecessors—the character of imagination as power of synthesis.[10]

The fifth thesis specifies the relation of imagination to sensation. Aristotle submits that the process of sensation involves a kind of movement ($\kappa i \nu \eta \sigma \iota \varsigma$) brought about by the actual operation ($\dot{\varepsilon} \nu \dot{\varepsilon} \varrho \gamma \varepsilon \iota \alpha$) of sensation and similar to that sensation. In addition to this movement of sensation, there is, then, imagination, itself also a kind of movement. To cite a few words extracted from Aristotle's very complex formulation: "Imagination appears to be some kind of movement and not to occur without sensation." He concludes: "Imagination must be a movement produced by sensation in actual operation."[11] The process of sensation—sensing or, as one might better say, perception or sense-intuition—is a movement brought about by the actual operation of sensation. Imagination is, then, another movement, a secondary movement generated from, if not simply by, the movement of sense.[12]

And yet, however much generated by the movement of sensation, imagination is in a significant regard a movement in precisely the opposite direction, a movement which, instead of drawing the soul toward things, involves a decisive withdrawal from them. The sixth thesis attributes to imagination this directionality and distance from what is present. Without ever quite formulating it explicitly, Aristotle develops it by means of a series of contrasts of imagination with other powers. Opinion, he observes, lacks detachment; in his words, "it is not in our power to form opinions as we want"—that is, we form opinions ($\delta o \xi \dot{\alpha} \varsigma \varepsilon \iota \nu$) in view of how things seem ($\delta o \kappa \varepsilon \tilde{\iota} \nu$) to us.[13] By contrast, writes Aristotle, "in imagination we are like spectators looking at something dreadful or encouraging in a picture."[14] Aristotle extends the contrast to include knowledge ($\dot{\varepsilon} \pi \iota \sigma \tau \dot{\eta} \mu \eta$), intelligence ($\nu o \tilde{\upsilon} \varsigma$), and of course sensation. In these instances there is even less detachment than in the forming of opinions. The index of such detachment is the capacity to be false, that is, the power not to be simply bound by what is present. Thus Aristotle writes: "All sensations are true, but most imaginations are false . . . . Nor is imagination any one of the faculties which are always true, such as knowledge or intelligence; for imagination may be false." Thus marking the detachment of imagination from what is present, Aristotle also indicates, on the other side, the distinctive connection of imagination with absence—writing, for example: "visions are seen by men even with their eyes shut." Still further, Aristotle refers to another moment of detachment at a quite different level, a detachment from its own being-present: "Sensation is always present ($\dot{\alpha}\varepsilon\grave{\iota}\ \pi\dot{\alpha}\varrho\varepsilon\sigma\tau\iota$) but imagination is not."[15] This is, then, the sixth thesis: the detachment of imagination from presence.

With this thesis a space is opened between imagination and presentation. It will be especially important to observe how Hegel elaborates that openness while at the same time sublating it in the comprehensive closure of spirit.

3. In the Hegelian system imagination belongs to spirit, is one of the activities of spirit. Without entering systematically into Hegel's discussions of spirit in general, let me simply note two determinations that are important for the issues to be raised with regard to imagination. I shall not attempt to mark at all the limits of these two determinations. The first is introduced through the discussion of spirit as sublating the externality of nature: "All the activities of spirit are nothing but various ways in which that which is external is lead back to internality, to what spirit is itself, and it is only by means of this leading back, this idealizing or assimilation of that which is external, that spirit becomes and is spirit" (*Enz.*, §381Z). In particular, then, imagination will be a way by which externality is assimilated to internality. The second determination pertains to the capacity of spirit to endure the pain of such assimilation. The formal essence of spirit is determined as freedom, the absolute negativity of the concept as self-identity. Hegel explains:

> "In accord with this formal determination, spirit can abstract from all that is external and even form its own externality, its determinate being. It can endure the negation of its individual immediacy, the infinite pain, i.e., in this negativity it can maintain itself affirmatively and be identically for itself (*Enz.*, §382).

Thus, spirit's endurance is such that it can survive all dismemberment, reemerging from its loss of self into a reaffirmation of its self-identity, indeed an affirmation that is richer as a result of the loss, which therefore is never, in the end, pure loss. Hegel will think imagination through to the end in the sense not only of filling out and completing the Aristotelian account but also of thinking it through to that point at which what was lost is recovered, to that end in which negativity comes to serve for reaffirmation, difference for self-identity, and absence for the recovery of presence.

Let me now narrow the focus to subjective spirit, the first, ideal moment in the development of spirit; and, still further, to the third moment within subjective spirit, the moment entitled simply "spirit" and designated as the subject of psychology. Though in fact several discussions pertaining to imagination are found in earlier stages, most notably in the anthropology (e.g., in *Enz.*, §408*Z*), it is within psychological spirit that imagination has, for Hegel, its place. Indeed, it will prove to be so secured to this place that the traces that it leaves behind in the anthropology will eventually become problematic.

Spirit, the subject of psychology, is the truth, the unity, of the first two moments in the development of subjective spirit. Like the second moment, consciousness, it stands as one side over against an object; and yet, like the first moment, the soul, it is also both sides and therefore a totality, not because, as with the soul, it fails to make the distinction of self from object, but because it has sublated that distinction. This result is expressed by saying that spirit is reason, the identity of subjective and objective. And yet, initially, in its immediacy, Hegel says,

> spirit is only the indeterminate certainty of reason, of the unity of the subjective and the objective. That is why at this juncture it still lacks determinate cognition of the rationality of the object. In order to attain it, spirit has to liberate the implicitly (*an sich*) rational object from the form of contingency, singularity, and externality which clings to it in the first instance, and so free itself from being related to something other than itself (*Enz.*, §441*Z*).

The various faculties of spirit with which psychology deals can be treated in a rational way only if they are regarded as stages in this liberating of spirit to itself. Imagination will prove to be one of the ways, one of the stages, in this self-liberation of spirit.

Let me narrow the focus still more so as to determine more specifically the place of imagination. That place lies within the first of the three moments of spirit, the moment of theoretical spirit. At this stage spirit involves a double determination: it both finds something within itself as a being and, on the other hand, posits it only as its own. Theoretical spirit, which Hegel also calls intelligence, is the transition from the first of these determinations to the second; that is, it is the activity by which the seemingly alien object comes by degrees to be assimilated,[16] by which spirit comes to posit the immediate affection as its own. Finding itself immediately determined, theoretical spirit comes to posit that determination as its own.[17] The course followed by such knowledge—or, more specifically, by what could be called cognition, thus translating *Erkennen*, which Hegel at this point distinguishes from *Wissen*—this course is described by Hegel as "a conceptually determined, necessary transition from one determination of intelligent activity (a so-called faculty of spirit [*Vermögen des Geistes*]) to another" (*Enz.*, §445). Imagination is, for Hegel as for Aristotle, one of these faculties and thus constitutes one stretch on the course of theoretical spirit.[18]

Anticipating this course, Hegel cautions against a certain way of regarding the faculties, namely, that in which each faculty is regarded as a fixed, independent determinateness and spirit therefore as a mere collection of isolated faculties. A similar caution is found in Aristotle (cf. 432a–b), also, Hegel suggests, a similar attempt to deal with the soul in terms of a series of progressive determinations, even though the attempt remained incomplete and the determinations were not entirely blended into a whole.[19]

Hegel formulates the issue also in terms of the relation between the activity proper to spirit, viz., cognition, and the various faculties or activities that are ascribed to spirit. In saying that intelligence cognizes, it is not to be understood that, along with its cognizing, intelligence also intuits, presents, imagines, etc. Rather, cognition is the actuality of spirit, and intuiting, presenting, imagining, etc., are simply moments of this actualization. Hegel explains regarding cognition:

> The moments of its realizing activity are intuiting, presenting, recollecting, etc.; the activities having no other immanent significance; their only end (*Zweck*) being the concept of cognition. It is only when they are isolated

> that they are presented as being useful for something
> other than cognition, as affording cognitive satisfaction
> by themselves, so that a fuss is made about the delights
> of intuition, recollection, phantasy, etc. (*Enz.*, §445).

On the other hand, Hegel grants that even isolated intuiting, imagining, etc., can afford a certain kind of satisfaction. Yet, having granted such diversion, he displaces it from the truth: "it will be admitted, however, that *true satisfaction* is afforded only by an intuiting pervaded by understanding and spirit, by rational presentation, by productions of phantasy, etc. pervaded by reason, exhibiting ideas, that is, by cognitive intuiting, presenting, etc." But will it be, must it be, admitted? Can imagining provide *true* satisfaction only insofar as it is pervaded by reason, only insofar as it serves the end of cognition, serves for spirit's coming to be present to itself in what initially seemed an alien object? Can imagination provide *true* satisfaction only by serving self-presentation? And even if so, must it be admitted that truth is the sole measure of satisfaction? Could one not ask, for instance, about that intrinsic connection, stressed by Aristotle, between imagination and falsity? Could one not wonder about the very appropriateness of truth as a measure of imagination?

Within theoretical spirit, presentation is the middle term, stretching between intuition and thought. Imagination, placed within presentation, will be, as with Aristotle, an intermediate faculty. Intuition, the first moment of theoretical spirit, has an immediate object; or, rather, it is the movement of coming to have such an object. Beginning as sensation of the immediate material, i.e., as feeling, it passes through the diremption brought by attention, which both fixes the object and separates the object from itself; thus it comes to posit the object as self-external, to project it into the forms of space and time (cf. *Enz.*, §445*Z*; §§446–448). The movement of presentation, beginning at this point, will be brought to completion at the stage of thought, where the immediate, implicit unity present in intuition will be restored out of the oppositions that will have arisen intermediately, in the movement of presentation. Beginning at that point at which the movement of intuition ends, presentation—hence also imagination—is, as in Aristotle, a secondary movement generated from the movement of intuition, of sensation. In the transition to thought, in the restoration of the unity that will have been disrupted, presentation—hence also imagination—will be thought through to the end.

Hegel outlines the course of presentation quite precisely: "The course taken by intelligence in presentations is to render the immediacy internal, to posit itself as intuiting inwardly (*in sich selbst*), while to the same extent sublating the subjectivity of inwardness, and so in itself externalizing that which pertains to it that it is in itself in its own externality (*Enz.*, §451)." As in intuition, there is a double movement, one directed inwardly, the other outwardly. But in the case of presentation the movements are not simple positings of internal and external in their opposition but, rather, a positing of external as internal and of internal as external. More specifically, it is a matter of internalizing the intuition while also in a sense positing in external form, as an outward double, what has been internalized.

At the threshold of presentation Hegel cautions again against taking the various forms of spirit to be independent faculties instead of grasping the rational connections between them and recognizing the sequence as the development of intelligence. At the standpoint of presentation there is, Hegel remarks, an even greater tendency than in previous stages to be diverted into such an ultimately irrational approach.

Within presentation, imagination is the middle term, stretching between recollection (*Erinnerung*) and memory (*Gedächtnis*). Recollection,[20] the first stage of presentation, is the moment of internalizing—that is, spirit's collecting, its gathering, to itself what has been yielded by intuition, its positing as its own a content now isolated from the external space and time of intuition, now deposited within spirit's own space and time. Though this content remains the same as in intuition, it now has the form not of intuition but of *image* (*Bild*) (*Enz.*, §452). Hence, in recollection, at the threshold of imagination, the image is born within us, even though it is only in imagination proper that it will become, in Hegel's sense, *for us*. Again it is an Aristotelian thesis that is being thought through to the end.

But the birth of image from intuition is only the first moment of recollection. Recollected within intelligence, transposed into the space and time of intelligence and the corresponding implicitness, the image is, Hegel says, "no longer existent but is *preserved* unconsciously" (*Enz.*, §453). Intelligence is thus "a nocturnal pit (*Schacht*) within which a world of infinitely many images and presentations is preserved without being in consciousness." But then, such images, slumbering within the nocturnal pit, can be recollected from the depths and brought into the light of determinate existence only through relation to an intuition. The third moment of recollection introduces therefore a certain movement of externalization, and what is properly called recollection is precisely the relating of the image to an intuition:

> The images of the past lying latent in the dark depth of our inner being become our *actual possession* in that they come before intelligence in the bright, plastic shape of an intuition, a *determinate being* of *equivalent* content, and we, helped by the *presence* of this intuition, recognize them as intuitions we have already had (*Enz.*, §454Z).

The image, thus called up from the pit by the intuition in such a way as to be separated from both pit and intuition, has come to be presented as image. This separation and the transition to imagination which it prepares mark the birth of the image *for us*.

Let me, then, finally narrow the focus to imagination itself. Hegel's treatment of it occurs in §§455–459 of the *Encyclopædia*, §460 providing then the transition to memory. Of the five sections devoted to imagination, all but one involve a supplementary remark by Hegel, amplifying the more concise statement in the section proper. All but one of the five sections also include *Zusätze* added to the text by Boumann in his 1845 edition of the 1830 version of the *Encyclopædia* and based on two of Hegel's notebooks as well as five sets of notes on Hegel's lectures.[21] Especially in the final section, where the discussion turns to language, the supplementary remark as well as the *Zusatz* are extended quite out of proportion to the section proper and to the remarks and *Zusätze* to most other sections of the *Encyclopædia*. I shall have to forego giving attention to this extended final section. The other sections must, however, be considered with some care and with attention to the difference between Hegel's own text and the *Zusätze*.

In §455 Hegel considers the first form of imagination. He terms it "reproductive imagination" and identifies it as "the issuing forth (*Hervorgehen*)[22] of images from the ego's own inwardness." The reference is to the pit from which, in the final stage of recollection, images were called forth by intuitions.

The *Zusatz* to §455 proceeds to outline quite distinctly the development of imagination even beyond this first form; in fact, it outlines the entire course of imagination right up to the transition to memory. Defining imagination in general as that which determines images, it proceeds to describe the three forms of imagination as three different ways in which images come to be determined. The first way is that of reproductive imagination, already identified in the section proper as the first form of imagination. In this case the determining consists in drawing images from the nocturnal pit out into determinate existence. The *Zusatz* adds something which, though briefly mentioned at the end of the final section on recollection, is not explicit in §455 proper: with the transition from recollection to imagination, the reproduction, the issuing forth of images from the pit, comes to occur voluntarily and without the aid of a corresponding intuition.[23]

The second form of imagination is, according to the *Zusatz*, associative imagination, which relates images to one another and in that way elevates them to universality. Thus in associative imagination that power comes into play that is expressed in another of the Aristotelian theses, that which ascribes to imagination the power of making one out of many, of bringing many images into a one. It is noteworthy, however, that the one is not itself simply another image, but, rather, is a representation elevated to the level of universality, thus directing the course of imagination toward an end in which the image will finally be sublated and imagination itself thought through to the end.

The third form of imagination enumerated in the *Zusatz* to §455 is phantasy. In this instance the universal presentation resulting from the previous form is what gets determined by imagination. Specifically, it gets determined as having over against itself a determinate being in which it is imaged and with which in that sense it is identical. This determinate being can assume two forms, that of symbol and that of sign; and so, the third stage of imagination consists of two types of phantasy, symbolic phantasy and sign-making phantasy.

Such is, then, the outline provided by the *Zusatz* to §455. It is important to observe, however, that in §455 itself Hegel does not venture nearly so far. Having identified reproductive imagination as the first form, he proceeds only to mention that there is a certain content deriving from spirit, set forth out of the pit, and providing a "general presentation for the associative relation of images." The supplementary remark following the section proper is largely devoted to criticism of certain views concerning association of ideas, and there is—quite remarkably—no mention of associative imagination as a second form of imagination in general.

In fact, in §456 associative imagination appears to be, rather, merely the transition to the second form. For association is, at the same time, "a *subsumption* of singulars under a universal which constitutes their connection." A difference is thus introduced between image and universality; yet, insofar as the universality comes to have a content derived not just from the stock of images but from intelligence itself as determinate concrete subjectivity, the movement between these moments becomes a recollecting of self by way of an imaging of intelligence back to itself. "Consequently it is inwardly and determinately recollected in this stock and informs (*einbilden*) the latter with its content—it is thus phantasy, the symbolizing, allegorizing, or poetical imagination." This form of imagination constituted in the movement of imaginal recollection, viz., phantasy, Hegel explicitly marks as the second form of imagination.

It appears that Hegel may have labored over this transition, specifically over the transition that the universal undergoes, since its presentation was thoroughly revised in the 1827 edition and again in 1830. In certain respects it is most directly expressed in §456 of the 1827 version: "Initially, this universality is the form of intelligence, and the *content* of the subsuming presentation belongs to what is found (*dem Vorgefundenen*). Intelligence however, (taken anticipatively) as *in itself determinate* subjectivity, has its own content, which can be thought, concept, or idea." It is, then, a matter of the images coming to be subsumed under the latter rather than the former content, a matter of a shift in the content of the operative universality. There is one quite significant indication that is missing in the 1817 edition, added in parentheses in 1827, and then expanded (without parentheses) in 1830, namely, the indication that this transition involves a certain exceptional anticipation of determinations of spirit far in advance of the form being presented here. To the degree that such an anticipation is operative, the character of the development as a thinking of imagination to the end becomes still more prominent.

The lack of correspondence between Hegel's own text and the *Zusatz* to §455 is now explicit. According to Hegel's text, reproductive imagination is the first form and phantasy the second; associative imagination, to the extent that one can consider it a distinct form, constitutes at most the transition from reproductive imagination to phantasy. The *Zusatz*, on the other hand, fixing associative imagination as the second form, displaces phantasy (specified as symbolic) into the third phase of imagination, compounding it with the form that Hegel's own text will place there. Though the significance of such enumeration clearly has its limits, especially given Hegel's strictures against isolating the forms of presentation as independent faculties, these forms can still be considered as stages in a development only if they are delimited; the enumeration belongs to that delimitation, and to this extent the confusion introduced by the apparent disorder in the *Zusatz* is a matter of serious concern.

Hegel's enumeration of the forms of imagination is somewhat more distinct within the simpler structure of the first edition, in which the treatment of imagination consists of three sections. In the second of these sections (§377), which corresponds to and to some degree is identical with §456 in the later editions, Hegel refers to the association of presentations—not to the associative imagination—but then introduces phantasy in such a way as to suggest quite strongly that it is to be considered the second form. On the other hand, in Hegel's lecture notes to §376 (corresponding to §455 in the later editions) the following enumeration is found: "*α*) *reprod[uctive] β*) *associirende—subj[ectiv] auflösend allgemeine γ*) *symbolisirend.*"[24] But it is not clear whether this is to be taken as an enumeration of the forms of imagination—the absence of sign-making phantasy would dictate against this supposition—or as merely tracing the movement from reproductive imagination to phantasy via association.

It is, of course, possible that the lack of correspondence between the enumeration in Hegel's own text and in the *Zusätze* reflects a certain development. In composing the *Zusätze* Boumann conflated the difference between notes based on several different lecture courses dating from 1817 up to 1830; and by his own testimony he gave "the comparatively raw material of these lectures the artistic form justifiably required of a scientific work."[25] Such a manner of composing could have resulted in covering over, yet retaining a trace of, a development in Hegel's way of presenting imagination. The problem is especially acute because it is virtually impossible now to analyze Boumann's editorial work, most of the notes he used being no longer available.

Having marked these textual problems, let me continue. The *Zusatz* to §456 begins by stressing the dependence of the universalizing operation on intelligence; universality could never arise by mere superimposition of similar images. However, the most important contribution of this *Zusatz* is the way in which it assembles the moments of phantasy into that movement as a whole. As a result of the role of intelligence in the generation of universality, the opposition between image and universal assumes within the present form the character of an opposition between internality and externality, which is then brought to unity as imaginal recollection, as the conjunction of an imaging of the universal with a universalizing of the image. Yet, this unity is no mere conjunction, no mere neutral product. Rather, the unity proceeds from the side of internality, from the activity of intelligence as the element of universality, proceeds, as the *Zusatz* expresses it, "by its activating and proving itself as the substantial power over the image, subjugating the image, making itself the soul of the image, coming to be for itself, recollecting itself, manifesting itself, in the image. In that intelligence brings forth this unity . . . , the presenting activity, insofar as it is the *productive imagination*, completes itself internally." This unity of internality and externality, this phantastical unity on the side of internality, constitutes the formal element of art, which, though at the level of absolute spirit, presents the universal in the image.

The *Zusatz*, though indeed amplifying the account of phantasy in §456 proper, at the same time introduces a designation that does not occur in Hegel's own text, viz., *productive imagination*. It is not clear how it relates to the enumeration given in the previous *Zusatz*, much less to that in Hegel's text proper. Is it simply to be equated with phantasy (in the sense specific to §456)? Or is it, as productive, to be contrasted with reproductive imagination and hence extended to cover all other forms? Is intelligence not productive in the generation of universality from the stock of images? Is it not productive especially in that third form of imagination that Hegel is about to introduce, that form in which occurs the making of signs?[26]

Section 457 introduces the third form of imagination as constituted by an addition to the subjective self-intuition achieved in phantasy, by the addition of the moment of being. It is a matter of movement of externalization by which that in which phantasy is imaged back to itself, the stock of images, comes to be determined *as being*. This occurs in what Hegel marks explicitly as the third form of imagination: sign-making phantasy (*Zeichen machende Phantasie*). Hegel's Supplementary Remark adds a clarification: "The image produced by phantasy is only subjectively intuitable. In the sign, phantasy adds proper intuitability."

The *Zusatz* to §457 is especially instructive in that it elaborates the character of that phantasy that constitutes the second form of imagination, distinguishing it, as a symbolic phantasy, from the sign-making phantasy to which §457 has just moved, and clarifying therefore that move. According to the *Zusatz*, symbolic phantasy is distinguished from sign-making phantasy by the fact that in it intelligence still pays heed to the given content of the images: "In order to express its universal presentations, this phantasy selects only that sensuous material which has an *independent* significance *corresponding* to the specific content of the universal to be imaged. The strength of Jupiter, for example, is represented by the eagle, since the eagle is supposed to be strong." Much the same can be said of allegorical and of poetic phantasy, that is, of all phantasy prior (at least in certain of its moments) to the inception of signs. This inception replaces the imaginal attestation of universality with an objective attestation: "Now in that the universal presentation liberated from the content of the image makes itself into something intuitable within an external material *voluntarily* selected by itself, it brings forth what has to be called—as specifically distinct from a symbol—a *sign*." As Hegel himself expresses it—symbolically—in §458A: "The *sign* is a certain immediate intuition, presenting a content which is wholly distinct from that which it has for itself;—the *pyramid* in which an alien soul is displaced and preserved."

In the transition to the final form of imagination it is, then, a matter of cancelling the internality, the subjectivity, that still belonged to that self-intuition constituted by the circuit of image and universal or of symbol and intelligence. To cancel that subjectivity requires that that in which intelligence intuits itself be no longer an image appropriated to subjectivity but rather an objective being, a being that remains objective, unappropriated, even as functioning to present spirit to itself. Hegel can thus write that phantasy—that is, sign-making phantasy—"is the central point in which the universal and being, one's own and what is merely found (*das Eigene und das Gefundensein*), the inner and the outer, are made completely one." It is also thus that he can write, even if with qualifications, that "phantasy is reason" (§457*A*).

4. If one could, even momentarily, withdraw from the incessant movement of presentation, if one could somehow detach oneself, then one might indeed wonder at this result, that phantasy is reason. One might wonder that the loss of self in phantasy comes thus to be recovered. One might wonder that the displacement of self into the play of images serves so entirely in the end to lead the self back to its proper place, to recover its presence.

Let me venture, then, a question. The question might read: Does phantasy exceed reason? Or, more generally, is imagination in excess of spirit? The question is difficult—excessively difficult—to sustain. The difficulty lies in the necessity of not understanding excess here in the sense that would be operative if one were to say, with Hegel—and as he in effect says—that reason exceeds phantasy, that it is a more central central-point. It is a matter of attempting to think excess non-dialectically, or rather— since this very formulation can so easily become dialectical—to think it in excess of dialectic.

Let me venture, then, this question of excessive imagination. Let me venture it, not in order to move on as economically as possible to an answer by which the interrogative loss of assurance would thus be recovered. Let me rather insist on the question, persist—even if only momentarily—in attempting to learn how, if at all, it can be asked with sustenance.

Along the way up to and through Hegel's presentation of imagination, I have marked those moments in which the various theses comprising Aristotle's theory of imagination are taken up and thought through. Thus imagination is for Hegel a faculty of spirit, as it was for Aristotle a faculty of the soul; Hegel, resuming an Aristotelian tendency, prohibits regarding imagination or any other faculty as something fixed and independent. It is of utmost consequence that what generates this prohibition is the demand that imagination (and all other faculties) be rigorously subordinated to cognition, that it be placed within presentation, retained in the service of absolute presentation. Thus placed, imagination is, then, as for Aristotle, an *intermediate* faculty; but that intermediate character is now thought through to the end, thought as mediation operating in spirit's discovery and recovery of itself in the image. As such, imagination belongs, as in Aristotle, to a secondary movement generated from the movement of intuition or sensation, a secondary movement which—for Hegel, thinking it to the end—resumes that movement of self-recovery that it was the function of intuition to begin. That resumption is broached by recollection, which gives birth to the image and recalls it from the nocturnal pit, letting it be reborn *for us*. Taking over the manifold of images, imagination proper then exercises that power that Aristotle ascribes to it, the power of making one out of many images. Yet the one is not an image but a one thought through to the end. Even in its more developed forms, as phantasy, imagination remains a certain drawing of the many back to the one—as indeed it must if it is to remain in service to self-presentation.

But what about the final Aristotelian thesis? What about the detachment of imagination from presence? Clearly Hegel also resumes this thesis: one could say that the entire movement of recollection leading up to reproductive imagination is precisely a matter of intelligence's detaching itself from the immediate presence of the intuition; one might also say that the transition to sign-making phantasy is a matter of detachment from presence in the form of the image or symbol. However, the question—the question I want to venture—is not simply whether there is such a detachment operative in imagination but rather whether that detachment disrupts to the end or only serves to prepare a new attachment, a new assimilation. The question is whether imagination can detach itself from presence so disruptively as to exceed being regathered into the circle of self-presentation. Can imagination be so disruptively detached as to be in excess of spirit?

In a certain sense it is perfectly obvious, as Hegel fully recognized, that there are certain forms of imagination that are quite disruptively detached, forms of imagination that break out of the movement of self-presentation, stationing themselves outside its periphery. What is especially noteworthy is the strategy that Hegel adopts in order, in a sense, to grant these forms their externality while ensuring that they pose no threat to the integrity of self-presentation. The strategy is one of systematic displacement and consequent repression. Certain forms of imagination are displaced from psychology to anthropology, to a phase where, as a result of the element of corporeality that still remains undetached from spirituality (*Geistigkeit*), the subject is susceptible to disease.[27] Disease means precisely being in opposition to the totality, opposing placement within it: "The subject therefore finds itself involved in a contradiction between the totality systematized in its consciousness and the particular determinateness which is not fluidified and given its place and rank within it. This is madness" (*Verrücktheit*) (*Enz.*, §408). In madness it is as though one made the futile attempt to remain outside a whole whose very nature is to have no outside. It is as though one sought vainly to lose oneself beyond all hope of recovery, as though one sought to exceed a totality whose very nature is such as to prohibit in the end all excess.

Hegel actually describes certain forms of imagination as madness. For example, madness is said to supervene upon a person when he "believes his simply subjective presentation to be objectively present and clings to it in spite of the actual objectivity by which it is contradicted." Such persons might, Hegel adds, "imagine that they are someone *else*" (*Enz.*, §408Z). Hegel mentions also several cases of imagined illnesses. Here especially his strategy becomes transparent. The madman's position outside the whole is either to be declared a matter of incurable disease, madness thus being isolated from reason and hence disarmed; or else, his position is to be reassimilated dialectically to that whole that it would then prove not to have exceeded. Of this second possibility Hegel writes as follows: "In the case of an imagined illness for example, it is often the case that the madman can be cured by appearing to adopt the person's distorted view, and then suddenly doing something which gives him a glimpse of what it is to be free of the malady." He illustrates this dialectical therapy with the following example:

> Another person, who considered himself to be dead, remained motionless, and refused to eat, recovered his understanding in the following manner. Someone else, pretending to share in his folly, placed him in a coffin, and took him to a vault where there was another person, also in a coffin, who pretended at first to be dead. After the fool had been there for a while however, the other person sat up and said how pleased he was to have company in death. Then he got up and ate the food he had by him, telling the astonished newcomer that he had been

> dead for some time and therefore knew how the dead
> went about things. The fool was taken in by this assur-
> ance, followed suit by eating and drinking, and was cured
> (*Enz.*, §408 Z).

Even the most extreme possible attempt in imagination to lose oneself—imagining that one is dead—can be dialectically reversed into a recovery of self, a resurrection; or else, it can, granted the displacement, be declared incurable disease.

Let me return to Hegel's psychological presentation of imagination in order now to let the question multiply. It is a question of the subordination of imagination to presentation—to presentation in all three senses but pre-eminently in that sense appropriate to spirit as such, presentation as the self-presentation of spirit, as absolute self-presentation. In its inception imagination takes over the stock of images issuing forth from the nocturnal pit, brings them forth voluntarily without the aid even of those corresponding intuitions that were still required for recollection. Here it is a matter of "dissolving (*zerteilen*) the nocturnal gloom enveloping its wealth of images and banishing (*verscheuchen*) it by means of the bright clarity of presence (*durch die lichtvolle Klarheit der Gegenwärtigkeit*)" (*Enz.*, §455 Z). The question is whether the nocturnal pit can be so thoroughly illuminated by the light of presence or whether even after the advent of reproductive imagination there do not remain withdrawn in its dark depths slumbering images that are not simply at the call of spirit. And does the nocturnal pit perhaps cast its shadow over the entire course of imagination? Do even those images brought forth from the pit by reproductive imagination not bring along something of its darkness, mixing it then into that play of images from which spirit would draw up universality? Is there in that play of images a dark residue, something not recoverable in universality, something resistant to that subjugating of images that would make them in the end only the mirror for spirit? Can one pass over that transition over which Hegel himself appears to have labored, the shift in the content of the universality operative in phantasy? What about this shift from a universality that would merely constitute the connection between the particulars belonging to the stock of images *to* a universality that would derive its very content from intelligence itself rather than from the stock of images from which it was first raised? What about this shift which allows intelligence then to subjugate the stock of images and to find in it only a mirror of itself? Is there a residue that it merely represses rather than sublating? Or, differently regarded, is there a residue that is absolutely lost beyond all hope of recovery? And would such a residue be, with still more finality, left behind, assimilated, in the transition from symbol to sign? Or might even the sign be drawn back toward the pit from which it would have emerged, drawn back to the symbol as its metaphorical supplement—as, for example, when the sign itself comes in Hegel's own sober text to be called a pyramid?

Near the threshold of Hegel's presentation of presentation there is a discussion (*Enz.*, §449*Z*) in which reference is made to Aristotle, to his saying that all knowledge has its beginning in *wonder*. A Hegelian interpretation of that saying is then offered: at the beginning there is tension between the irrationality with which the object is burdened and the merely indeterminate certainty that spirit has of finding itself in that object; it is precisely because of this tension that one is at the beginning inspired with wonder. But then the self-presentation of spirit is to resolve that particular tension and thus "philosophical thought has to raise itself above the standpoint of wonder." The question is whether on the way from pit to pyramid, the way of imagination, there is not an excess, a darkness, that is irreducible to mere irrationality, that cannot be merely coaxed back to the life of spirit, like the madman who imagined that he was dead. Such excessive imagination, such phantasy drawn back toward the pit, toward a withdrawal from presence, could perhaps broach a wonder that one could never aspire to surpass.

Notes

1. The following discussion is limited almost exclusively to the philosophy of spirit as expressed in the Third Part of Hegel's *Encyclopedia of the Philosophical Sciences*, some account being taken of the differences between the three editions of this work (1817, 1827, 1830). In particular, it has not been possible to include within the present framework a discussion of the development of the philosophy of spirit during Hegel's Jena period. As regards the problem of imagination Petry points to a certain continuity:

"by 1805/6, he was already treating imagination in a way which was not so very different from that of the mature Encyclopedia [*sic*]" (M. J. Petry, *Hegel's Philosophy of Subjective Spirit* [Dordrecht: D. Reidel, 1978], vol. III, p. 408). But clearly this development needs to be thoroughly investigated now that the texts of the Jena period have been issued by the Hegel-Archiv.

2. Cf., for example, Hegel's description of the *Phenomenology of Spirit* as "*die Darstellung des erscheinenden Wissens*" (*Phänomenologie des Geistes* [Hamburg: Felix Meiner, 1952], p. 66).

3. J. G. Fichte, *Werke*, ed. I. H. Fichte (Berlin: Walter de Gruyter, 1971), vol. I, p. 284.

4. "The spirit which, so developed, knows itself as spirit is *science*. Science is the actuality of spirit and the realm that spirit builds for itself in its own element" (*Phänomenologie des Geistes*, 24).

5. Aristotle, *Metaphysics* 982b 11–14; *Enz.*, §449Z.

6. *Kehler* Ms., p. 56, as cited in Petry, I, p. 11.

7. The quotations suggest that Hegel especially admired Aristotle's recognition of the soul's progression in degree of complexity (cf. Petry, I, p. 145; also G. W. F. Hegel, *Vorlesungen über die Geschichte der Philosophie* [Frankfurt: Suhrkamp, 1971], vol. II, p. 203).

8. As Hicks observes, one would have expected Aristotle to use $\delta\iota\acute{\alpha}$-$\nu o\iota\alpha$ (instead of $\dot{\upsilon}\pi\acute{o}\lambda\eta\psi\iota\varsigma$) in the second clause as he did in the first. Hicks proposes the following connection: "Thus $\delta\iota\acute{\alpha}\nu o\iota\alpha$ is the process of which $\dot{\upsilon}\pi\acute{o}\lambda\eta\psi\iota\varsigma$ is the result" (Aristotle, *De Anima*, ed. R. D. Hicks [Cambridge, 1907], p. 457.

9. Aristotle explicitly excludes here "what we say metaphorically" about $\varphi\alpha\nu\tau\alpha\sigma\acute{\iota}\alpha$. According to Hicks the wider, metaphorical sense is based on the felt connection of $\varphi\alpha\nu\tau\alpha\sigma\acute{\iota}\alpha$ with $\varphi\alpha\acute{\iota}\nu\epsilon\sigma\theta\alpha\iota$. In this wider sense "$\varphi\alpha\nu\tau\alpha\sigma\acute{\iota}\alpha$ means presentation, appearance, and any of the cognitive faculties, or again even sense-perception, may be described as presentative; that is, the result they produce is something present to the soul, something that appears ($\dot{o}$ $\varphi\alpha\acute{\iota}\nu\epsilon\tau\alpha\iota$)" (*ibid.*, 460–461). Hegel would no doubt have found very pertinent the way in which the Greek language thus identifies and yet distinguishes imagination and presentation.

10. This character is considered by Aristotle, not in the principal account of imagination (Book III, chapter 3), but in a supplementary account dealing more generally with the role of imagination in the origination of movement and of action. Specifically, the statement "$\dot{\omega}\sigma\tau\epsilon$ $\delta\acute{\upsilon}\nu\alpha\tau\alpha\iota$ $\acute{\epsilon}\nu$ $\acute{\epsilon}\kappa$ $\pi\lambda\epsilon\iota\acute{o}\nu\omega\nu$ $\varphi\alpha\nu\tau\alpha\sigma\mu\acute{\alpha}\tau\omega\nu$ $\pi o\iota\epsilon\tilde{\iota}\nu$" (434a 10) occurs within the framework of a distinction introduced in that context between sensible imagination ($\alpha\dot{\iota}\sigma\theta\eta\tau\iota\kappa\grave{\eta}$ $\varphi\alpha\nu\tau\alpha\sigma\acute{\iota}\alpha$) and deliberative imagination ($\beta o\upsilon\lambda\epsilon\upsilon\tau\iota\kappa\grave{\eta}$ $\varphi\alpha\nu\tau\alpha\sigma\acute{\iota}\alpha$). The power of combining many images into one is explicitly ascribed only to the latter.

Cf. the discussion in D. A. Rees, "Aristotle's Treatment of Φαντασία," *Essays in Ancient Greek Philosophy*, ed. John P. Anton with George L. Kustas (Albany: State University of New York Press, 1971), vol. I, pp. 500–501.

11. This formulation (428a 1–2) is repeated in somewhat different form in *On Dreams*, 459a 18.

12. Cf. Hicks, pp. 467–468.

13. *Ibid.*, p. 459.

14. Cf. *Poetics* 1448b 2–3.

15. 428a.

16. In his lecture-notes on the corresponding section of the 1817 edition, Hegel writes: *"der Intelligenz ist inhalt gegeben, macht ihn zu demihrigen.producirt denselben in sich. Assimilation."* See *"Hegels Vorlesungsnotizen zum subjektiven Geist,"* ed. F. Nicolin and H. Schneider, *Hegel-Studien* X (1975): 53.

17. On the other hand, practical spirit or will proceeds in the opposite direction, beginning with its own aims and interests and proceeding to make these objective. Free spirit unites theoretical and practical, eliminating the one-sidedness of each.

18. Hegel's use of the title "psychology" (which did not appear until the 1827 edition) could be taken to suggest that what Aristotle treats in his work *"Περὶ Ψυχῆς"* is the same as that which Hegel treats under the rubric "spirit." But this cannot be entirely or simply the case in view, for example, of Hegel's statement that the soul as dealt with in his anthropology is "the passive νοῦς of Aristotle" (*Enz.*, §389). Without proposing any detailed correspondence between Aristotle's treatise and all or part of Hegel's philosophy of subjective spirit, it suffices to observe that spirit (as the subject of psychology) is the *truth* of soul, suffices for establishing that in conceiving imagination as a *faculty of spirit* Hegel is thinking through to the end the Aristotelian determination of imagination as a *faculty of the soul.*

Hegel's placing of imagination on the side of *theoretical* spirit would also appear to be prepared by the Aristotelian analysis which, distinguishing practical thinking (φρονεῖν) from intelligence (νοεῖν), then places imagination in relation to powers associated with νοεῖν. One difficult passage even suggests that φαντασία is a kind of νοεῖν, along with ὑπόληψις (cf. 427b).

19. *Vorlesungen über die Geschichte der Philosophie*, II, p. 199. In the first edition of the *Encyclopedia* (1817), Hegel points out that "as regards faculty, the *dynamis* of Aristotle has an entirely different meaning" (§368)—that is, Aristotle understood faculty (δύναμις) in a way entirely different from those who take a faculty to be a fixed, isolated determinateness.

20. It is important to bear in mind that *"Erinnerung"* has for Hegel

not only the sense of remembrance but also of inwardizing or collecting into oneself. In fact, in its first two moments it has almost exclusively the latter sense, coming to have the sense of remembrance only in its third moment. "Recollection" has the advantage of preserving both senses and also, not inappropriately, of alluding to ἀνάμνησις.

21. Boumann's Foreword to his edition is reprinted in Petry, I, pp. *cl–clvii.*

22. In the first edition (1817): *Hervorrufen.*

23. In §454: "Intelligence is therefore the power of being able to express (*äussern*) what it possesses, and of no longer requiring external intuition in order to have this possession existing within itself." This is also confirmed in Hegel's lecture-notes: "*reprod[ucirende Intelligenz] bedarf der Empf[indung] Unm[ittelbarkeit] der Ansch[auung] n[icht] mehr*" ("*Hegels Vorlesungsnotizen,*" p. 62).

24. "*Hegels Vorlesungsnotizen,*" p. 62.

25. Petry, I, p. *cliii.*

26. At the end of §457 proper, at precisely the point where he introduces that form, he characterizes intelligence thus determined as "*producirend.*"

27. It is not without significance that, in the *Philosophical Propadeutic* (1808ff), these forms are not displaced, but treated under the heading of "Imagination" along with the other forms such as reproductive and productive imagination. Cf. Hegel, *Werke in zwanzig Bänden* (Frankfurt am Main: Suhrkamp, 1970), vol. IV, pp. 46ff.

Commentary on "Imagination and Presentation"
In Hegel's Philosophy of Spirit

Daniel J. Cook

In his essay, Professor Sallis has demarcated a small but central segment in Hegel's philosophy of spirit as it is adumbrated in the *Encyclopædia*. While the section on imagination (*Einbildungskraft*) stretches from §455 to §460, Sallis concentrates his attention almost exclusively upon §455 through §457, avoiding any discussion therefore of over half the material (if one includes the *Zusätze*) that Hegel devotes to the category of imagination, including all the material on language. Sallis has also avoided incorporating the Jena writings into his discussion, though (as he says in his first footnote) he does believe such an investigation is warranted. I think that Sallis is wise to narrow his focus in this way, so that we can benefit from the wealth of detail and scholarship that he is able to bring to bear on the specific issue at hand. His analysis of the Aristotelian background to Hegel's theory of imagination and of Hegel's other remarks (in the *Encyclopædia* and elsewhere) on this topic have enriched his presentation greatly. However, I will concentrate primarily on his interpretation of the specific texts in the *Encyclopædia*.

First and foremost, the question arises: is Hegel's treatment of imagination significantly different from that of his contemporaries, or in any way particularly original or at least distinctive? Petry, whom Sallis cites with approval, equivocates on this issue. He does find that some of the distinctions Hegel draws in this section "constitute an *advance* upon the ordinary thinking of the time, [and are] not, as is often the case in Hegel, a re-statement within the overall dialectical pattern, of generally accepted analyses."[1] But in talking of Hegel's treatment of language, a central issue in this section on imagination, Petry claims that its "most important feature ... is its systematic placing as a level of *psychology*. This is to be found in the 1794 text, and remains unaltered throughout the whole of his career."[2] This "1794 text" (entitled "*Zur Psychologie*") as well as the "*Materialien zu einer Philosophie des subjektiven Geistes*" of the same period,[3] are not original essays of Hegel, but represent notes and outlines taken from other sources.[4] In these, as well as earlier juvenilia copied by Hegel (e.g., "*Philosophie.Psychologie.Prüfung der Fähigkeiten.*")[5], imagination and language are prominently mentioned. But is Hegel's *general* treatment (as opposed to some specific aperçus or comments) of imagination, especially the roles of *Vorstellung*, sign and language therein, novel, or is it simply, to quote Petry, "a re-statement within the overall dialectical pattern, of generally accepted analyses"?

Thus, while agreeing with Sallis, who cites Petry, that "by 1805/06, Hegel was already treating imagination in a way which was not so very different from that of the mature Encyclopedia [*sic*]."[6] the question remains whether his earlier treatment was significantly different from that of other eighteenth century philosophers, either in form or content. Perhaps the problems that Hegel had in setting up a proper expositional framework for his psychology, as pointed up in the inconsistencies of organization between as well as within various editions of the *Philosophy of Spirit*, (including the *Propadeutik*), which Sallis has so ably expounded, reflect a struggle on Hegel's part to get beyond the traditional format. The question is: did he succeed? I am inclined to think not, but there is certainly much room here for further investigation and discussion.

Second, I think it is important to understand somewhat more clearly what the developing notion of freedom is for *Geist* in these sections of the *Encyclopædia*. Let us begin by quoting from Hegel, at the outset of the whole section on *Vorstellung* (of which imagination forms the middle segment):

> ... intelligence is immersed in the external material, is one with it, and has no other content than that of the intuited object. Therefore, in intuition, we can become unfree [*unfrei*] in the highest degree. But ... intelligence is the *self-existent dialectic* of this immediate asunderness. Accordingly, mind posits intuition as its own, per-

vades it, makes it into something inward, recollects (in-
wardizes) itself in it, becoming present to itself in it, and
hence free [*frei*] (§450*Z*).[7]

The words Hegel uses here are "*unfrei*" and "*frei*," but in his discussion in the following sections he uses words like "*Willkür*" and "*willkürlich*" more often, and at one point revealingly uses the words "*willkürlich*"
and "*zufällig*" synonymously (§452). The freedom developed at this stage
is not so much a freedom of choice, i.e., the freedom of *voluntarily* choosing a certain *Vorstellung*, be it a *Bild* or a *Symbol*—but a freedom that
stresses the progressive arbitrariness and thoroughgoing conventionalism
(the absolute power or whim, if you will) that intelligence creatively displays
in choosing which *Vorstellungen* it happens to find (its *Gefundensein*,
as Hegel calls it in §457), to represent the content of its consciousness.
Thus, when Sallis translates "*willkürlich*" as "voluntarily" (in §457*Z*), an
important dimension of the freedom Hegel is protraying here is slighted.
A better word might be "freely" (Miller's choice, which at least preserves
the Hegelian ambiguity)—if not "arbitrarily." We would not want to say
that until now intelligence has not *voluntarily* chosen the *Bild* or *Symbol*
through which it wishes to express itself, for though the range of choices
may be more restricted, surely Hegel believed that intelligence is free to
choose one image rather than another: for example, a lion to symbolize
strength, instead of an eagle.

Symbols and even images, as well as signs, are voluntarily selected,
so that cannot be what distinguishes one from the other. To preserve the
meaning of Hegel's point as Sallis quotes him, it must be stressed that the
free assignment of a sign as opposed to a symbol means that one is no
longer at all bound by any *bildlich* connection to the object so designated.
Signs are purely *for us*—they serve *ad libitum*, at our pleasure, and are
purely arbitrary or conventional in their meanings. The vessel *per se* has no
meaning; one arbitrary sign would be as good as another. The important
thing is that we see the system of signs only as a medium, one that is
immediately *aufgehoben*, and the sooner the better. This, by the way,
accounts for Hegel's preference for a spoken, phonetic language (whose
existence, in his words, "vanishes in the moment of being") over a written
or hieroglyphic one, which indeed is the whole topic of §459, by far the
longest in the section on imagination.

Let me introduce my final point by noting that, like many dialectical processes in Hegel, the dialectic of imagination is a paradoxical one because through the process of imagination, images as images are *aufgehoben* into signs. They are no longer really images, when they become *for us*, because they are no longer simply mirroring or picturing objects in the external world. In Hegel's words, *"Die Einbildungskraft erarbeitet sich einen ihr eigentümlichen Inhalt dadurch, daß sie sich gegen den angeschauten Gegenstand denkend verhält,—das Allgemeine desselben heraushebt—und ihm Bestimmungen giebt, die dem Ich zukommen"* (§451*Z*). By "relating thinkingly (*denkend*)" to the intuited object, it becomes clear that the process of imagination is indeed through and through a *thinking* one. Being the first stage of thinking, it prefigures in many ways the later ones, thus explaining why, in Sallis' words, "this transition involves a certain exceptional anticipation of determinations of spirit far exceeding the form here being presented." In its final form as sign-making phantasy, imagination *is* reason, albeit only formally.

I stress this intellectualized treatment of imagination to show, as Sallis already has, that Hegel is intent upon ignoring any subjective, irrational, or unconscious elements lurking in the imagination. Only the cognitive implications of this process directly interest Hegel because, in Sallis' words, "imagination [must] be rigorously subordinated to cognition." Consequently, irrational, or rather non-rational, elements in man's consciousness are not relevant, since they cannot be brought to presence, objectified, because they cannot be *vorgestellt*. If they cannot be so represented, they are not amenable to dialectical thinking for Hegel and consequently cannot be thought or known at all.

If Professor Sallis wishes to develop the idea that imagination can be detached from presence, from the process of objectification, as he thinks Aristotle implies, then he is "throwing out the baby with the bathwater"; he must also give up the whole basis of the section in which imagination appears, that is *Vorstellung*. Hegel's whole argument in this section, as well as in others, is premised on the idea that anything to be thought, even in the weakest sense, must be represented—*vorgestellt*. Whatever else *Vorstellung* means—and goodness knows a veritable cottage industry of scholarship has grown up explicating this term—it includes minimally the notion that a mental construct represents or stands for the experience of *something* rather than pointing up an absence of *something else*, a *something else* that by its very nature cannot be objectified or represented.

By redefining the concept of presence in representation, by translating the former, for example, as *Anwesenheit*, a word Hegel never used in this context, and thus downplaying the "movement towards objectification" or *Gegenwärtigung*," Sallis is clearly invoking the non-objectivist thinking of Heidegger. It is equally clear to my mind that such a thinking is totally foreign to Hegel. Whether Hegel's thinking, in Heidegger's words, "summons thought of another kind of thinking into the clarity of its own thinking,"[8] is an interesting question. But in any event, such a process does not "set that other thinking [i.e., Hegel's] free into its own nature,"[9] as Heidegger claims; it totally distorts it. Sallis has shown us that, like Heidegger, he can understand and clearly expound Hegel's position, if he wishes, but it also appears that he wishes to use the thinking of Hegel that he has so ably presented as a vehicle for overthrowing that very objectivity which is the soul of his philosophy.

Notes

1. G. W. F. Hegel, *Hegel's Philosophy of Subjective Spirit*, M. J. Petry, ed. and trans., Vol. 3 (Dordrecht: D. Reidel, 1978), p. 409.

2. *Ibid.*, p. 415.

3. *Dokumente zu Hegels Entwicklung*, ed. by J. Hoffmeister, 2nd ed. (Stuttgart-Bad Canstatt: Frommann-Holzboog, 1974), pp. 195–217.

4. See, for example, Hoffmeister, pp. 448–454; also H. S. Harris, *Hegel's Development: Towards the Sunlight:* 1770–1801 (Oxford: Clarendon Press, 1972), p. 73, n. 5.

5. Hoffmeister, pp. 113–136.

6. Petry, p. 408.

7. *Hegel's Philosophy of Mind*, trans. W. Wallace, with Boumann's *Zusätze* translated by A. V. Miller (Oxford: Clarendon Press, 1971), p. 201.

8. M. Heidegger, *Hegel's Concept of Experience* (New York: Harper & Row, 1971), p. 70.

9. *Loc. cit.*

Natural Life and Subjectivity

Am Bewußtsein des Lebens aber zündet sich das Selbstbewußtsein an.

—G. W. F. Hegel

Murray Greene

What does Hegel mean by saying that it is in consciousness of life that self-consciousness kindles itself?[1] Most directly, the "kindling" refers to a moment in the phenomenological development of self-consciousness, whose essence is self-relation or self-reference.[2] The self-reference "I am I," however, is an empty tautology until the "I" determines itself, which entails its negating itself by referring itself to an other, or not-I. In this self-relating via a relating to other, self-consciousness is for Hegel first of all "desire" (*Begierde*). The desiring self-consciousness's object or not-I is *das Lebendiges*, or what I shall call a "natural life." Thus it is as concupiscence that self-consciousness first experiences itself, and as a natural life: it desires itself as a life in the guise of a living creature standing opposite it. But what is there about a natural life that self-consciousness should first kindle itself in desiring it?

Self-consciousness is for Hegel the appearing of Spirit and the direct precursor of reason; the desiring self-consciousness deals with two great principles of metaphysical philosophizing, natural life and mind. Traditionally, natural life as soul ($\psi \upsilon \chi \acute{\eta}$ [*psyche*]) is viewed as the mediator of the selfless materiality within nature and the pure self-active $No\tilde{\upsilon}\varsigma$ (*Nous*). In this mediating role in Aristotle, for example, natural life is conceived as a circular motion: in its aspect as spatial motion ($\kappa \acute{\iota} \nu \eta \sigma \iota \varsigma \ \kappa \alpha \tau \acute{\alpha} \ \tau o \pi \acute{o} \upsilon$ [*kinesis kata topon*]), natural life embodies the universal natural principle of change or becoming other; but in its aspect as a return to self, natural

94

life comes as close as possible to the self-relating perfect substance that is God. Thus the sheer other-becoming of motion is subordinated to the return to self, and thereby the identity of beginning ($\grave{\alpha}\varrho\chi\acute{\eta}$ [arche]) and end ($\tau\acute{\epsilon}\lambda o\varsigma$ [telos]), in the concept of substance.[3]

The main part of our chapter, however, deals with Hegel's connecting of natural life and mind. Hegel too conceives natural life as a self-relating circular movement; but this he comprehends not as an Aristotelian $\kappa\acute{\iota}\nu\eta\sigma\iota\varsigma$ but as a movement (*Bewegung*) of the Notion, which is ultimately subject. $No\tilde{\upsilon}\varsigma$, says Hegel, obtains a deeper comprehension in the modern concept of Spirit (*Geist*)[4] and Spirit as subject is the higher truth of substance.[5] Thus, in comparing the Aristotelian and Hegelian connecting of natural life and mind we are comparing the subordination of physical motion to the principles, respectively, of substance and subject, $No\tilde{\upsilon}\varsigma$ and Spirit. In both thinkers, however, natural life attains its perfection in knowing, so that we may refer to the two thinkers' conceptions of natural life by the term "noetic living."

1. As in the case of Plato's concept of nature, circular motion is for Aristotle the best possible kind of motion and the one that enables nature to be as good as possible.[6] For Aristotle, however, circular motion does not render nature a one Living Creature fashioned in the likeness of the divine $No\tilde{\upsilon}\varsigma$;[7] in the first place, nature is not at all a one living creature. Rather, circular motion constitutes for all living creatures their ways of attaining the perfections possible for their specific natures. But perfection in the full sense belongs to God, and it is in Aristotle's separating and connecting the divine perfection of $\nu\acute{o}\eta\sigma\iota\varsigma$ (noesis) from the perfections of natural life that we shall see how the latter is conceived as a circular motion and a noetic living.

Being simply, or life most complete, is God, who is cause of nature insofar as He is "first in complete reality."[8] God is substance in the complete sense, not a natural substance containing matter and thereby unrealized potentiality. God is $No\tilde{\upsilon}\varsigma$, an eternal self-sufficing thinking of thinking—not a motion, which is incomplete, but an actuality, hence pure form without matter and therefore without possibility of being otherwise. In the sense that He cannot be other than He is, God is necessary, hence good and the object of desire and thought; in this way He is the ultimate cause of nature's unfailing motion.

To be natural is to be something less than "first in complete reality," although this does not mean for Aristotle that nature is not fully real or is merely phenomenal in a Kantian sense. Not to be first in complete reality means above all to be subject to change or becoming other; in the first place, subject to change in place, i.e., locomotion, which is the basis for all natural change. All things in nature, including the imperishable heavenly substances, in some way become other; nothing natural remains eternally selfsame, nothing is in every sense a one in actuality, nothing is wholly self-sufficient, nothing is self-active or necessary with a necessity all its own. In all of these ways natural substances fall short of the perfection of God. At the same time, however, these ways mark the perfections of living beings ($\varsigma \tilde{\omega} \alpha$ [*zoa*]) that pertain to them *qua* natural: for example, to be self-sufficient, self-active, and a one apply most of all to living beings, which for that reason most especially of all natural things deserve the name "substance." But how do we distinguish the perfect self-activity of the unchanging Divine Life from the self-activity of a changing natural life? Like his teacher Plato before him, Aristotle puts forward the concept of circular motion: unlike rectilinear motion, which proceeds up to one point and then beyond it to another and so on into the infinite ($\epsilon i \varsigma \ \H{\alpha} \pi \epsilon \iota \varrho o \nu$ [*eis apeiron*]), circular motion encompasses a changing and a return upon self of the same.[9] As Aristotle contrasts rectilinear and circular motion within a problematic of substance, Hegel will contrast the spurious and the genuine infinite in his problematic of subject.[10]

As capable of being otherwise, natural substances are said by Aristotle to be at "too far remove" from their originative source to possess perfect being; but through God's goodness they are able to attain to "the next best thing," namely, that their coming to be ($\gamma \acute{\epsilon} \nu \epsilon \sigma \iota \varsigma$ [*genesis*]) remains unceasing and uninterrupted.[11] Most important for our particular purposes is why the unceasing coming to be is closest to perfect being; not as an ongoing succession but as a continuity, or rather, self-continuity, is this $\gamma \acute{\epsilon} \nu \epsilon \sigma \iota \varsigma$ closest to eternal being. Such a coming to be, says Aristotle, must take the form of a circular movement; for only that which is moved in a circle is continuous in the sense that it remains "with itself" through the movement.[12] Can this Aristotelian circular movement—as a maintaining of self-continuity in change—stand comparison with Hegel's desiring self-consciousness that relates itself to itself in its relating itself to its other? For any such comparison there arises the question of whether a main Hegelian category of subjectivity, namely, being-for-self (*Fürsichsein*), is in some way operative in Aristotle's conceiving a natural life as a substance and a circular movement.

Aristotle uses the concept of circular movement not only for the life-activity of living beings but also for the ongoing transformations into one another of the terrestrial elements.[13] These take place mechanically and hardly seem to require or afford a notion of being-for-self.[14] In this circular return of the same, what returns is said to be the same specifically ($\varepsilon'\iota\delta\varepsilon\iota$ [*eidei*]), i.e., not this bit of fire or water but some other of the same nature. In the circular motion of the immortal heavenly beings, what returns is the same specifically as well as numerically ($\dot{\alpha}\varrho\iota\theta\mu\tilde{\omega}$ [*arithmo*]), since each is unique of its kind. The heavenly beings are sensible (ethereal) substances as well as intelligences, and their life activity is physical as well as noetic. Their circular motion is uniform, uninterrupted, and necessary, and only in respect to place is it a becoming other. But since this becoming other is their being drawn towards their source and perfection through their own desiring, their circular movement is a return upon self of what is numerically the same. Nature, we are told, is the realm of motion and becoming other; but a natural thing, we are also told, is that whose source of motion lies within itself.[15] The circular return upon self of the heavenly substances, I believe, can be regarded as a kind of paradigm, in the ontology of substance, of the being-for-self in other exhibited in natural life generally, including the life of perishable beings. Hence, while Aristotle expressly says of the mortal life that what returns in the circular movement is the same not numerically but specifically,[16] I shall interpret him to mean not merely the kind of return as with the simple natural bodies, but rather a return to self of the perishable creature as this living particular ($\tau\acute{o}\delta\epsilon\ \tau\iota$ [*tode ti*]).

In the case of perishable natural creatures, we are dealing with things that are not eternal and necessary like the celestial beings, but "admit alike of being and non-being."[17] As a $\tau\acute{o}\delta\epsilon\ \tau\iota$ the mortal creature cannot partake of the divine perfection through a movement that is eternal and self-continuous, but only as a member of a class, or in its universal species-nature.[18] Taken in the narrowest sense, return of the same in species means simply that the mortal creature's life-activity culminates in its replacing itself by another of its kind. But reproduction is not a faculty separable from or addable to an otherwise complete creature. Rather, it determines the life of the mortal creature from the beginning, as in the connection between division into male and female, and the faculty of sense perception ($\alpha\check{\iota}\sigma\theta\eta\sigma\iota\varsigma$ [*aisthesis*]).[19] Hence a mortal life is not only a circular return of the same by way of a succeeding of the generations; the life-processes of the $\tau\acute{o}\delta\epsilon\ \tau\iota$ represent a return of the same, as pleasure in copulation, for example, is the sentient creature's continuity with self or being for itself in its relation to its other. In the case of the mortal life the continuity with self means a far more contingent self-sufficiency and a far greater dependence on other than for the celestial beings; nevertheless, in the main life-activities and kinds of soul we see an ascension in self-continuity towards a noetic living that constitutes the Aristotelian connecting of natural life and mind.

That the circular return of the same, in the case of the mortal creature, consists not only in the production of another of its kind is indicated from the first in the fusing of nutrition and reproduction in the concept of "the primary soul" as that which "can generate something like itself."[20] In nutrition, which is a self-preserving by way of an ongoing self-reproduction, the living creature transforms its "other"[21]—in Aristotle's ontology of substance, that which is actually unlike itself but potentially like—into what is actually like itself; literally, it assimilates its other unto itself, whereby it preserves itself "qua individual and substance" ($\tau\acute{o}\delta\epsilon\ \tau\iota$ and $o\mathring{\upsilon}\sigma\acute{\iota}\alpha$ [*ousia*]).[22]

In nutrition the creature is agent, assimilating to itself its other, which is patient; in its sustaining itself thereby, we see the relating to other as the dependent and perishable creature's way of relating to itself. At first this seems not to be the case in sense perception, where the agent is the object acting upon the sense organ of the perceiver as patient. Sense perception is termed by Aristotle a change of state or "becoming other" ($\mathring{\alpha}\lambda\lambda o\acute{\iota}\omega\sigma\iota\varsigma$ [*alloiosis*]) and not a circular motion.[23] The becoming like of agent and patient seems not to be a return to self as in nutrition; for the sense organ, far from assimilating the object to itself, takes on the latter's qualities. Could it be then that, while nutrition is a return to self from other, sense perception, which is the higher function, is simply a becoming other, like a stone's taking on the warmth of the fire?

It is speaking mainly as a physicist, however, that Aristotle views sense perception merely as a becoming other. The sentient soul is by no means a passive recipient like a *tabula rasa*. In the first place, the single sense organ itself is affected through a medium and is in its own nature a mean containing potentially the whole spectrum of qualities within its own domain of colors, tastes, etc.[24] In this way the sentient creature is able to receive the sensible form of the object without the matter, which the nutritive soul cannot do. As the "common sense" ($\kappa o \iota \nu \dot{\eta}\ \alpha \ddot{\iota} \sigma \theta \eta \sigma \iota \varsigma$ [*koine aisthesis*]), the sentient soul takes the object not as white or sweet merely but as a thing of many qualities.[25] Retaining the immaterial form, the common sense gives birth to other faculties: memory, recollective and associative imagination, appetite, and pleasure and pain. Thus, by receiving the object's form without the matter, the creature indeed does not come back to itself directly as in nutrition; but its indirect coming back to self constitutes it a higher form of life. Capable of experiencing the object at an interval of space and retaining the image over a period of time, the animal is able to apprehend a rudimentary universal, and thereby to learn, to anticipate, and to select. Thus the agent-patient relation of an $\dot{\alpha} \lambda \lambda o \acute{\iota} \omega \sigma \iota \varsigma$ is essentially superseded: through a largely self-constituted cohesive experience, the animal assimilates the object to its own life-purposes, as in nest-building. In sentience, therefore, is a self-continuity in otherness that renders the being of the animal closer to $\tau \grave{o}\ \pi \varrho \tilde{\omega} \tau o \nu\ \dot{\varepsilon} \nu \tau \varepsilon \lambda \acute{\varepsilon} \chi \varepsilon \iota \alpha$ (*to proton entelecheia*), or perfect substance, than the plant. Not only does the sentient creature partake of the Divine Life in its coming back to itself in its feeling of pleasure, but animals, as Aristotle tells us, can also be said to have knowledge.[26]

Taking together in ascending series the nutritive, sentient, and rational souls,[27] we best see Aristotle's connecting of natural life and mind through the notion of self-continuity in change—or the circular return to self through relation to other. "Ascending" here signifies that the successive souls or ways of natural life more and more approach a noetic living. For the animal possessing mind ($No\tilde{v}\varsigma$) and speech ($\lambda \acute{o} \gamma o \varsigma$ [*logos*]) as well as sense perception, noetic living means the active life of virtue. This requires the governance of reason over the passions, and entails a circular return to self on a new level, namely, that of the $\pi \acute{o} \lambda \iota \varsigma$ (*polis*). The nature of man, the $\pi o \lambda \iota \tau \iota \kappa \grave{o} \nu\ \varsigma \tilde{\omega} o \nu$ (*politikon zoon*), is "to live with others";[28] his faculties are not merely biological, but realizable only in mutual relations with others of his kind. In the life of friendship, the highest ethical virtue, the self-relation of the $\tau \acute{o} \delta \epsilon$ $\tau \iota$ is through "another self."[29] In man's theoretical knowledge—his most self-sufficient, self-continuous, and least impeded activity[30]—mortal life comes as close as it can to the eternal self-activity of the Divine Life, wherein "thought and the object of thought are the same."[31]

Thus Aristotle's connecting of natural life and mind is through a conceiving of the former as the living being's self-continuous circular movement of return to self through other. On ascending levels of the living being's actualization of itself through assimilating its other, i.e., in nutrition, perception, and the activity of reason, it approximates in the best way possible for natural life the complete self-activity of the Divine Life. "And life also belongs to God; for the actuality of thought is life, and God is that actuality; and God's self-dependent actuality is life most good and eternal. We say therefore that God is a living being ($\varsigma \tilde{\omega} o \nu$ [zoon]), eternal, most good, so that life and duration continuous and eternal belong to God; for this *is* God.[32]

2. Spirit being for Hegel the modern and more profound expression of the ancient $No\tilde{v}\varsigma$, Hegel's philosophizing through the modern concept of subjectivity represents at once a departure from and a going back to the Platonic and Aristotelian comprehension of natural life. For Hegel, too, natural life can be termed a noetic living, inasmuch as it embodies principles of self-relating activity that are perfected in knowing. Life, more especially sentient animal life, is the highest attainment of nature, wherein nature surpasses itself to attain its own truth and source as self-knowing Spirit. Thus, in the movement from natural to spiritual life, we see part of the whole Hegelian system as a circular return to self of Spirit. The Absolute Idea of the Logic is an "imperishable life";[33] and Absolute Spirit is likened to the Aristotelian $\theta \epsilon \acute{o}\varsigma$ (theos) as the "actuality of thought" and an immortal life.[34]

But Hegel's view of natural life is also in fundamental ways different from that of Plato and Aristotle. With the new science's "destruction of the cosmos and the geometrization of space,"[35] it was no longer possible to see in the heavenly movements a circular return to self that is nature's closest approximation to the pure self-activity of the Divine Life. The concept of a good and beautiful κόσμος (*kosmos*) could no longer provide a ground or model for the good life for man.[36] The new ground, beginning with Descartes, became man himself as thinking ego and free will, distinct in being from a mechanical nature. For Hegel, too, man must fashion his good from within himself rather than look to nature. But man does this, according to Hegel, not by separating himself from nature in Cartesian or Kantian fashion, but in accepting his continuity with, as well as difference from, universal nature.

To be sure, nature is the realm of the self-external (*Außersichsein*) and therefore of unfreedom and blind necessity;[37] and nature's motion is certainly not to be viewed as in the primary sense circular and the closest approximation to the divine self-activity. But nature's self-externality is the contradiction within itself that impels it to inwardize itself on succeeding levels of mechanics, physics, and organics; the culmination of this inwardization in the sentient animal organism prepares the natural ground from which emerges the spiritual life of freedom and knowing.

But if in one sense nature moves towards the subjectivity of Spirit and the Notion, in another sense its movement presupposes the logical notion. The inwardization of nature is for Hegel a notional movement, and is shown, as Hegel emphasizes, not as an evolutionary development in time but "according to the logical Idea."[38] To this movement the nearest equivalent in Aristotle that we have had occasion to note is the "series" of souls, or ways of natural life, as ascending modes of relating to self through relating to other. But this is not claimed by Aristotle to be any sort of a movement, let alone one necessitated by an "idea" of nature. In the present section of our chapter we shall view Hegel's distinguishing of the plant and animal subjectivity as stages in nature's inwardization. In the concluding section we shall note Hegel's treatment of animal life as a return to self through the processes of shape, assimilation, and genus.

As individual and "concrete subjectivity," writes Hegel, natural life (*Lebendigkeit*) is first instantiated in the animal or "veritable" organism.[39] The reason first given why the animal is "individual" and "concrete" subjectivity—as distinguished from the merely "formal" subjectivity of the plant—is that the differences of shape (*Gestalt*) in the animal are not parts merely but an articulation (*Gliederung*) of the animal body as concrete totality. But are not the parts of the plant also organs, members of a concrete totality? In order to see the difference between the formal subjectivity of the plant and the genuine subjectivity of the animal, we need to look briefly at Hegel's meaning of an organized body as "the first ideality" of nature.

In entering into chemical and other relations with diverse natural powers wherein it "kindles and sustains itself," says Hegel, the organic body is "self-related *negative* unity"; it has "essentially developed the nature of *self* and become *subjective*."[40] Hegel's "first ideality" as subjective may be compared with Aristotle's soul as "first actuality" of a natural organized body.[41] Does the latter contain anything comparable to Hegel's "negative unity"? We recall Aristotle's characterization of nutrition as the organism's rendering like of the unlike but potentially like; is this akin to Hegel's meaning of subjectivity as self-related negative unity?

We need to see first of all that what, for Aristotle, is the unlikeness but "potential" likeness of organism and nutriment is, in Hegel, to be understood as a necessary relation deriving from the very emergence, notionally speaking, of the organized body in nature's own process of inwardization. The organism's becoming the ideality of nature is *eo ipso* the latter's becoming the organism's "inorganic nature." To take but one example by way of anticipation: locomotion is seen by Hegel as the animal's freedom from gravity,[42] i.e., the animal's positive negating and assimilating unto itself this universal natural power. So is nature generally the organism's "own" other: not a relation of potential likeness merely, but a being bound together in the negative tie of opposition. That the organic body sustains itself in negating its other as its inorganic nature is the "ideality" of the life-process. "The perpetual action of life is thus absolute idealism; it becomes an other which, however, is always sublated ...; it always inhibits the reality of the other and transforms it into itself."[43]

But the organic body is not only "self-related negative unity" *qua* sublating its other. It is also negatively related to itself in a way that seems affordable only through the negative self-relation of subjectivity: namely, the organism's sublating of the external other is simultaneously a sublating of the particulars within itself to "moments" of its concrete totality. As Aristotle tells us, a hand severed from the body is no longer a hand; it is a hand only through its organic function within the living whole. Hegel conceives this relationship in terms of negativity. Life "perpetually brings forth its infinite form" through a negating of the particulars of organic shape, which particulars, *qua* organic, are negatively related to one another and to the living whole.[44] It is "in this negative of the negative, in this absolute negativity alone" that the living creature is 'the movement of its own becoming."[45] Since life's "principle determination is subjectivity," we need to see further the differences between the negative self-relation of subjectivity and the kinds of self-relation we saw in the circular movement in Aristotle. The ground of the negative self-relation of the living creature is the movement of self-diremption wherein the creature is subjectivity and Notion: this is its self-oppositing, or opposing of itself to itself, for which we have no analogue in an ontology of substance. "Since life, as Idea, is the movement of itself whereby it first constitutes itself subject, it converts *itself* into its other, into its own obverse (*Gegenwurf*): it gives itself the form of object in order to return to itself and be the accomplished return-into-self."[46]

Here we see how Hegel views natural life in overall terms as a subject-object relation—to the extent, at any rate, of viewing the living creature's relation to its other as deriving originally out of the self-dividing of the living subject. This is the original dividing (*Urteil*) of the Notion as such, for which the phenomenological paradigm is the *Urteil* of the individual consciousness.[47] Just as the original self-dividing of consciousness establishes the subject-object opposition as well as the ground of its overcoming, so the original self-dividing of life constitutes the creature's relation to its other from which it returns mediately to itself. In the original self-dividing, says Hegel, the organism "makes itself into its own presupposition." We see this first in the vegetative organism as "formal" subjectivity:

> ... This is the subjectivity which immanently (an *ihr selbst*) differentiates itself into members and which excludes from itself the merely *implicit* organism, physical nature in its universal and individual forms, and confronts it. But at the same time, it has in these natural powers the condition of its existence, the stimulus, and also the material of its process.[48]

This is the initial op-positing (*Gegenüberstellen*) by the *Lebendiges* of its own implicit being—meaning, what it has become or as it has emerged in the whole preceding inwardizing development of nature. Just as the animal in its limbs and structure generally "confronts" physical nature in its universal form of gravity, the plant in its own shape and capacities confronts its "own" other in which it has the condition of its existence. Now the life-process can begin as that of the *"singular* individual," although, just as in Aristotle the nutritive and reproductive soul coincide, the process of the plant individual for Hegel "coincides with the process of the genus and is a perennial production of new individuals."

Finally, we are in a position to see why for Hegel the plant is only formal subjectivity. While the process of inner articulation—governed by the original self-dividing and confrontation with other—is the singularity's coming forth from itself and its self-sustenance, the plant's growth, says Hegel, is at the same time a falling apart into a number of individuals, the whole plant being their "basis" (*Boden*), rather than a "subjective unity" of the members. For this reason the plant subjectivity is merely formal: not yet the "genuine infinity" or coming back to self as "negative, simple unity," but rather a proliferation and branching out into members which are themselves wholes. In other words, the plant subjectivity is somewhere between the spurious infinite of becoming an other and an other, etc., and the coming back to self in the genuine infinity. In the plant the return to self from assimilating its own other "...does not have for result the *self* as inner subjective universality over against externality, does not result in self-feeling."[49]

In the animal as veritable organism, says Hegel, the subjectivity of the Notion is first actualized concretely in the realm of nature. Not only is the animal's outward process of formation (*Gestaltungsprozeß*) an idealization into members, but, in contrast with the plant's ramifying into other individuals, it is in the animal a preserving inwardly of "the unity of the self." "This is the *animal* nature which, in the actuality and externality of immediate singularity, is equally, on the other hand, the *inwardly reflected self* of singularity, *inwardly* present *subjective* universality."[50]

In Hegel's distinguishing of the "formal" subjectivity of the plant from the animal's "concrete" subjectivity, we may note several differences from the Aristotelian approach to natural life through an ontology of substance. For Hegel, the ascension from plant to animal constitutes a notional development of greatest importance in nature's inwardizing movement, all structural and other differences between plant and animal being seen in light of this movement. Such a movement can hardly be detected in Aristotle, whose ascending series of kinds of soul is not offered as an immanent development of natural life *per se*. Distinguishing animal and plant, Aristotle tends to stress physical considerations, e.g., that the plant lacks in its composition "the mean" that enables the sense organ of the animal to receive the sensible form of the object without the matter. That the animal is "inwardly reflected self of singularity" is a terminology that one would certainly not expect to find in Aristotle, although the concept, as we shall note shortly, is implicitly present in the Aristotelian common sense. For Hegel, the superiority of the animal is in the first place its consummated return to self as subjectivity, as compared with the plant. In this connection we may note that certain distinguishing features of the animal nature, e.g., locomotion, which Aristotle takes up partly empirically—albeit connecting teleologically with sense perception—are derived by Hegel from the notion of the animal as natural subjectivity: "The animal has spontaneous (*zufällige*) *self-movement* because its subjectivity is, like light, ideality set loose (*entrissen*) from gravity, a free time which, as removed from real externality, *of its own inner impulse determines its place.*"[51]

Thus animal locomotion is not taken by Hegel as a given, as is the case more or less in Aristotle, but derived from nature's inwardizing of its self-externality in the modes of space, time, and gravity; this inwardizing of the self-external is a beginning of self-determination that will constitute freedom on the level of Spirit proper. Hegel sees the possession of voice, animal heat, and interrupted intussusception "as a self-individualizing relationship to an individual non-organic nature," whose notions are derivable from animal selfhood (*Selbsttischkeit*). But the essential distinguishing mark of the higher animal nature is for Hegel, as for Aristotle, sentience, here termed "feeling" (*Gefühl*); in Hegel it belongs to the animal because "in the animal the self is for the self." "But above all, as the individuality which in determinateness is for itself, immediately *universal*, simply abiding with itself and preserving itself, it has *feeling*—the *existent* ideality of being determined.[52]

In Aristotle, we recall, there were two considerations regarding sense perception as a circular return upon self: first, the perceiver's being affected by the object and becoming other; and second, the perceiver's return to self through assimilating the object into its total life-purposes. For the second the concept of the common sense is put forward by Aristotle as a self-relation that makes possible the discriminating upon which is based all perception, memory, and imagination. This fundamental faculty, which has been compared with a concept of consciousness and self-consciousness,[53] must in its discriminating be a one and somehow also not a one. How is this possible? Aristotle suggests the analogy of a mathematical point, which is one "numerically" (ἀριθμῷ) but divisible "in being" (τὸ εἶναι [*to einai*]).[54] Here I believe we see a limitation in the concept of substance for a comprehension of sense perception, and an advantage in Hegel's being-for-self of subjectivity. The mathematical point is no doubt one and also divisible—not, however, for its own self but for a third party, namely, we who conceive the point as such. The point is not for itself the end of one length and the beginning of another; the one instant is not for itself the end of time past and beginning of time future. In asking how it is that we not only see and hear but "we perceive that we see and hear," Aristotle is asking, how can a one be so divided that what are separated are at the same immanently connected? But is this the case for the point, the instant? These and other analogies Aristotle offers in his writings do not divide themselves and remain for themselves a one precisely in the dividing.

For Hegel, immanent connectedness can only be that of the subjectivity which divides itself, e.g., into subject and object, and remains "for itself" precisely in the division. In conceiving the living creature as subjectivity, Hegel seeks to combine oneness and divisibility as moments in the self-activity of a subject which divides itself "in order to return to itself and be the accomplished return-into-self." The notional moments of self-dividing, self-oppositing, and return to self—what we have been terming a "circular movement" in order to compare Aristotle and Hegel—make possible the concept of the living creature, in Hegel's comprehension, as "inwardly re-flected self of singularity, inwardly present subjective universality." Out of the self-dividing and return to self of natural life in its notion, according to Hegel, derive the dialectical relationships of the living creature, in the first place, to its determinations of bodily shape as its immediate "objective being"; to its external environment as its own "inorganic nature" or its outer objectivity; and, finally, to an other of its own kind (*Gattung*) in the sex-relationship and death. To these we now turn in our concluding section.

3. In approaching animal life through the Notion, Hegel distinguishes the total life-process into three syllogistic movements, on different levels, of self-relation through relation to other. The first is the structural process (*Gestaltungsprozeß*) wherein, through the original dividing contained in the notion of natural life as subjectivity, the animal relates itself initially to its own body as object. In this process each determination of shape *qua* particularity maintains itself through the others "and in opposition to them." Of itself each particular can neither maintain nor negate itself; rather, each brings itself forth at the expense of and in opposition to the others, so that the self-maintenance of each is at once its self-effacement within the whole. But in this seeming war of all against all of the particulars, the organic totality remains "in every determinateness the same one universal, so that in the animal body the complete untruth of asunderness is revealed." This thorough idealization of the particulars to moments of the organic unity, says Hegel, "is the process which as for result the simple immediate *feeling of self* (*Selbstgefühl*).[55] Thus sentience is initially conceived by Hegel as the organism's relating itself to its own body as an other in the negating of whose every corporeal particularity to a moment of an ideal unity of the organism comes back to itself as subjective one.

But as "simple, immediate feeling of self," says Hegel, the animal subjectivity is "also immediately excluding (*ausschließend*)." The "excluding" is again the subjective self-dividing, but on a new level. Having sublated its immediate relating to self in its structural process, the subjectivity in its *Urteil* directs itself against its other as an externality opposed to it but also comprising its "external condition and material." The creature's inwardizing of this external other and its making it unto its own comprises the second syllogistic movement of the life-process. This is an "assimilation," a making like of the unlike, which Aristotle, as we saw, conceived by way of a circular motion.[56] In Hegel the movement, which is syllogistic or notional, proceeds initially from the structural process as the subjectivity's being "immediately reflected into self"; wherefore the first moment of assimilation is the "ideal" attitude towards externality. This Hegel terms the "theoretical process," which, however unusual-seeming for a notion of animal life, is consistent with our theme of noetic living. The animal subjectivity, says Hegel, intuits what is "distinct from itself, an other, yet which is immediately not an other." Hegel takes the opportunity to characterize "the universal element of sense": "... the vanishing of determinateness into pure ideality which, as soul or ego, remains at home with itself in the other: the sentient subject is thus the self which is for the self."[57] While both plant and animal appropriate to themselves the external world, the animal's sentient appropriation is one where "the other is left free, remains in existence, and withal is still in relation with the subject, without remaining indifferent to it."[58] Here, says Hegel, the relation of the animal subjectivity to its other is not motivated by appetite but is, nevertheless, a source of "inner" satisfaction in the animal and a kind of freedom. Thus we see in animal sentience elements of continuity with Spirit proper; and, notes Hegel, since the animal preserves itself as inwardness in its outer process, the rest of nature is for the first present "as outward."

While sentience as such is ideal and theoretical, the "real" process of the organism with external nature is termed by Hegel a "practical" relationship. Here the process begins with the creature's feeling of "lack" (*Mangel*) and the urge (*Trieb*) to get rid of it: "... the feeling of externality as *negation* of the subject, which is at the same time positive self-relation and the certainty (*Gewißheit*) thereof in face of this its negation ...."[59] Appetite or desire (ὄρεξις [orexis]) in Plato and Aristotle starts from the fact that the natural being's good lies outside itself, whereas the starting point for Hegel is "the diremption of the organism within itself." Lack is for Hegel not a negation merely but "posited as contained in the affirmation of the subject itself." Like the "privilege" of pain,[60] the feeling of lack is a prerogative of the sentient nature.

> Only what is living feels a *lack*; for in nature it alone is
> the *Notion*, the unity of itself and its specific opposite.
> Where there is a *limit* (*Schranke*), it is a negation only for
> a third, for an external comparison. But it is a *lack* only
> in so far as the lack's overcoming is equally present in
> the same thing, and contradiction is, as such, immanent
> and posited in it. A being which is capable of containing
> and enduring its own contradiction is a subject ....[61]

Lack and its satisfaction are for Hegel "infinite self-reference"—or, rather, a first suggestion thereof. The satisfaction of the lack, consisting in the organism's assimilating of the individualized external things, is a "consuming them, and destroying of their own qualities." This appears similar to the Aristotelian rendering of the unlike like in nutrition, but it possesses for Hegel a dimension not present in Aristotle. Since the real process outwards is one where the animal comports itself as "immediate singularity," its overcoming of the inexhaustible singular forms of its other can never be a return to self adequate to its notion as "inwardly present subjective universality." As on the phenomenological level of the desiring self-consciousness, the animal "perpetually returns from its satisfaction to a state of need." Thus for Hegel the very success of the assimilation means a new contradiction and notional impetus towards a higher form of return to self than in consuming the other as an unending series of natural singularities. This higher form and consummation of natural life, indeed the consummation of nature's inwardizing movement generally, Hegel calls the "genus-process" (*Gattungsprozeß*).[62]

It is perhaps Hegel's concept of the genus-process that best exemplifies our themes of circular return to self and noetic living, wherein we have sought to compare the Aristotelian and Hegelian approaches to natural life. The third and concluding syllogistic movement of natural life in its notion, the genus-process weaves together motifs of self-feeling, sexual union, and death. As elsewhere in our discussion, we shall focus here on aspects of Hegel's comprehension of natural life as subjectivity.

The genus-process entails the notion of the living creature as "subjective One," the subjectivity existing "as the One which pervades the whole." The subjective One was indeed present in the two previous processes but in incomplete fashion. From the simple immediate self-feeling of the self-enclosed structural process, the subjective one became in assimilation the subjectivity that returned to itself from its real process outwards, a return wherein the living creature "gives its self-certainty, its subjective notion, truth and objectivity as a *single* individual." In thus assimilating its universal nonorganic nature in its own self-maintenance, the subjective One has become the universal ground of itself as singularity: the "concrete universal, genus, which enters into relationship and process with the singularity of subjectivity." The genus or universal, says Hegel, is hereby the "concrete substance" of the singular subjectivity and in "implicit simple unity" with it.[63] Thus we need to see the genus *qua* substance not as emerging of a sudden but as the subjectivity's obverse, i.e., the side of objectivity, initially in the form of the body and its particular structural process; next, the universal external nature as the other in which the subject had its condition and material of existence and which it assimilated in the process outwards; and finally, as the universal ground of the subjective One that has come back to itself in those processes.

As concrete substance of the singularity, the genus is ground not only of the singularity's negating but also its affirmative self-relating. But now the singularity's self-relating is through an other not as its external nonorganic nature but of its own concrete substance; the subjective One, being "excluding," excludes from itself another individual into whom it also "continues itself" and in whom it "feels its own self." Like the previous process, this too begins with "need"; for as singularity the animal subjectivity does not measure up to the genus. Within the singularity, therefore, the genus is present as a "straining" (*Spannung*) of the subjective One, the urge "...to obtain its self-feeling in the other of its genus, to integrate itself through union with it and through this mediation to close the genus with itself and bring it into existence—copulation (*Begattung*)."[64]

With Hegel's comprehension of the animal sex-relationship we may compare the viewpoints in Plato and Aristotle. In the *Symposium* of Plato ἔρως (*eros*) derives from the singular creature's feeling of lack *vis-à-vis* its own universal being, i.e., its craving for everlasting possession of the Good. In Aristotle the universal is not transcendent of the singularity or τόδε τι but its immanent and indwelling form: the drive for sexual union is not viewed as a contradiction within the singular creature but as a motion (κίνησις) motivated by the orectic soul. From the Hegelian point of view, each of the earlier thinkers possessed part of the truth; but the full truth is neither the Platonic transcendence nor the Aristotelian immanence. The universal as genus is not prior to or transcendent of the singularity, nor is the latter prior to it. The two are opposites—the subjective and objective sides of the natural creature—developing in dialectical interrelationship in the three-stage syllogistic movement of natural life in its notion. In sexual union with another of its kind the subjective One reaches its actualization, which is simultaneously the bringing into existence of the genus.

For Hegel, the animal's sexual drive is the urge of the subjective One to overcome its onesided subjectivity—to obtain its self-feeling as totality, i.e., objectify itself in the genus as universal and concrete substance of the individual. The objectifying, however, is not a digesting of the other, as in the real process outwards; for the two sides are not now related as organism and external nonorganic nature, but rather as "totalities of self-feeling," where "the nature of each permeates both."[65] Thus the sexual relationship, in Hegel's concept of natural life, exhibits the negative self-relation of subjectivity wherein both sides of the relation—each relating itself to itself in relating itself to the other—posit what they are implicitly: "one genus, the same subjective vitality (*Lebendigkeit*)."

> Here, the Idea of Nature is actual in the male and female couple; their identity and their being-for-self, which up to now were only for us in our reflection, are now, in the infinite reflection into self of the two sexes, felt by themselves. This feeling of universality is the highest to which the animal can attain; but its concrete universality never becomes for it a theoretical object of intuition; else it would be Thought, Consciousness, in which alone the genus attains a free existence.[66]

The concept that in sexual union the "feeling of universality" is the highest to which the animal can attain is crucial for Hegel's comprehension of natural life as circular return to self and noetic living. Even in the sexual union, wherein each singularity finds itself within the sphere of the genus, there remains an incommensurateness (*Unangemessenheit*) between the subjective One and the genus in its own nature that is its universal being and substance, i.e., its objectivity. Not in the natural subjectivity of feeling, according to Hegel, but only in the rational self-consciousness of Spirit is the subjective One identical with the universal. Though nature's highest inwardization, the natural creature's return to self as subjectivity is still a self-externality, and, says Hegel, once again a contradiction. From the incommensurateness of the subjective One and its own universal being, Hegel seeks to show the necessity of the natural creature's demise.

The product of the sexual union, notionally speaking, is the different individuals' negative identity *qua* "genus become" (*gewordene Gattung*): an overcoming of onesided subjectivity that takes the form not of an objective knowing but an "asexual" life. The genus here is not the concrete universal that on the level of Spirit is identical with the individual. Rather, this genus is only in principle more substantial than the singulars whose negative identity it is: on the natural side, or as having "become" as a result of the sexual union, the genus is itself an immediate singularity developing into the same natural individuality whose cycle was just gone through.

This is the succession of generations as a spurious infinite progress: "the genus preserves itself only through the destruction of the individuals who, in the process of generation, fulfil their destiny and, in so far as they have no higher destiny, in this process meet their death."[67] Since natural life is "tied to one singular," the animal subjectivity can approximate noetic living, or the fulfilled return to self, only to the point of sensing its own universal being to which it cannot prove equal but only succumb.

> ...As animal, it stands *within Nature*, and its subjectivity is only *implicitly* (*an sich*) the Notion but is not *for its own self* the Notion. The inner universality therefore remains opposed to the natural singularity of the living being as the *negative* power from which the animal suffers violence and perishes, because natural existence a such does not itself contain this universality and is not therefore the reality which corresponds to it.[68]

The contradiction of the sexual union is never truly resolved, not only because its natural result is the spurious infinity of one generation's succeeding another, but because the union of the sexual couple means that each as subjectivity "is itself the unity of both sexes." This asexuality in the natural creature, however, is but an "abstract" and formal overcoming of the onesidedness of the subjective One that has attained its highest self-feeling in its sexual act. Asexuality is but a husk of objectivity, lacking the enlivening tension of subject-object opposition. The asexual mask of the genus is the creature's own death mask: "...its activity has become deadened and ossified and the process of life has become the inertia of *habit*; it is in this way that the animal brings about its own destruction.[69] Within the plant, as we noted, nutrition and reproduction are hardly distinguishable, and in this formal subjectivity there is no subjective One of self-feeling. The self-feeling of the animal subjectivity, nature's highest attainment, drives the subjective one outside itself to objectify itself in an other of its kind. The union that gives the subjective One the feeling of its universality is also an extinguishing of the opposition within itself that constitutes it a natural life. The singular animal subjectivity passes away in the power of the universal, but not without having a presentiment of itself in its universality.

Notes

1. *Hegel's Philosophy of Subjective Spirit*, ed. and trans. M. J. Petry, 3 vols. (Dordrecht: D. Reidel, 1978), vol. 3, *Phenomenology and Psychology*, p. 312. See also *Hegel's Philosophy of Mind*, trans. William Wallace and A. V. Miller (Oxford: Clarendon Press, 1971), p. 165.

2. *Hegel's Phenomenology of Spirit*, trans. A. V. Miller (Oxford: Clarendon Press, 1977), pp. 105ff.

3. It is living beings that "are substances most of all" (*Metaphysics* 1034a 4).

4. G. W. F. Hegel, *Enzyklopädie der philosophischen Wissenschaften im Grundrisse* (1830), ed. Friedhelm Nicolin and Otto Pöggeler (Hamburg: Felix Meiner, 1959), §8*A*; hereinafter referred to as *Enz.* See also *The Logic of Hegel*, trans. William Wallace (Oxford: Oxford University Press, 1892), p. 15.

5. *Hegel's Phenomenology of Spirit*, p. 10. "Further, the living Substance is being which is in truth *Subject*, or, what is the same, is in truth actual only in so far as it is the movement of positing itself." In all passages quoted, emphasis is Hegel's. Wherever I have altered a word or phrase of the translation, I have provided the German original in parentheses.

6. For circular motion as the motion "which above all belongs to reason and intelligence," see Plato's *Timæus* 34a and following, *Laws* 897d and following; also, Aristotle's *On Coming-to-Be and Passing Away* 336b 25 and following for circular motion as the best in nature. Hereafter the latter work will be cited as *GC*.

7. For Aristotle's criticisms of Plato's concept of the circular motion of the World Soul, see *De Anima* 406b 27ff [hereafter *De An.*].

8. *Metaphysics* 1071a 37.

9. *GC* 338a 6; *Physics* 264b 10.

10. See *Enz.*, §93ff. To be sure, the spurious and the genuine infinite are in the logic of Being and not yet the subjective logic of the Notion; but from the genuine infinity emerge the categories of Being-for-self, of which "the readiest instance," says Hegel, "is found in the 'I'" (*The Logic of Hegel*, p. 179).

11. *GC* 336b 33; see also *De An.* 415a 30; *Generation of Animals* 731b 24ff [hereafter *GA*].

12. *GC* 337a 33.

13. *GC* 337a 5.

14. Yet the concept of being-for-self is important in Hegel's concept of matter as "sundered being-for-self" (*Hegel's Philosophy of Nature*, trans. by A. V. Miller [Oxford: Clarendon, 1970], §262—hereafter *PhN*).

15. *Physics* 192b 14.

16. *GC* 338b 13; *GA* 731b 34.

17. *GA* 731b 25.

18. *GA* 732b 35.

19. "In practically all animals which can move about the male and the female are found separate ..." (*GA* 732a 14). All creatures that have locomotion have sense perception (*De An.* 434a 35).

20. *De An.* 416b 23.

21. The nutriment of the animal is termed the contrary of the flesh (*GC* 322a 1).

22. *De An.* 416b 14.

23. *De An.* 415b 24, 407a 5. Sense perception consists "in being moved and acted upon" (416b 33).

24. *De An.* 423b 7, 424a 5. Plants possess no mean for receiving the form of sensible objects, hence "are affected by the matter at the same time as the form" (*De An.* 424b 3).

25. Aristotle's concept of the common sense is of great interest in comparing substance and subject: see above, p. (XXX), and below, n. 61. As regards the circular movement, we may note that for Aristotle sense-perception must be a self-relation: "we perceive that we see and hear" (*De An.* 425b 12); and if our perceiving were a mere becoming other, then the process of perceiving that we perceive, etc., would go on to infinity; hence we conclude that "a sense must perceive itself (*De An.* 425b 17).

26. *GA* 731a 34.

27. *De An.* 415a 1. If nutrition and reproduction constitute the "most natural" of life-functions (*De An.* 415a 27), and thinking the most divine-like, then we would expect to see, in the three levels of soul, an ascension in ways of return to self.

28. *Nicomachean Ethics* 1169a 17.

29. *Nicomachean Ethics* 1166a 32; on friendship and selfconsciousness, see 1170a 29ff.

30. *Nicomachean Ethics* 1177b 20ff.

31. *Metaphysics*1072b 22; *De An.* 430a 4.

32. *Metaphysics* 1072b 26ff.

33. G. W. F. Hegel, *Hegel's Science of Logic*, trans. A. V. Miller (New

York: Humanities Press, 1969), p. 824.

34. *Enz.*, §577. Hegel terms the Idea "a circle of circles" (*Enz.*, §15), and natural life as notional return to self is thus a circle within a circle. This is not the case for the circular movement in Aristotle, for whom the concept of God does not entail, as for Hegel's Spirit, a coming back to self from self-externalization in nature.

35. Alexandre Koyré, *From the Closed World to the Infinite Universe* (Baltimore: Johns Hopkins Press, 1957; reprint, Harper Torchbook), p. *vi*.

36. See Plato's *Timaeus* 46c.

37. *Enz.*, §248.

38. *Enz.*, §§249, 252.

39. *Enz.*, §337.

40. *Enz.*, §337; *PhN* p. 273.

41. *De An.* 412a 28.

42. *Enz.*, §351. Gravity would be part of the animal's *anorganische* (inorganic or nonorganic) nature; the animal's shape, and more especially the limbs, constituting the organic embodiment of that universal natural feature.

43. *PhN* p. 274.

44. In a natural organized body, Kant said, the mutual generating of the parts in their relation to one another and to the whole cannot be comprehended mechanically, but only teleologically, and not through a constitutive, but only a reflective, judgment. (See *The Critique of Judgment*, trans. James Creed Meredith [Oxford: Clarendon Press, 1961], Part II, p. 22.) Hegel applauded Kant's notion of inner design (*Endzweck*) but rejected the onesided subjectivity of Kant's teleological judgment. (See *Enz.*, §57ff.)

45. *PhN* p. 275.

46. *PhN* p. 275.

47. *Enz.*, §166A; *Hegel's Phenomenology of Spirit*, p. 102.

48. *Enz.*, §342; *PhN* p. 299.

49. *Enz.*, §347; *PhN* p. 336.

> It is only when the self exists *qua* self that it is exclusive (*ausschließend*) in its relationship to the outer world and, precisely as such, is the soul of this relationship as reference-to-self: and since in this self-reference the self forms both sides of the relation, this latter is a circle within the soul which holds itself aloof from its own nonorganic nature. But as the plant is not such a self,

it lacks the inwardness which would be free from the relationship to the outside world (*PhN* p. 308).

50. *Enz.*, §350; *PhN* p. 351.

51. *Enz.*, §351; *PhN* p. 352.

52. In dealing with the human soul in Spirit proper, Hegel makes a distinction between "sensation" (*Empfindung*) and "feeling" (*Gefühl*) as different levels of psychical life. (See *Enz.*, §§399, 403; and Murray Greene, *Hegel on the Soul* [The Hague: Nijhoff, 1972], pp. 81ff and pp. 103ff.) I do not find such a distinction in his concept of the animal subjectivity.

53. See, for example, John I. Beare, *Greek Theories of Elementary Cognition* (Oxford: Clarendon Press, 1906), pp. 288ff; and D. W. Hamlyn, *Aristotle's De Anima* (Oxford: Clarendon Press, 1968), p. 122.

54. *De An.* 427a 9ff.

55. *Enz.*, §356; *PhN* p. 377.

56. In Hegel the two "unlikes" would be the organism and its excluded other as its own inorganic nature; these no doubt can be said, in Aristotelian fashion, to be "potentially like". Such an expression, however, would only make sense in Hegel in light of the animal subjectivity's original self-dividing, which, as we saw in the case of the common sense, has no place in the Aristotelian concept of substance.

57. *PhN* pp. 381–382.

58. *PhN* p. 353.

59. *Enz.*, §359; *PhN* p. 384.

60. *Hegel's Science of Logic*, p. 135.

61. *Enz.*, §359A; *PhN* p. 385. Since Hegel here refers to "limit" (*Schranke*) as a negation "for an external comparison," we may refer again to Aristotle's analogy of the common sense to a point. Aristotle says that insofar as the common sense uses the same "limit" ($\pi\acute{\epsilon}\varrho\alpha\varsigma$ [*peras*]) twice, it is divisible (*De An.* 427a 13). If Hegel is correct in his concept of limit, then it is evident that the point is not for itself a one and also divisible, but only so for the common sense; wherefore Aristotle's showing by analogy with the point how the common sense can be one and also divisible is a begging of the question.

62. *Enz.*, §367ff. Genus here does not have the same meaning as in present-day biology's taxonomic classification. Logically, genus is for Hegel "the universality which is in its own self a concrete"; and he gives "man" as an example (*Science of Logic*, p. 649).

63. *Ibid*.

64. *Enz.*, §369; *PhN* p. 411.

65. Each sex "negates its being-for-self" as singularity and posits itself as identical with the other (*PhN* p. 347). Since the being-for-self of the plant does not reach that of self-feeling, there is in the plant only an "analogue" of the sex relationship (*PhN* p. 344).

66. *PhN* p. 412.

67. *Enz.*, §370; *PhN* p. 414.

68. *Enz.*, §374; *PhN* p. 440.

69. *Enz.*, §375; *PhN* p. 441.

Commentary on "Natural Life and Subjectivity"

John McCumber

Profesor Greene shows with instructive detail how Hegel, not bound as were Plato and Aristotle to unchanging εἴδη (*eide*), is able to bring thought and reality much closer together than they could do. But that very immanence of thought to reality, Greene argues, binds Hegel's system to the science of its time. Since that science was (eminently) falsifiable, Hegel's thought remains, like that of his Athenian prececessors, a "likely story" about the universe. I would like here to follow Greene by sketching in, a bit more than he has done, the relation which may hold between such "likelihood" and demonstrative necessity in Hegel's system; I will also follow Greene on that part of his pathway which leads through Aristotle.

Desiring soul is, for Aristotle, an efficient cause of animal motion through the σύμφυτον πνεῦμα (*symphuton pneuma*), and, as Greene argues, this is suspiciously *ad hoc*. But the soul also operates as final cause: the good person acts for the sake of his or her soul, and more particularly of its νοῦς (*nous*).[1] These two causal roles are related, I suspect, only by analogy;[2] in any case, they explain wholly different things. Material and efficient causes explain the *necessity* of the world according to blind κίνησις (*kinesis*). Final causes explain the goodness of the world, and how things come to be for the best.[3] That the world is both good (ἀγαθόν [*agathon*]) and beautiful (καλόν [*kalon*]) is for Aristotle absolutely certain. As a brute datum the world's goodness showed the early philosophers that material and efficient causality were not enough;[4] in more reflective form, the goodness-and-beauty of the world is a metaphysical or theological fact, established in *Metaphysics* XII.

Human life is there shown to be part and parcel of the beauty and goodness of the universe, and it is thus certain for Aristotle that human life has a good and noble τέλος (*telos*)—which he refers to as nobility, or perhaps "moral beauty:" τό καλόν again. But the propositions of ethics, which show how that τέλος can be realized in human life, are not certain for Aristotle; they are at best rules of thumb, or as Plato would say, likely stories.[5]

Thus the account of a τέλος can, it seems, be certain, while the subsidiary accounts of how it is realized and what this implies about the world are not. It is this insight which I would like to apply to Hegel, via Aristotle's characterizations of τό καλόν as "harmony over size."[6]

In his *Aesthetics*, Hegel refers to philosophical truth as a kind of intellectual beauty.[7] I do not think that he is wholly wrong in this, and suggest that we spell it out in terms of two better-known claims Hegel makes for his system: that it be *necessary*, i.e., that all its contents be generated immanently from the Notion, and that it be *comprehensive*, in that only the "impotence of nature" escape it.[8] It is not difficult to see in these requirements radicalizations of the components of Aristotle's καλόν: harmony and size. It seems that Hegel's system might qualify as a supremely καλòς λόγος (*kalos logos*): a discourse exhibiting the maximum of harmony and magnitude.

Consider, now, a sentence such as "in the male, the uterus is an indifferent generality."[9] This, Hegel tells us, is a sentence from a natural science—from Jakob Ackermann's "*infantis androgyni ....*" As such, it is what empirical sentences have since Plato been generally recognized to be: a likely story. It is induced from fragments of experience (here the observation of a single child), themselves open-textured and underdetermining; it is open to refutation by subsequent fragments.

But the sentence is also, presumably, a moment of Hegel's system. As such, it occupies a fully-determinate place within what Hegel regards as a rigorously-developed whole of thought. This is not, for Hegel, merely a likely circumstance. Though the sentence's empirical truth—its relation to sensory reality—is at best likely (and today is hardly even that), its relation to other moments of the system is demonstrably certain: the demonstration is the development of the system itself.

I do not see why such a sentence should lose its place in the system

119

if, for various reasons, scientists should cease to assert it. If the system is truly immanent in its development, why should the replacement of one likely story by another one matter to it? The sentence, even if no longer warranted by scientific discourse, remains a part of the intellectual potential of mankind—of our spiritual gene pool, as it were. The system claims, I suggest, not that its individual component assertions are true, or even warranted—those are matters for scientists—but that they are warrantable: that, as *Denkformen*, they can be assigned a definite and determinate place within a comprehensive whole of thought.[10]

Hegel recognized that the progress of the sciences would continually produce new representations (*Vorstellungen*), which presumably would furnish new matter to be taken up by the activity of philosophical thought. He also recognized (in 1812) that his system itself—not merely his presentation of it—had many defects; and a cursory glance at the tables of contents for the various versions of his *Logic* shows that he revised without compunction.[11] To some people, these facts may bespeak a fundamental lack of rigor. To me, they suggest simply that the system, like any modern formal language, can warrant at any point more than is actually said. Just as a logician, having proved Theorem 35 in a deductive system, has a choice of what to make Theorem 36 (and often has several ways to prove it), so Hegel's system has at any point a variety of thought-contents that could be expressed. Those currently being asserted by scientists would presumably have priority, but others asserted in the past could in principle be reconstructed, as could still others which might be asserted in the future.

That Hegel's system is harmonious and comprehensive does not mean, then, that it is irretrievably bound to the empirical truth of its particular components—any more than the metaphysical certainty of Aristotle's noble τέλος stands or falls with the fate of his ethics. It also follows that Greene's conception of "noetic living" works both ways in Hegel: as life is comprehended through noetic categories, so νόησις (noesis) is comprehended in terms of life.

True, the accent is on the νόησις: man achieves his well-being not from nature, as for the Greeks, but from himself. But he does not achieve it as an entity separate from nature—as, for example, a Kantian moral being which is somehow to be conceived as the final cause of nature. Νόησις is not for Hegel, as for the Greeks, eternally invariable and unmoving. It is, like a living animal, able to absorb new contents and adjust to them without losing its own center of unity. The parallels between Greene's treatment of αἴσθησις (aisthesis) and *Gewohnheit* illustrate this: just as αἴσθησις for Aristotle has an active component in that it incorporates a received sensible form into the sensing animal's whole βίος (bios), so the system does not simply restate previous discussions of habit but appropriates the category for its own purposes.

Finally, in being taken out of the discourse of the natural sciences and placed into that of the system, a sentence is of course changed. It is carried over (μεταφέρειν [metapherein]) from an empirical, piecemeal discourse and placed into a totalistic one. This may require revision and redefinition, as is again evident from Greene's discussion of *Gewohnheit*. It is partially through such revisions that the system relates to sensory reality, and to the scientific understanding of that reality. These "metaphors" are, on the one hand, flexible and "likely"; on the other, they are dynamic and principled, because their direction is distracted by the developing needs of the system itself. That system is thus a fully-determinate τέλος into which empirical discourse is transformed. But the τέλος itself need not dictate the specific "hows" and "whiches" of that transformation.

If "natural" language and empirical discourse are the sole measure of meaning, then Hegelian discourse is often not literal. But if rigorous and comprehensive determinacy of meaning is our standard, then empirical discourse is often obscure and disconnected from larger issues. To sharpen it is to render it (in some sense) falsifiable. The seeds of its death are within it, and only the Hegelian καλὸς λόγος can—metaphorically speaking—save it. In so doing, the τέλος may reformulate itself: it is not an unmoved mover, but a self-moving one.[12] But that brings us back to Professor Greene's triple theme: noetic living, lively νόησις, and subjectivity.

Notes

1. *Nicomachean Ethics* 1094a, 1095a, 1098a; in general, happiness, the

aim of intentional action, is the well-being of the rational principle in man.

2. The argument for this would be that soul is essentially unmoved, and exercises final causality in virtue of its essence, or κατ'οὐσίαν (kat'ousian); it is incidentally moved, and its efficient causality would lie in the category of ποιεῖν (poiein), or action: cf. *De Anima* I.3 *passim* and 433b; *Physics* 212b, 259b; *Categories* 4.

3. *De Generatione Animalium* 717a, 731b, 789b; *De Partibus Animalium* 642a, 645a; *Metaphysics* 1078b, *Politics* 1326a.

4. Apart from some observations that the φυσιολόγοι (*physiologoi*) were unable to agree with one another about the nature of the material cause, this is in fact the first refutation in the *Metaphysics* of materialism (*Metaphysics* 984b). Aristotle's later arguments against it (988b and following) are more from his own philosophical standpoint; here he seems to be reporting a discovery of the φυσιολόγοι themselves.

5. *Metaphysics* 1072a. Cf. *Nicomachean Ethics* I.3 *passim*, 1098a/b, 1113b, 1115b, 1116a, 1117a/b, 1120a, 1122b, 1155a; *Politics* 1281a, 1326a, 133a; etc.

6. *Metaphysics* 1078b; *Politics* 1326a; *Poetics* 1450.

7. More strictly, Hegel refers to beauty as the immediate sensory presentation of truth: *Ästhetik*, 3 vols., Eva Moldenhauer and Karl Markus Michel, eds. (Frankfurt: Suhrkamp, 1970), I, pp. 151f, 205; for the rejection of "theoretical" or subject/object truth—mere "correctness"—cf. *loc. cit.*, 152f. Hegel's point, we may suspect, is derived from Kant's conception, in the second part of the *Critique of Judgment*, of a discipline which would look at nature from a teleological perspective but would be forbidden to make truth-claims. Hegel's point, as I take it, would be that philosophy does not make truth-claims as Kant understood them—i.e., it does not claim that its content corresponds to reality—but does make a higher truth claim: that its content *is* reality, when that term is properly understood. Cf. Hegel's remarks on the *Critique of Judgment* at *loc. cit.*, pp. 85f.

8. For sample statements of these claims, cf. Hegel, *Wissenschaft der Logik*, 2 vols., hrsg. Georg Lasson (Hamburg: Meiner, 1932), I, pp. 9, 16, 19.

9. *Enz.*, §368*Z*; also cf. M. J. Petry's note at Petry (trans., ed.), *Hegel's Philosophy of Nature*, 3 vols. (New York: Humanities Press, 1970), III, pp. 353f.

10. See Hegel, *Logik*, *loc. cit.*, for references to *Denkformen*.

11. Cf. *Enz.*, §459*A*; *Wissenschaft der Logik* I, p. 36.

12. For Hegel's "howler"—actually a significant reinterpretation of Aristotle—in making the "true essence" of the universe self-moved rather than

unmoved, cf. Haldane's note to his translation, with Frances H. Simson, of the *Lectures on the History of Philosophy*, 3 vols. (New York: Humanities Press, 1974), II, p. 145.

The "Spirit" of Hegelian Politics: Public Opinion and Legislative Debate from Hegel to Habermas

Harry Brod

Any valid interpretation of Hegel's *Philosophy of Right* must bear in mind that it is an elaboration of §§483–551 of his *Philosophy of Spirit* (or *Mind*), the section designated as "Objective Spirit."[1] To situate his political philosophy as part of the unfolding of his philosophy of spirit is to recall that Hegel's political philosophy is an *idealist* one, in that its primary concern is with the development of the *consciousness* of the citizens of the Hegelian state, rather than with their material well-being, as would be the focus of any materialist or economistic political theory. In designating his political theory as *objective* spirit, however, Hegel is also insisting that this political consciousness must not merely exist in the minds of the citizens, but that it must also be demonstrably embedded in the workings of the political institutions of the Hegelian state. Situating politics as "Objective" Spirit, between "Subjective" and "Absolute" Spirit, means that for Hegel the essential task of politics is to mediate and facilitate the transition between two dimensions of human life: first, human beings as simply "natural" entities, given over to their particular desires, abilities, idiosyncratic predilections, etc. (i.e., human beings as conceptualized by classical political economy or a Hobbesian *homo œconomicus*), and second, human beings as purely "cultural" entities, given over to the universal truths of art, religion, and philosophy. Students of Hegel are aware of the great value he placed on self-consciousness, on the idea that there is an intrinsic value in, and one might say an innate drive towards, persons coming to full consciousness of the totality of their situations. The underlying thrust of the institutions of the Hegelian state, properly understood as part of his philosophy of spirit, is to create an ever greater consciousness in the citizens' minds of their nature as political agents.

The political institutions of the Hegelian state can be divided into two types: objective institutions—i.e., the legislature, bureaucracy, and monarchy—and subjective institutions—i.e., patriotism, religion, and public opinion. Of these, one in each category has as its particular function the inculcation and propagation of an appropriate public political consciousness. Hegel's conceptualizations of public opinion and the legislature are expressly designed to mediate between objectivist and subjectivist, or, as I shall come to call them, cognitivist and voluntarist strains of political thought. Carefully tracing out Hegel's analyses in these sections of his *Philosophy of Right* is essential to understanding the important and distinctive contributions of Hegel's theory, both because it aids in understanding Hegel's own philosophy, and because it points to an important affinity and indebtedness of important contemporary theorists, such as Habermas, to Hegel. The bulk of this paper shall be devoted to this exegetical task, coupled with an analysis of the significance of the issues Hegel raises.

1. As part of his philosophy of mind, Hegel develops his *Philosophy of Right* as an explication of the concept of the will, in which the concept of right has its "point of origin."[2] To elucidate the philosophical presuppositions of this concept of the will, Hegel in the *Philosophy of Right* refers the reader back to his *Encyclopædia*, where the concept of the will, as an aspect of mind, is situated as the transition between the concepts of cognition and volition.[3] Accordingly, Hegel develops this concept in a way which allows him to mediate what are, on his analysis, two distinct tendencies in the history of ethical and political philosophy regarding the problem of the freedom of the will—on the one hand a cognitivist, objectivist, universalist approach, and on the other hand a voluntarist, subjectivist, particularist approach.[4]

The cognitivist approach leads to a justification of political authority in terms of rationality or knowledge. The prime historical example here is Plato's philosopher-rulers. The voluntarist approach leads to a justification of political authority in terms of volition or desire. The paradigm here is liberal, majoritarian-democratic theory, represented for Hegel by contractarianism. As is his wont, Hegel opts for neither of these positions absolutely, but rather attempts to synthesize the two into a concept of the rational will which preserves that which is valid in each conception. The success of Hegel's political philosophy in the later sections of the *Philosophy of Right* depends on his ability to delineate political institutions which will manifest this kind of rational will in citizens who will self-consciously reach a level of rationality by reflecting upon the political institutionalizations of their volitions. As alluded to earlier, the legislature and public opinion are centrally important to this task. It is noteworthy that an interpretation which emphasizes the importance of these particular branches of the Hegelian state, as this one does, contradicts much of the standard commentary on Hegel, much of which, in some cases under Weberian influence, looks to the bureaucracy as the major institution in the Hegelian state, as the key agent of Hegelian rationality. Thus George Sabine, for example, writes:

> The key to ... Hegel's constitutionalism was the high importance that he attached to an official governing class, the "universal class" as he called it ... it represents the general will and the "reason" of society .... . In comparison with the part assigned to officialdom, both representative institutions and the monarchy played a minor role in Hegel's theory of constitutionalism.[5]

Similarly, Georg Ahrweiler in *Hegels Gesellschaftslehre* writes, "die für *Realisierung politischer Automonie gegenüber sozialer Interessen und Interessengruppen wichtigste Instanz is zweifellos die Bürokratie* (the bureaucracy is without a doubt the most important authority for the realization of political autonomy against social interests and interest groups)."[6]

As I shall attempt to demonstrate, interpretations of Hegel's political philosophy along these lines miss the importance Hegel attaches to the spiritual, subjective dimension of political life. This is not to say that the material well-being and the economic activities of the citizens are disregarded in the Hegelian state. On the contrary, these aspects of life are the chief concern of the entire sphere of civil society, and of the bureaucracy within the state proper. But it is to say that when Hegel posits the political state as a sphere higher than civil society, he is indicating that these materialistic concerns are secondary to the more important question of the political consciousness and identity of the citizens in the modern political world. This line of interpretation is corroborated by the relative amounts of space Hegel devotes to the three branches of the state in the *Philosophy of Right*, as well as by his statements in the *Philosophy of Right* regarding the specific functions of these institutions, which we shall examine shortly.

2. A useful way of approaching Hegel's analysis of public opinion is through reference to parts of one of Jürgen Habermas' earliest works, *Strukturwandel der Öffentlichkeit* (*Structural Transformation of the Public Sphere*), which contains an intellectual history of the concept of public opinion.[7] One of Habermas' crucial concerns is to differentiate between cases where opinion is conceptualized as "public" or as "private." For example, in Plato's opinion, "$\delta\acute{\omega}\xi\alpha$" (*doxa*) is sharply differentiated from true knowledge. Opinions—held by ordinary people, expressed in everyday speech, naïve, biased, and incomplete—do not entitle one to input into the political process, which should be the sole province of those who have true knowledge, the philosophers. With this as one's point of departure, no concept of "public opinion," of a politically relevant sphere of the opinions of ordinary citizens, can emerge. For Hobbes especially, and for Locke as well in the final analysis, opinions remain private, and count primarily only in the "inner court" of conscience.

Only in the late eighteenth century does one see the emergence of a concept of "public" opinion. Only then do the collective opinions of the citizenry begin to be conceptualized as a political force, and not merely as a private domain.[8] This change in the concept of public opinion reflects a change in the actual composition of the public. The eighteenth century saw the emergence of a literate, politically active public in the new institutions of political journals and pamphlets and salons. To be politically efficacious, public opinion must be articulated through some collective institutions. At the same time, the concept has always retained some reference to the immediate, unformed opinions of people.

Habermas traces the dynamics of these aspects of "public opinion" through various theorists. To do no more than allude to key figures, Rousseau's concept of the "public spirit" for the first time combines both subjective and objective components—the general will infallibly expresses the people's natural wisdom, but it is present only in the properly constituted general assembly. Kant, despite his emphasis on individual autonomy, holds out more hope for the enlightenment of an entire public than of separate individuals. Burke's "public opinion" is found in the "real public wisdom and sagacity in shops and manufactories."[9] Bentham emerges as the first to discuss the formation of public opinion as a result of the public debates of Parliament.

With this background in mind, we may now turn to Hegel's own theory of public opinion. Given the issues raised by Habermas' historical overview, what stands out most clearly in Hegel's approach is his emphasis on the "public" nature of public opinion. This is what lies behind what would be, according to the traditional liberal logic, the anomaly of Hegel dealing with the issues of freedom of speech and the press as the concluding segment of his discussions of the political institutions of the state, rather than under the heading of the individual freedoms stemming from civil society.

To many thinkers, raising the issue of the expression of public opinion in the politicized way that Hegel does also raises fears that what is being discussed is not the freedom of expression so much as the limitation of expression. For example, Ernst Bloch writes that the whole manner in which the will of the people is treated in Hegel's *Philosophy of Right* "has the sole task of letting the people know that they are ruled well; it [the manner in which the people are represented] is not an instrument for improving the will, but solely the point at which objective spirit is mediated to subjective consciousness."[10]

For Bloch, as well as for those who subscribe to the classical liberal individual rights defense of rights of expression, discussing public opinion in the context of the functions of the state and the political formation of opinions means that one is more interested in the formation and control of public opinion, as dictated from above, than in the expression of popular sovereignty from below. There is much in Hegel to support such an estimation. Especially in his attitudes towards the French Revolution, Hegel is indeed no champion of direct popular sovereignty, and he does say that public opinion contains so much that is false that much of it must be disregarded by any able legislator.[11] But a fairer estimation of Hegel's philosophy requires an understanding of the positive reasons why Hegel situates his discussion of public opinion in this context, in addition to seeing the drawbacks of this approach. The standard individualist approach to defending freedoms of expression continues to treat political views as the private affairs of those who hold them. As Habermas' historical account of the concept of public opinion shows, on this view the right to express one's views belongs to a separate sphere from any considerations of the possible impact of those views on actual political affairs. The right to speak is systematically separated from the right to be listened to, which does not enter into the picture at all. However, when public opinion is treated not as a question of private right but as a question of public welfare, then the right to speak carries with it the right to speak in forums which have access to real political power. The rights to the expression of public opinion follow not from individual, natural rights, but from the demand of modern consciousness to have input into and find recognition of itself in modern political institutions.

Hegel's understanding of the rights of modern political consciousness leads him to affirm the necessity of a free press and public education, as well as the necessity for institutionalized access to policy makers by ordinary citizens, so that everyone can feel that they have had their say and been heard. At the same time, policy makers must not let such a system of citizens' input into the system degenerate into a system of government by plebiscite or referendum, because public opinion is too unstable for such a system to achieve the necessary political stability. Indeed, in a comment reflecting the most disparaging aspects of Hegel's attitudes towards public opinion, Hegel offers as a supporting argument for full freedom of expression the idea that in a well-run political system, much of what is said by public opinion is rendered superfluous and innocuous by the rationality of the debates and decisions of public officials.

> Freedom of public communication . . . is assured indirectly by the innocuous character which it acquires as a result principally of the rationality of the constitution, the stability of the government, and secondly of the publicity of Estates Assemblies. The reason why the latter makes free speech harmless is that what is voiced in these assemblies is a sound and mature insight into the concerns of the state, with the result that members of the general public are left with nothing of much importance to say, and above all are deprived of the opinion that what they say is of particular importance and efficacy.[12]

Hegel's attitudes towards public opinion share the same ambivalence evident in his attitudes towards the general political consciousness of his day. It is the repository of valid truths, yet these truths are lost in a mass of scattered opinions. It is the task of philosophy to sort out what is true and deserving of being preserved from what is not. Here Hegel has added to his analysis of the relationship between the ordinary discourse of everyday life and the task of the philosopher the insight that this confrontation between philosophy and ordinary language can successfully take place only when the encounter is mediated through established institutional recognition of public opinion. This recognition brings articulated public opinion into the light of the public forum. This forum itself then plays a pedagogical role in further refining public opinion because all political deliberations must be open to the public and publicized.

It may be well at this point to call attention to the deepest significance of what is at stake here in Hegel's analysis of public opinion, and to suggest why it is appropriate that it is the last topic he deals with in discussing the institutions of the state. We have emphasized the importance of the *consciousness* of the citizens in Hegel's political philosophy, an emphasis which results from Hegel developing his political philosophy as part of a philosophy of spirit. What Hegel's political idealism successfully captures about the modern state is that modern politics, like no earlier political system or theory, is founded on the consciousness of the citizens. This is what for Hegel is correct about contractarian political theory, which bases political legitimacy on the will. But contractarian theory incorrectly conceptualizes this will as a private, individual will, and thus fails to do justice to the need for this will to be an internal part of the political system in which it finds recognition of its efficacy. Individualistically based political theory leads either to a system in which each individual feels that their will must be immediately and directly active and effective in ordering political life (Hegel has in mind here the Terror which followed the French Revolution), or to a system in which the essential element in politics is seen to be the private, personal interests of individuals, and the whole political sphere is seen as simply a means to that end (Hegel's target here is the liberalism of his day). The creation of an integrated, satisfying political system which is subject to neither anarchy nor alienation, argues Hegel, depends on a social, universal conception of the will which can serve as a foundation for politics, and not a private, particularist conception of that will.

Ultimately at issue here is the Hegelian notion of recognition as a basis for the legitimacy of political authority, in contrast to the liberal notion of consent. Hegel finds the standard liberal notion of consent, as paradigmatically expressed in classical social contract theory, too volitional for it to play the foundational role assigned to it in these theories. He attempts to found political legitimacy on a more complex sociological analysis of the institutional arrangements required for individuals to identify with and find an expression of their will in political institutions.

The liberal contractarian notion of consent places individuals in a hypothetical state of nature outside the actual societies in which they live, and asks what institutions they would validate from this exterior vantage point. Similarly, the liberal defense of freedoms of speech and expression also marks out a private sphere to be held inviolate and outside the sphere of social regulation. In contrast, the Hegelian notion of recognition situates the rights of freedom of speech and expression as political, not civil, rights. That is to say, they are rights of participation in political power, rights to find one's will reflected in the social process of political decision-making, not rights to exemption from the exercise of political power. Further, the Hegelian state is legitimated, on the Hegelian political logic, to the extent that citizens of the Hegelian state would actually, and not only hypothetically, affirm the institutions of their society. A proper understanding of the sphere of public opinion as the locus of these affirmations is thus essential to the Hegelian political enterprise.

A crucial element in this Hegelian conception of politics is this conceptualization of public opinion in political terms which has just been presented. Thus, while Hegel's concept of public opinion does carry with it the risk of authoritarian overtones which threaten to limit the free expression of opinion, it also carries with it the possibility of much greater integration of public opinion into the political process than the individualistic alternative. Indeed, it should be noted that the liberal defense of free speech usually put forward as the preferred alternative to Hegel's view has always recognized the right of the state to limit threatening speech. Radical critics of liberalism have even argued that in varying historical periods the degree of toleration of radical political speech in liberal societies seems to vary in inverse proportion to the degree of effectiveness of that speech.[13]

The importance of the idea that the modern state bases its legitimacy on the consciousness of the citizens can be illustrated by reference to Habermas' development of this concept. We noted that the historical overview of the concept of public opinion cited earlier appears in one of Habermas' earliest works. This political concept of public opinion is crucial to understanding the concepts of political legitimacy and of the legitimation crisis of the modern state which Habermas develops in his later work.[14] It is only because the modern state depends for its legitimacy in its own self-understanding on the principle of the rational will of its citizens that a crisis of confidence in the system becomes a serious *internal* problem for the system itself, and not a threat from without by a competing system. The "legitimation crisis" of modern states is differentiated from all previous forms of failures in the legitimating arguments of the system (e.g., religion, tradition, etc.) by the way in which the crisis of legitimacy enters into the logic of the system itself. By way of contrast, the denial of the divine right of kings was an external denial of the entire form of legitimating arguments of an earlier period, and not an immanent critique and challenge to the authority of this or that monarch from within the religious authoritarian paradigm of argument. The universal rise of the principles of the modern state, however, means that all arguments for the legitimacy of one state over another remain within a logic which holds that the legitimacy of the political order is founded in the rational will of the citizens.

The point can be put in other idioms as well. It is commonly argued that around the mid-nineteenth century the term "democracy" shifted from a primarily descriptive to a primarily emotive meaning. That is to say, prior to this period, "democracy" was more or less consistently used to refer to a system of direct rule by the majority of the people, and was as such argued for or against. After the mid-nineteenth century "democracy" lost this specific cognitive content, and diverse political systems from representative democracy to communism all advanced arguments designed to put forth their claims to the title of being a true system of democracy. The principle underlying this change is what Hegel has in mind when he declares that in the modern world politics must be based on the will of all, and all that remains is to work out the more precise meaning of this principle. The unchallenged, universal acceptance of this very basic principle is what Hegel has captured in the basic principles of his political philosophy and in his claim that the modern era has reached this decisive stage from which there can be no retreat. Hegel's attention is on the underlying deep level of continuity and agreement in the foundations of political discourse in the modern world which makes it possible, for example, to take competing systems like capitalism and communism and cast the arguments for each in terms acceptable to the other system; to speak of competing claims to realize political and economic democracy; and to construct a dialogue in a way in which a dialogue with shared basic assumptions could not have been constructed between monarchists and republicans, for example, in an earlier period. Every modern political system must in some sense claim to express "the voice of the people" and give at least lip service to the idea of "popular sovereignty," while classical or medieval political systems had no such obligation.

Public opinion is the sphere in which the universal truths of the age find their particular voices to articulate them. It is here that what one commentator calls "the ascending and descending power structures,"[15] the voices of the many seeking political power from below and the voice of the state conferring legitimacy from above, most clearly meet in the consciousness of the citizens. This is the closest Hegel comes to answering a key question which has troubled many commentators on Hegel's political philosophy, the question of precisely how much knowledge of the principles of political philosophy do the claims of Hegel's philosophy require one to attribute to the citizens of the Hegelian state.[16] Between the extreme poles of the claim that all Hegelian citizens must essentially be Hegelian philosophers and the claim that only the few true Hegelian philosophers in the state possess a satisfied consciousness lies the Hegelian middle, which claims that these principles are embodied in the institutions which constitute the Hegelian state, and that these institutions are structured with an eye towards the creation of a rational sphere of public opinion open to all. All Hegelian political institutions are evaluated by Hegel with their effect on the consciousness of those who participate in them as a key criterion in this evaluation. There is, it should be noted, a necessary indeterminacy in the empirical application of these principles. That is to say, Hegel does not need to show that every empirical individual in the Hegelian state can give a full account of the rationale behind all political institutions and practices. To make such a demand misunderstands the nature of philosophy, which needs only provide the general principles on which the society is to be ordered.

In modern terms, the public opinion which, for Hegel, testifies to the political freedom and involvement of the citizenry is not that which is registered by random surveys or public opinion polls, but rather that public opinion which is reflected in such forums as public media political commentaries, resolutions of social, civic, and religious bodies, the formation of citizens' groups, etc. This is public opinion as publicly articulated, not simply as privately held. Hegel looks to one particular branch of the state to serve as a vehicle for the translation of this public opinion into the laws of the state. In the following section, I shall not be so much concerned to argue that Hegel succeeds in delineating structures which will consistently uphold a free sphere of public opinion (such an evaluation would have to systematically address issues such as the apparent elitism of Hegel's position, and is beyond the scope of this essay), as I shall be concerned to show that this is the problematic which motivates important aspects of the construction of the Hegelian state. I believe that, aside from the question of Hegel's success at instantiating his principles, his unique approach to the question of public discourse is an important contribution to political theory.

3. The institution which deals most directly with the formation of public consciousness in the Hegelian state, and which in fact leads Hegel into his discussion of public opinion in the first place, is the legislature, and so it is necessary to turn to an examination of the Estates Assembly. The most important aspect of the Estates is their role in the formation of public political consciousness, rather than their role in taking care of the material interests of the citizens. Though the latter is an important function of the legislature, and, as we shall see, Hegel has definite ideas as to how this should best be carried out, it is not to the legislature but to the bureaucracy that this latter function is assigned as a primary task.

> The purpose of the Estates as an institution is not to be an inherent *sine qua non* of maximum efficiency in the consideration of state business, since in fact it is only an added efficiency that they can supply (see §301). Their distinctive purpose is that, in their pooled political knowledge, deliberations, and decisions, the moment of formal freedom shall come into its right in respect of those members of civil society who are without any share

> in the executive. Consequently, it is knowledge of public
> business above all which is extended by the publicity of
> the Estates debates.[17]

While unorganized public opinion threatens to become mob rule and would be a force in opposition to the state (as in the extremes of Jacobinism), the Estates turn this potentially oppositional into an integrative force in the society. "They [the Estates] prevent individuals from having the appearance of a mass or an aggregate and so from acquiring an unorganized opinion and volition and from crystallizing into a powerful bloc in opposition to the organized state."[18]

Note that Hegel does not argue that an *independent* volition is harmful to the state, but only that an unorganized one is. The point here is not to stifle or co-opt dissent, but to create an institutional channel for public dialogue. Lack of a channel for input into the political system is far more alienating and disruptive of political harmony than dissident opinions themselves.

> In France freedom of speech has turned out far less dan-
> gerous than enforced silence, because with the latter the
> fear is that men bottle up their objections to a thing,
> whereas argument gives them an outlet and a measure
> of satisfaction, and this is in addition a means whereby
> the thing can be pushed ahead more easily.[19]

Given that in the modern world people demand that the political system fulfill their demands for the recognition of their subjective consciousness, the alternative to a representative Assembly is violence. "When the multitude enters the state as one of its organs, it achieves its interests by legal and orderly means. But if these means are lacking, the voice of the masses is always for violence."[20]

The public business conducted by the Estates includes not only the passing of laws serving the "well-being and happiness"[21] of the citizens, but also the extracting of services from the citizens towards the state. It is a mark of the modern state that these services, with the exception of military service, which is a uniquely personal form of service, are all extracted through the medium of taxation, rather than through tasks directly performed for the state by the citizens. This permits one's service to the state to be mediated through one's subjective consciousness, since in the modern state one is essentially free to choose the means through which one earns the money which goes to the state. The state does not infringe on the sphere of personal dignity by deciding for the individual what kind of work is to be done by the individual for the public welfare, argues Hegel.

> In these circumstances [e.g., Plato's *Republic*, feudal monarchies, Egyptian and Eastern public monuments] the principle of subjective freedom is lacking, i.e., the principle that the individual's substantive activity ... shall be mediated through his particular volition. This is a right which can be secured only when the demand for service takes the form of a demand for something of universal value, and it is this right which has brought with it this conversion of the state's demands into demands for cash.[22]

Hegel proposes that the legislature should consist of two houses. In this way, each of the classes of civil society can attain their appropriate political significance. One house is to represent the agricultural class, and membership in this body is fixed by birth. It is here that the social, political concept of private property developed by Hegel in abstract form in the "Abstract Right" section of the *Philosophy of Right* has its most explicit direct impact on the form of institutions in the Hegelian state.[23] The idea that property is family property comes in this class to mean that this property is not subject totally to the individual prerogative of any member of the landed class, and must be handed down according to the rules of primogeniture in order to assure that there is in the state a fixed, substantial class which comes into direct relation to the state, without having its fortunes depend on "the state's capital, the uncertainty of business, the quest for profit, and any sort of fluctuation in possessions. It is likewise independent of favour, whether from the executive or the mob."[24]

Seen in historical perspective, this is the same kind of nostalgia for which Hegel criticizes Plato when he attempts to conceptualize a form of the Greek πόλις (*polis*) already rendered obsolete in some ways by the growing commercialization of Athens. The non-commercial aristocracy on which this description of Hegel's depends was already a rapidly vanishing breed when this was written. Nonetheless, Hegel's underlying principle, that in the interest of greater social stability a way should be found to have at least one segment of the government not committed to the proposition that the business of government is business, can be separated from the specific class Hegel pinpointed to embody this idea. In any case, Hegel's most distinctive contribution to the question of how legislative representation is best to be achieved comes in his discussion of the other house of the Estates, whose members are elected by the business class. While the members of the landed class are directly present in the Assembly in their own persons, the members of the commercial class are represented by their deputies, and Hegel's doctrine of the nature of this representation is key to understanding how the Estates are to facilitate the growth of political reconciliation and identity out of the economic diversity of civil society.

Hegel's doctrine of representation is derived from his concept of political mediation, which holds that in order to prevent the alienation and anomie which continually threaten to dominate modern political life, it is essential that individuals interact with the state not as isolated individuals, who would be overwhelmed by the scale and complexity of the modern state, but as members of organizations which ensure that their members have attained a stable political identity. The state is thus not a conglomerate of individuals, but "an organization each of whose members is in itself a group."[25] Hegel argues that the representative of the commercial class must be chosen through the organizations which give that class social cohesion and enable it to have political status and impact. To disperse these associations at election time by having each individual vote for deputies at large would lose the political integration which the corporations have achieved in civil society and through their role in making the transition from civil society to the state. Representatives are elected as representatives of specific corporations and other associations.

> Since these deputies are the deputies of civil society, it follows as a direct consequence that their appointment is made by the society as a society. That is to say, in making the appointment, society is not dispersed into atomic units, collected to perform only a single and temporary act, and kept together for a moment and no longer. On the contrary, it makes the appointment as a society, articulated into associations, communities, and corporations, which although constituted already for other purposes, acquire in this way a connexion with politics.[26]

Hegel's concept of representation mediates between what Hannah Pitkin, in an insightful analysis, calls the "Burkean" and "liberal" concepts of representation.[27] In terms of the discussion here, these correspond respectively to cognitivist and voluntarist conceptions. What is striking about Hegel's theory is his use of a non-liberal schema for the attainment of the ends of liberal doctrine. On the Burkean model: "The member [of Parliament] is to pursue the interest of his constituency rather than do its bidding; the characteristic feature of the Burkean approach is that such a contrast is possible and even highly meaningful."[28]

Hegel's doctrine of election to the Assembly through corporations rather than through direct universal suffrage assumes this Burkean distinction. Like Burke, he argues that representatives are chosen for their insight into the affairs of the nation as a whole, seen from the perspective of the interests of their constituency. While they are elected because the electors have confidence in their judgment, once they are in office they are not bound by the will of their constituency, but are to follow their own judgment. The Assembly is not a congregation which simply records the votes of delegates delivering opinions developed in separate political bodies in isolation from each other. It is a deliberative body whose rationality emerges from the discussions in its chambers. Consequently, the delegates must have the freedom to have their insight shaped by parliamentary debate.

> Since deputies are elected to deliberate and decide on *public* affairs, the point about their election is that it is a choice of individuals on the strength of confidence felt in them, i.e., a choice of such individuals as have a better understanding of these affairs than their electors have and such also as essentially vindicate the universal interest, not the particular interest of a society or a Corporation in preference to that interest. Hence their relation to their electors is not that of agents with a commission or specific instructions. A further bar to their being so is the fact that their assembly is meant to be a living body in which all members deliberate in common and reciprocally instruct and convince each other.[29]

For Burke and Hegel, it is essential that all branches of society have their interests represented, and Hegel argues that leaving the matter simply to universal suffrage not tied to already organized interests does not insure that this will happen. For both, the essential element is that each particular point of view on the universal be represented in public deliberations. The point is not a competition of power among different interests, but the completeness of public debate, and therefore both are not so much concerned with the numerical distribution of representatives among different groups as they are with the simple requirement that each constituency be represented.

> It is obviously of advantage that the deputies should include representatives of each particular main branch of society (e.g., trade, manufactures, &c, &c.)—representatives who are thoroughly conversant with it and who themselves belong to it. The idea of free unrestricted election leaves this important consideration entirely at the mercy of chance.[30]

Taken in this context, it becomes clear that Hegel's criticism of direct universal suffrage is that it does not assure sufficiently equitable representation of all elements of society, not that it gives too great a voice to the people. In fact, Hegel argues that one of the flaws of undifferentiated universal suffrage is that in large states it will encourage political abstention and apathy, "since the casting of a single vote is of no significance where there is a multitude of electors."[31] As Shlomo Avineri points out, "Hegel is thus among the first political theorists to recognize that direct suffrage would create a system very different from that envisaged by the advocates of such a system of direct representation."[32]

> Thus the result of an institution of this kind is more likely to be the opposite of what was intended; election actually falls into the power of a few, of a caucus, and so of the particular and contingent interest which is precisely what was to have been neutralized.[33]

These same concerns figure prominently in Hegel's other political writings, in which he often criticizes what are to him simply abstract age and property qualifications for voting, qualifications which do not take into account the properly political concerns which Hegel's theory addresses. In the "Proceedings of the Estates Assembly in the Kingdom of Wurtemberg, 1815–1816," Hegel writes:

> Provisions of the kind which presuppose a nation as a mass rather than a state and divide it generally by numbers into particular masses and by age and a specified

> property qualification into two classes cannot possibly
> be called *political* institutions. They do not suffice to
> strip the people's share in national affairs of its demo-
> cratic formlessness or to attain the end of not leaving
> to chance the acquisition of fit deputies for a National
> Assembly. A political institution cannot be content with
> the mere demand that something ought to happen, with
> the hope that it will happen, with barring certain factors
> which might impede its happening. It deserves its name
> only when it is so organized that what ought to happen
> does happen.[34]

The same ideas figure in Hegel's criticisms of the proposed reforms in "The English Reform Bill" of 1831,[35] and it is these passages in which Sidney Hook so erroneously sees something "ominous."[36]

Hegel's concern that the Estates continue to function as a vehicle to channel the consciousness and input of the citizens into the political system is why the Burkean model does not exhaust Hegel's doctrine of representation. This concern motivates the element of Hegel's doctrine which corresponds to the "liberal" or voluntarist concept of representation. On the logic of the dominant aspect of Burke's concept of representation which we have been discussing, the process of electing representatives seems almost superfluous. What matters here is that their objectively measurable interests are being advanced, not that their subjectively held opinions are being validated. As Pitkin describes the interest which the Burkean representative is said to represent, "these interests are largely economic .... To a very great extent, these interests are conceived of as 'unattached'; it is not the interest of farmers but the agricultural interest— an objective reality for Burke apart from any individuals it might affect."[37]

It is this distance from the consciousness and lives of the individuals affected themselves which Hegel cannot accept in the Burkean doctrine. As we have seen, for Hegel the primary task of the Estates Assembly is to ensure the identification of the citizens with the political process, to be the institutionalization of the citizens' active role in politics. Hegel sides with the liberal concept of representation in insisting that what is being repre-sented is not "unattached interests," but "people who have interests."[38] For Hegel, the chief qualifying asset that representatives bring to their de-liberations is not any privileged insight into the general welfare, though it is to be hoped that electors are looking for this quality in their representatives, but the confidence of their constituency, who feel that their interests are being looked after. This is a decidedly subjective criterion, in contrast to Burke, who argues that the representatives should be demonstrably better educated, cultured, etc., than their constituents. In the final analysis, no political theory so thoroughly based on the will as is Hegel's can result in a Burkean conservatism. In this way, the legislature secures the institutionalized recognition of the importance of the subjective consciousness of the citizens essential to the proper functioning of the Hegelian state. Representatives validate the public opinions, and not merely the interests, of their constituencies.

To conclude by returning to the theme enunciated at the outset of this essay, that of interpreting Hegel's political philosophy as part of his philosophy of spirit, one may say that Hegel's unique modes of conceptualizing public opinion and legislative institutions—as integral and essential parts of the ladder spirit must ascend on its way from immersion in nature to free participation in culture—are the best examples of the Hegelian project to attempt to "spiritualize" politics in the positive Hegelian sense, that is to say, to see political affairs as a manifestation of a collective, social mind or intelligence, without "spiritualizing" politics in a negative, overly romantic sense, that is to say, seeing political consciousness reduced to the internal subjective states of mind of individuals, with insufficient attention being paid to this consciousness' institutional embodiment. These often neglected dimensions of Hegel's political philosophy are thus essential moments of his philosophical system.

Notes

1. G. W. F. Hegel, *Philosophy of Right*, trans. T. M. Knox (Oxford: Oxford University Press, 1952) [hereafter *PR*], and Hegel, *Philosophy of Mind*, trans. William Wallace and A. V. Miller (Oxford: Oxford University Press, 1971).

2. *PR*, p. 20.

3. G. W. F. Hegel, *The Encyclopædia of the Philosophical Sciences*, Part I, *Logic*, trans. William Wallace (Oxford: Oxford University Press,

1972), pp. 370–373.

4. *PR*, p. 23. While Patrick Riley, in his *Will and Political Legitimacy: A Critical Exposition of Social Contract Theory in Hobbes, Locke, Rousseau, Kant and Hegel* (Cambridge, Mass.: Harvard University Press, 1982), correctly identifies these two strains in Hegel's concept of the will, he errs in concluding that Hegel minimizes the voluntarist strain to such an extent that for him "consent, contract, election, and opinion, so important to social contract theorists, are of little value." Chapter 5, "Hegel on Consent and Social Contract Theory: Does He 'Cancel and Preserve' the Will?", p. 173.

5. George Sabine, *A History of Political Theory*, Third Edition (New York: Holt, Rinehart & Winston, 1961), pp. 662–663.

6. Georg Ahrweiler, *Hegels Gesellschaftslehre* (Neuwied: Luchterhand, 1976), p. 147.

7. Jürgen Habermas, *Strukturwandel der Öffentlichkeit* (Neuwied: Luchterhand, 1976), p. 115.

8. Habermas is not alone in placing the rise of "public opinion" in this period. A contemporary, C.-C. de Rulhière, is approvingly quoted by Crane Brinton in placing the rise of "the empire of public opinion" in pre-Revolutionary Paris. See "Reflections on the Alienation of the Intellectuals," in *Generalizations in Historical Writing*, ed. Alexander V. Riasanovsky and Barnes Riznik (Philadelphia: University of Pennsylvania, 1963), p. 213. For a survey of the influence of that aspect of Habermas' work under discussion here, see Peter Uwe Hohendahl, "Critical Theory, Public Sphere, and Culture. Jürgen Habermas and his Critics," *New German Critique* 16 (Winter 1979): 89–118.

9. Habermas, *op. cit.*, p. 118.

10. Ernst Bloch, *"Der Schwur auf den Styx. Der zweideutige Kosmos in Hegel's Rechtsphilosophie,"* in *Materialien zu Hegels Rechtsphilosophie, Band 2*, ed. Manfred Riedel (Frankfurt am Main: Suhrkamp, 1974), pp. 433–434.

11. *PR*, pp. 204–205.

12. *Ibid.*, pp. 205–206.

13. See *A Critique of Pure Tolerance*, Robert Paul Wolff, Barrington Moore, Jr., and Herbert Marcuse (Boston: Beacon Press, 1965). The earlier, contractarian version of liberalism with which Hegel was familiar is more susceptible to this strain of criticism than some later versions, though the individualist base is never abandoned. For example, some of Hegel's suggestions come close to John Dewey's "social conception of intelligence" in works like *Liberalism and Social Action* (New York: Capricorn, 1963).

14. See Jürgen Habermas, *Legitimation Crisis* (Boston: Beacon, 1975),

and *Communication and the Evolution of Society* (Boston: Beacon, 1979), Chapter 5. For a sociological analysis which expressly links the Frankfurt School's analysis of the concept "public opinion" to Hegel's concept of "Objective Spirit," see Friedrich Pollock, "Empirical Research into Public Opinion," trans. Thomas Hall, in *Critical Sociology*, ed. Paul Connerton (Harmondsworth, England: Penguin, 1976).

15. G. Heiman, "The Sources and Significance of Hegel's Corporate Doctrine," in *Hegel's Political Philosophy*, ed. Z. A. Pelczynski (Cambridge: Cambridge University Press, 1971), p. 135.

16. See Robert Pippin, "Hegel's Political Argument and the Problem of *Verwirklichung*," *Political Theory* 9, 4 (November 1981): 509–532.

17. *PR*, p. 203.

18. *Ibid.*, p. 197.

19. *Ibid.*, p. 294.

20. *Ibid.*, pp. 292–293.

21. *Ibid.*, p. 194.

22. *Ibid.*, p. 195.

23. *Ibid.*, pp. 37–57. This point is discussed at length in my unpublished manuscript, "Property, Poverty, and Personhood: Hegel on Economics and Freedom," prepared for the 1982 Roe Foundation Prize.

24. *PR*, p. 199.

25. *Ibid.*, p. 198.

26. *Ibid.*, p. 200.

27. Hannah Pitkin, *The Concept of Representation* (Berkeley: University of California Press, 1972), *passim.*

28. *Ibid.*, p. 176.

29. *PR*, p. 201.

30. *Ibid.*, p. 202. Cf. Pitkin on Burke, p. 187:

> The interests are only discovered in Parliament, through debate. But their discovery presupposes the participation of representatives of every interest so that all considerations will be brought to light in the debate. For Burke this has nothing to do with compromise among the wishes of conflicting groups; government is a matter of reason and not of will. But reason needs deliberators from every relevant point of view.

31. *PR*, p. 203.

32. Avineri, *op. cit.*, p. 163.

33. *PR*, p. 203.

34. G. W. F. Hegel, *Hegel's Political Writings*, trans. T. M. Knox (Oxford: Oxford University Press, 1964), p. 256.

35. *Ibid.*, pp. 295–330, especially 317–321.

36. Sidney Hook, "Hegel Rehabilitated?" in *Hegel's Political Philosophy*, ed. Walter Kaufmann (New York: Atherton, 1970), p. 61.

37. Pitkin, *op. cit.*, p. 174.

38. *Ibid.*, p. 190.

Commentary on
"The 'Spirit' of Hegelian Politics: Public Opinion
and Legislative Debate from Hegel to Habermas"

Florindo Volpacchio

Professor Brod tries to locate the characteristics of Habermas' public sphere in Hegel's discussion of public opinion and in the debates of the Estates Assemblies. He attempts to show how public opinion in Hegel serves the same purpose of developing a collective identity and of integrating the individual into society. Habermas himself notes how, at first glance, it appears that Hegel retains the eighteenth century notion of the public sphere.[1] But the actual political role of public opinion in Hegel is different from the liberal model of the public sphere.

Hegel's rejection of the liberal public sphere is best summed up in his statement "public opinion . . . deserves to be as much respected as despised . . . ."[2] On the one hand, it is a repository of the genuine needs and practices of common life as well as the principles, duties, and loyalties which bind society and the state; on the other hand, public opinion is determined by the accidents of opinion, ignorance, perversity, and false judgments.[3] Thus, despite its glimmer of truth, it should be despised for indulging and acting on the peculiarity of its own convictions, and for priding itself on the private and personal against the rational and universal.[4] The problem with public opinion is the same problem with the standpoint of morality: it tries to generate truth out of the strength of its personal conviction, rather than locate the truth in the norms of ethical life.[5] Public opinion then should not be equated with the standpoint of reason (*Vernunft*). As Habermas

145

himself notes, by presenting public opinion as the self-deception of the public, Hegel has rejected the right of the public to reason for itself.[6]

For Hegel, public opinion does not truly stand for the public's general will; it usually only represents a narrow particular interest. After all, public opinion emerges out of civil society as a product of the self-defining interests developed within the "system of needs."[7] Thus, according to Habermas, the source of Hegel's degradation of public opinion lies in the Hegelian understanding of civil society, where the transactions of all private individuals are not emancipated from domination or neutral with respect to power. The existence of classes, competition, and poverty causes public opinion to lose its basis in unity and truth, and it discredits public opinion's capacity to reason politically. This destroys the liberal fiction of a self-understanding public.[8] The excesses of the marketplace are in part controlled by the corporations. But, as Habermas notes, this is a concept of a public dimension within a private sphere which is no longer a liberal one. With the concept of society held in check by the corporation, Hegel has definitively surmounted the tradition of liberalism.[9]

Furthermore, in Hegel's understanding of civil society, not everyone has equal access to the public or participates in public opinion. Hegel derides all those who make appeals to the universal will based on public opinion for ignoring the fact that the public excludes women and others traditionally disenfranchised.[10] Even if everyone did have access to the public, it would still be dangerous to base the state on the collective wills of individuals. Such a mass would be merely an undefined collection of individuals.[11] Their moralistic standpoint would only lead to barbarous behavior and romantic political terrorism.[12]

Hegel takes up public opinion in the context of the state because the political nature of public opinion, bound by the particular self-interests of civil society, turns it into a threat which must be checked. Public opinion must not be controlled in civil society; to do so would mean the annihilation of the principle of subjective freedom. But to introduce public opinion directly into the state would mean transferring the conflicts of civil society into the state.[13] For public opinion to be an effective and controlled form of political expression, especially within the modern state where the direct political participation of everyone is impossible, it must be mediated.[14] This mediation is provided by the Estates Assemblies.

The Estates introduce the private will and judgment of civil society into the state. But they do so in such a way that they prevent individuals from appearing as an oppositional mass or from acquiring an unorganized opinion.[15] The deputies of the Estates Assemblies are to be highly qualified, experienced politicians who judge critically the particular interests which they represent and do not factionalize the legislature.[16] Since not everyone can participate in the affairs of state, those best qualified to become deputies, especially in the second chamber of the Estates Assemblies, are to be found among managers and businessmen, for their occupation allows them to develop the managerial and bargaining sense necessary for governing.[17] Thus, even in the Estates Assemblies, one form of opinion predominates, that of the middle class, "the class in which the consciousness of right and the developed intelligence of the mass of the people is found."[18]

The legislative process that goes on in the Estates Assemblies should be open and publicized. This appears to coincide with the principle of public information that defines the liberal public sphere for Habermas. But, for Hegel, what is more important about public proceedings lies in how they educate the public to the affairs of state.[19] Thus the Estates Assemblies are not an outlet for public opinion in the state; rather, "it is through them that the state enters the subjective consciousness of the people ...."[20] This process, as Habermas says, undermines the original notion of public opinion. A public dimension degraded to a sphere of education no longer has any value as a principle of enlightenment and as a sphere of reason to be realized.[21] The dominion of the personal then is refrained from directly affecting the state. Having turned public opinion into an ideological component of the state, it is not too difficult for Hegel to tolerate the freedom of public communication. Even so, it is protected primarily as a safety valve for releasing dissatisfaction and dissent, rather than as a way in which the public develops a rational will through discourse.[22]

As noted earlier, Hegel does detect a glimmer of truth in public opinion for which it must be respected. But this truth is discovered by not clinging "simply to the words in which public opinion is directly expressed."[23] Public opinion, then, should not be judged by what it thinks of itself. It is only the great man, says Hegel, who can find the truth in public opinion. "The great man of the age is the one who can put into words the will of his age, tell his age what its will is, and accomplish it. What he does is the heart and the essence of his age, he actualizes his age."[24] Thus the glimmer of truth that is to be found in public opinion is another manifestation of the cunning of reason at work.

If Hegel preserves any characteristics of the public sphere, it is within his conception of the corporation. The corporation is part of civil society where public opinion rightfully should pursue its freedom. It is a public organization accessible to everyone and open in its proceedings. Through a process of rational decision making, the members express the needs of their group to other social organizations and to their political representatives. Thus it ensures a realm in which private individuals may assemble to participate in a public body without being public officials. The corporation, then, is also involved in the political education of the citizenry, but this time it occurs through the direct involvement of the members themselves within the decision making process of the corporation.[25] What makes the corporation significant is that it involves the moral interaction of individuals. Like the liberal model of the public sphere, it is the one area where the moral and the political coincide in Hegel. For this reason, Hegel calls it the second ethical root of the state after the family, the one in civil society.[26]

Hegel's conception of public opinion anticipated the disintegration of the public sphere by the self-interest of civil society; through the corporation Hegel tried to bring about its structural transformation in light of the responsibility delegated to the public authority of the modern state to control the excesses of the marketplace.[27] Yet even Hegel did not expect the degree to which the economic and technological subsystems would penetrate all aspects of public life and overwhelm the normative institutional framework of the state; for him, the economic system retained its connection to ethical life through the mediation of the legal system.[28] The domination of instrumental reason, coupled with the current levels of public lack of interest in criticizing and effecting political decisions through public participation, means more than inefficacy of public opinion; it leads to the loss of the principle of subjective freedom. This is the problem confronting Habermas. Through the concept of public opinion, Habermas tries to recover the principle of subjective freedom which Hegel took for granted because he considered it inherent to civil society. As Hegel says, public opinion is a great power, but only to the extent that the principle of subjective freedom remains important and significant.[29] Despite his criticism of public opinion, even Hegel would have found the current lack of interest in questions of power and politics among the public deeply disturbing.

Notes

1. Jürgen Habermas, *Strukturwandel der Öffentlichkeit: Untersuchungen zu einer Kategorie der bürgerlichen Gesellschaft* (Berlin: Luchterhand, 1962), p. 144.

2. G. W. F. Hegel, *Philosophy of Right*, trans. by T. M. Knox (London: Oxford University Press, 1942), §318.

3. *Ibid.*, §317.

4. *Ibid.*, §§317–18.

5. In §337 of the *Philosophy of Right*, Hegel discusses the separation of politics and morals. Habermas specifically notes how Hegel thinks the reconciliation of the political with the moral in general is a false problem; this is characteristic of Hegel's rejection of the liberal model of the public sphere (Habermas, *op. cit.*, p. 147).

6. Habermas, *op. cit.*, p. 147.

7. Habermas also points out how, for Hegel, public opinion emerges out of the system of needs to crystallize into a powerful bloc in opposition to the organized state (Habermas, *op. cit.*, p. 146). However, even in his own presentation of the liberal public sphere, Habermas argues that in the eighteenth century "society had become a concern of public interest to the degree that the reproduction of life in the wake of the developing market economy had grown beyond the bounds of private domestic authority" (Jürgen Habermas, "The Public Sphere: An Encyclopedia Article [1964]," trans. by S. Lennox and F. Lennox, *New German Critique* 3 [Fall 1974]: 52).

8. Habermas, *op. cit.*, pp. 145–6, 149.

9. *Ibid.*, p. 147.

10. Hegel, *Philosophy of Right*, §301A.

11. *Ibid.*, §308A.

12. *Ibid.*, §303A. In the preface to the *Philosophy of Right*, Hegel attacks Jacob Fries for his populist views (pp. 5–6). The movement which Fries represented, however, turned out to be racist, nationalist, violent, and a threat to liberty—the necessary consequence of emotional political movements among the masses for Hegel. For a discussion of Fries, see

Knox's "Translator's Notes," *Philosophy of Right*, pp. 299–300; and Shlomo Avineri, *Hegel's Theory of the Modern State* (Cambridge: Cambridge University Press, 1972), pp. 119–21, 130.

13. Habermas, *op. cit.*, p. 146.

14. Hegel, *op. cit.*, §308*A*. Hegel argues that, in states where there is no mediating organ present between the government and the people, the tendency of the people will always be towards mob action. In such an order, it is not possible for a unity of interests to emerge between the people and the ruler. Violence can be the only outcome (Hegel, *op. cit.*, §302*Z*).

15. *Ibid.*, §302.

16. *Ibid.*, §309.

17. *Ibid.*, §310.

18. *Ibid.*, §297.

19. *Ibid.*, §315.

20. *Ibid.*, §301*Z*.

21. Habermas, *op. cit.*, p. 147.

22. Hegel, *op. cit.*, §317*Z*, §319.

23. *Ibid.*, §317*A*.

24. *Ibid.*, §318*Z*. Cf. Marx, from *The Holy Family*: "It is not a question of what this or that proletarian or even the whole proletariat momentarily *imagines* to be the aim. It is a question of *what* the proletariat *is* and what it *consequently* is historically compelled to do" (L. D. Easton and K. H. Guddat, eds., *Writings of the Young Marx on Philosophy and Society* [Garden City, N.Y.: Anchor Books, 1967], p. 368).

25. Hegel, *op. cit.*, §§252–256.

26. *Ibid.*, §255.

27. Habermas has argued that the dissipation of the public sphere itself within the social welfare state has led to the extension of its principles to social organizations dealing with the state. His characterization of such organizations have a great resemblance to Hegel's structure of the corporation. See Habermas, "The Public Sphere," p. 55.

28. Jürgen Habermas, "On Social Identity," *Telos* 19 (Spring 1974): 98.

29. Hegel, *op. cit.*, §316*Z*.

Hegel, the Old Secularism, and the New Theocracy

Merold Westphal

Arthur Danto began his presidential address to the Eastern Division of the American Philosophical Association last December with the observation that one normally comes to such occasions inexperienced and thus in something of a quandary about how to begin. Under such circumstances, he surmised, one could do worse than begin by quoting Hegel. If in no other respect, I am at least Danto's equal in inexperience, and, given both the setting of this address and the spirit of one-upmanship which pervades American philosophy as the spirit of thoroughness once pervaded German philosophy, I propose to begin with *two* quotations from Hegel. First, "religion is the foundation of the state." Then, "the state is the foundation of religion."[1]

Hegel makes both of these statements repeatedly, sometimes in just these words, using the crucial term *Grundlage*, sometimes in a variety of clearly equivalent locutions. Sometimes the latter statement is subsumed in the claim that ethical life (*Sittlichkeit*) or the spirit of a people (*Volksgeist*) is the foundation of religion, while at other times precisely the state is picked out as playing this role. Hegel can do this without conflict inasmuch as the state is the culmination of ethical life just as ethical life is itself the culmination of objective spirit.

Each of these statements is of interest in its own right. That interest is increased by the tension of their co-assertions. But neither by themselves nor in their dialectical unity am I interested in these statements *an-und-für-sich*, but rather *für uns*. That is to say that I am less interested in giving a critical exposition of Hegel's views because they are there, so to

151

speak, than in asking what light they throw on our contemporary situation, about which, accordingly, something needs to be said.

The two features of our world most worthy of note here might be called the old secularism and the new theocracy. By calling the old secularism "old" I mean simply to indicate that the forces and tendencies in question have been effectively at work among us for longer than those of the (consequently) "new" theocracy. By calling them "secular" I mean to suggest that the movement of these forces and tendencies is toward the absolutizing of pre-ethical goods.* Aristotle once summarized the goods I have in mind quite nicely as pleasure, wealth, and honor.[2] By pleasure Aristotle seems to have had in mind especially the sensual pleasures of food, drink, and sex. So we can call the tendency to absolutize these pleasures sensualism, just as materialism is the obvious name for the absolutizing of wealth. By honor Aristotle seems to have meant what we call status or prestige. The cult of this goddess has no common name (a fact worth noting, but not being fooled by). I fear we shall have to speak of statusism, hoping that this linguistic grotesquery will not inspire others.

Each of these "isms" involves two distinct but functionally inseparable processes. The first is that escalation of expectations in which what can be hoped for from each of these goods rises to the place where it begins to make sense to identify its possession with happiness, the answer to the question of the meaning of human existence. Individually or in combination they come to define the good life. Although the "old" secularism is at least

---

* This is not, of course, the standard definition of secularism. But it is not difficult to observe that with the decrease in the influence of religious ideas and institutions comes an increase in the tendency to absolutize pre-ethical goods in the manner subsequently specified. It is as if to a significant degree society acted on the principle, "if God is dead everything is permitted." To observe this empirical phenomenon is neither to validate the inference in question nor to deny the presence of those who repudiate it, who seek to preserve at least significant portions of traditional morality apart from the metaphysical support to be found in theological ideas and from the sociological support to be found in communal religious practice. Far from being a challenge to standard definitions, mine is only meant to call attention to an important observable feature of the secularization process.

as old as Aristotle, perhaps we hear its secularity best when we contrast the meaning of the phrase "the good life" on Aristotle's lips with its meaning in a phrase like "the good life at Malibu." It is the latter rather than the former which is promised to us by the politicians and the advertisers, if only we leave the driving to them.

The flip side of this escalating of expectations is the autonomy of these goods from moral constraints. If it is in them that happiness, the good life, and the meaning of human existence are to be found, then the placing of ethico-religious restrictions on their pursuit and enjoyment must be, from the prospective of the old secularism, either old-fashioned, kill-joy puritanism or naïve, adolescent idealism, neither of which can win its case in the Supreme Court of Realism. Thus the sexual revolution which plays such a key role in modern sensualism has consisted almost entirely in deactivating earlier moral constraints on the pursuit of sexual pleasure. There are those who note, with a sense of irony, that the moral constraints are regularly replaced by technical limits, so that the less it comes to be that we *ought* not to have all the sexual pleasure we would like to, the more we find that we *cannot* have all the sexual pleasure we would like to, in spite of all the manuals. Be that as it may, the point for emphasis here is the growing disappearance of moral constraints.

While the sexual revolution has received the most public attention, the same movement toward insulating pre-ethical goods from ethical criticism is found in other realms as well. The consumption of food and drink is by no means free from constraints today, as is clear in our preoccupation with cholesterol and calories. Anything that threatens my health or sex appeal may need to be sacrificed. But if one tries to move from this narcissism to a genuinely ethical question, by, for example, raising the question of the relation of our consumption patterns to global justice and world hunger, one immediately faces the most ultimate of all refutations the old secularism has to offer—boring. Preachers may talk about such issues (at their peril), but those who really make things happen, the politicians and the advertisers, will find other things to talk about. (The really smart preachers, and educators, who understand the importance of being effective, will catch on quickly to what it is we want to hear. Religion and liberal education will offer themselves—sell their souls—as handmaidens of secular success.)

Perhaps the most succinct expression of the autonomy motif in the old secularism comes from the economic sphere. When one of the most powerful bankers in the world was asked by church groups to discontinue making loans to the government of South Africa, providing both respectability and capital to its morally reprehensible system of apartheid, he did not debate the morality of apartheid. He only noted that his bank had but two criteria for investment, legality and profitability. His only concern with the moral issue was to make clear its irrelevance to the pursuit of profit.[3]

If we turn from the matter to the form of the old secularism, we find that it pursues its pre-ethical goods both individually and collectively. Whether one speaks of narcissism, the cult of the self, or simply individualism, the posture is as familiar as its slogans, "looking out for Number One," and "each one for him- or herself and the devil take the hindermost." Of course, in an age which no longer believes in the devil, the latter must be demythologized. It now appears in a number of new translations, among which are "each one for him- or herself, and perhaps a little will trickle down to the hindermost," and "each one for him- or herself, and herpes for the unlucky."

If individualism and collectivism are opposites, this does not mean, as the propaganda of the understanding would suggest, that they are alternatives. They are rather dialectical opposites, inseparable from each other. So we should not be surprised to find that the self whose interest (read: immediate desire) is absolutized in the old secularism is the corporate self as well as the individual self. While corporate or collective selves come in many sizes, it is the national self which is of particular importance here. It does not play a particularly important role in the pursuit of pleasure, but it is central to the pursuit of wealth and status.

In the case of wealth the nation's role is a real one, for the level of my affluence is not determined just by personal effort and by my place in the national economy but also by the health of the national economy and by the share of the world's resources over which it presides. In short, you can understand as much about my economic situation by knowing that I am an American as you can by learning about my own personal talents and efforts.

In the case of status the nation's role is a symbolic one, for the benefit of belonging is not tangible, as previously, but psychological. I participate vicariously in national victories and bask in a glory I may have done nothing to earn. We have ritualized this same phenomenon on a smaller scale in competitive sports, and perhaps no clearer insight into the essence of nationalism can be gained than by watching thousands of fans who have been nothing but spectators standing with upraised index fingers and screaming "we're Number One!"

In speaking about the old secularism it has been natural to speak of goddess and cult, of ritual and sacrifice. Is this language accidental, or should we ironically find the old secularism to be itself a kind of established religion? The latter is, I think, quite clearly the case. The escalating importance of pleasure, wealth, and status to positions of centrality in the human enterprise and the corresponding absolutizing of them, along with the individual and collective selves who seek to possess them, mean that for the old secularism these things above all else are sacred. They are ultimate as the goals to be pursued, the criteria of all value, and the selves to be served.

The religion in question is polytheistic, to be sure. Sensualism, materialism, statusism, individualism, and nationalism are not so much the names of denominational differences in serving the same God, analogous to Methodism, Presbyterianism, Catholicism, etc. They are rather the names of different cults in which various members of the pantheon, e.g., Zeus, Athena, Apollo, Hermes, etc., are worshiped.

Perhaps the religious character of the old secularism is nowhere clearer than in its nuclear nationalism. Consider what we are prepared to do on behalf of the nation, or at least on behalf of what its leaders declare to be the national interest. We are prepared to incinerate millions of innocent men, women, and children, simply because they happen to belong to another people. Though Russians have been substituted for Jews, it is appropriate that this slaughter is still referred to as a holocaust. But the world holocaust is rich enough to do more than link the "Final Solution" with the nightmare of nuclear exchange. Originally the term referred to a burnt sacrifice offered in worship to a god. If we ask who is the god to whom human life on this unprecedented scale, along with human civilization and the earth's biosphere, are to be sacrificed, the answer is clear: the nation.

The morality that goes with this religion is simple. The end justifies the means, any means. In this context the abandonment of chemical weapons or the disavowal of a nuclear first strike are plainly not moral imperatives but tactical stupidities. When practiced by others this morality is sometimes called "Bolshevik morality," but it is plainly the morality adopted by the West in its effort to keep the world safe from communism. It is the morality of the Mafia, but also of law-and-order respectability in the service (and worship) of the nations.

Now a wide variety of ethico-religious traditions would agree, in spite of important differences between them, that this religion is idolatry and this morality the heart of immorality. So it is not surprising that we should find ethico-religious protests against the old secularism. Sometimes these protests have the flavor of the political left, but when they do they tend to have little effect (in North America, that is—in Latin America the situation is just the opposite). This protest tends to reside in religious hierarchies and bureaucracies and to separate religious leaders from their people more than uniting them in a challenge to the reigning secularism.

But in recent years the story has been quite different when the ethico-religious critique of "secular humanism" has had the flavor of the political right. Through a combination of charismatic television personalities and massive, computerized, direct-mail fund raising, a movement has arisen which has shaken the complacency of the old secularism rather considerably. The movement as a whole is most often designated by the name of one of its constituent organizations, the Moral Majority. This designation by reference to morality rather than religion corresponds to the earlier definition of the old secularism as the absolutizing of pre-ethical goods. The battleground is the ethical, though in the final analysis the combatants are, like Moses and Pharaoh, David and Goliath, representatives of different gods.

In calling this protest from the right the new theocracy I am not unaware of the differences between its posture and the dictionary definition. This movement does not advocate an established state church, nor, more importantly, does it propose government by clergy. That is to say that it does not suggest that religious officials should hold government office by virtue of their ecclesiastical office.

But the spirit of theocracy is present. While religious leaders do not claim the right to government office, they do claim the right to political authority and influence on the grounds of the religious authority they claim to embody. Furthermore, the religious authority to which they appeal and which they would make the foundations of the political order is epistemologically sectarian. A point of view is epistemologically sectarian, regardless of whether it is shared by a minority or majority, if the criteria by which it seeks justification are privately owned, either by being secret, as in the case of an oracle, or by being public without being universal. This latter condition exists when the criteria of justification can be expected to make sense or ring true only to those already socialized into a distinctive sub-community of the larger community whose life is to be governed by those criteria. Thus, for example, the dictatorship of the proletariat would be another example of a politics which rests on an epistemologically sectarian basis.

During the Viet Nam and civil rights era an ethico-religious protest against the old secularism from the left made itself felt briefly. The impact of the new theocracy may be as brief, but then again, it may not be. Prophecy would be foolish. In any case, the present situation is anything but attractive. The old secularism and the new theocracy may be dialectical opposites, but their dialectic is not that of the Idea, where difference is *aufgehoben* (preserved and transcended) in organic harmony. It is rather the dialectic of finite things whose internal incoherence carries the seeds of their own destruction. The fragmentation of our society is at least as serious as during the earlier protest period just mentioned.

Nor is it easy to hope for harmony and reintegration by the victory of one party over the other, for each is seriously flawed. It is far from clear how any politics which rests on an epistemologically sectarian basis can be compatible with the principles of a free society. So it is not surprising that the new theocracy's concept of freedom is simply unacceptable, a fact best illustrated by its designation of those who imposed Somoza's reign of terror on Nicaragua and who now seek to reinstate themselves in power as "freedom fighters." Whatever we may think about the Sandinistas, this is a use of language which reminds us that we are living in 1984. And on the home front it looks as if the new theocracy is prepared to give back any number of hard-fought victories for toleration and freedom of conscience.

The old secularism, child of the Enlightenment that it is, has sought to avoid epistemological sectarianism. Instead of trying to base politics on a particular world-view among others, it has appealed to the universal.

There is nothing sectarian about the desire for pleasure, wealth, and honor, nor about the willingness to place self-interest (of either the personal or corporate self) above the interests of other selves. The problem is that the old secularism appeals to our lowest common denominator, rather than to what is best in us. As a result its view of freedom is also unacceptable, for it is freedom without responsibility, freedom, for example, to pursue profits in South Africa without responsibility for the human victims of that pursuit.

Furthermore, the old secularism cannot easily defend itself against the charge of idolatry. No nation is worthy of the sacrifices we are prepared to offer as a holocaust to ours. Nor are pleasure, wealth, and status worthy of being treated as the content of true happiness and the meaning of human existence. If Kierkegaard is right in seeing at the heart of the comical the confusion of the finite and relative for the infinite and absolute, then the old secularism must be the laughing stock of our time. But this is the unity of the tragic and the comic, for what could be more tragic than to make human existence into a joke?

It is on this point of idolatry that we ought to find the new theocracy most appealing. But it looks as if the majority can be enlisted only in the cause of a very selective morality. For while the new theocracy is prepared on a number of fronts to challenge the old secularism's attitudes toward sex as idolatrous, it is more inclined to reinforce than to challenge the other idolatries. It accepts without reservation its alleged enemy's definition of success in terms of wealth and status. It accepts without challenge the secularist identification of freedom with individualism and the dialectically corresponding nationalism in its military dress uniform. But it does not suffice to say positively that it accepts or negatively that it does not challenge most of the old secularism's world-view. It seeks to enshrine all this under the sacred canopy of divine approval. Thus, God wants us to be rich, personally and nationally, and God wants us to have a bigger military budget, for we are the shining city set on a hill to save the world from the evil empire. Apart from a few issues like school prayer and abortion, the new theocracy looks just like the old secularism in its Sunday go-to-meetin' clothes.

It would be foolish, of course, to read Hegel as if he were a contemporary journalist commenting on these circumstances. Yet his views about the relation of religion and the state are by no means irrelevant to them, and, just because he is operating at the level of basic principles, he may help us to get closer to the heart of the matter than the best of journalists. From the Hegelian perspective on religion and the state, both the old secularism and the new theocracy will have to be abandoned. They turn out to be opposed to each other not as contradictories, one of which must be true, but as contraries, both of which may be, and in this case are, false. If these are the operative alternatives which our society offers us, this only shows how irrational is our world, both in its reality and in its self-understanding.

At first glance it might appear that Hegel and the new theocracy are allies of principle. His claim that religion is the foundation of the state could be taken as support for its position on issues like abortion, and his claim that the state is the foundation of religion could be taken as support for its position on school prayer. But this would be a superficial reading. In fact, Hegel's views imply a threefold critique of the new theocracy. This is not surprising in view of his strong commitment to the separation of church and state.

Since it is the genius of Hegel's view, and also the source of its greatest difficulty, that it affirms both the separation of church and state and the inseparability of religion and state, it is important to be clear that Hegel has no qualms about holding these views simultaneously. It is tempting to attribute the separation motif to the early Berlin years surrounding the *Philosophy of Right* and the inseparability motif to the later Berlin years. If the two were incompatible such an expedient would be necessary, keeping Hegel coherent by having him correct himself. But Hegel himself surely thought that, far from being incompatible, the two motifs were indispensable to each others' proper interpretation, and he affirms them both throughout the Berlin years. In doing so he is but recapitulating the position of his "early theological writings," where the separation motif in "The Positivity of Christianity" is sandwiched in between the inseparability motif in the "Tübingen Fragment" and "The Spirit of Christianity and its Fate."[4] The Hegelian critique of the new theocracy arises from the dialectical union of these motifs in the claim that religion is the foundation of the state.

Hegel is as eager to tell us what this formula does not mean as to tell us what it does mean. High on the list of what it does not mean is theocracy, either literally or in spirit. Whether in the form of tribal patriarchy, oriental despotism, feudal absolutism, Cromwellian radicalism, or romantic nostalgia for one of these earlier theocracies, Hegel consistently repudiates the attempt to wed religious and political leadership. The first problem with theocracy is the epistemologically sectarian basis on which it rests. The state's *raison d'être* is freedom, the union of the universal and the subjective will which is recognized as such. Because the recognition is as important as the union, blind obedience cannot be the principle of true patriotism. Hence the principles upon which the socal order is based must be in principle accessible to all. Like Descartes at the beginning of the *Discourse on Method*, Hegel is convinced that reason is the epistemological common denominator.

This means, on the one hand, that religion is the foundation of the state only when interpreted in the light of reason, a fact which explains the frequency with which Hegel identifies *philosophy* with worldly wisdom when discussing the religious foundation of the state. The translation of religion from *Vorstellung* (pre-philosophical idea) to *Begriff* (philosophical concept), which lies at the very heart of Hegelian methodology and metaphysics, also lies at the heart of his politics.

On the other hand, to put it negatively, religion has no political authority when it appeals to faith or feeling, authority, and tradition as its foundation. Neither the intensity of its subjective certitude nor the sincerity of its piety can legitimate its claims to steer the ship of state, for all of these are quite compatible with both shallowness and immorality. As Jesus might have put it, not all who say, "Lord, Lord," are doing the work of the kingdom. We might make the point more concretely by noting that all the religious devotion in the world on the part of practitioners and defenders of slavery and apartheid cannot make these racist social institutions just.

The point, of course, is not that theocracy is inherently racist, but rather that its epistemological sectarianism is an open invitation to the ideology of oppression, that is, to the religious legitimation of the imposition of the particular interests of one group upon another. Even if, by accident, this does not happen at the level of social $\pi\varrho\tilde{\alpha}\xi\iota\varsigma$ (*praxis*), it has always already happened at the level of theory and of "truth" insofar as the foundations remain epistemologically sectarian. Society as a whole is subjected to rules which can be expected to make sense only to those socialized into one of its sub-cultures.

The second reason why Hegel refuses to give a theocratic interpretation to his claim that religion is the foundation of the state is ontological. The spirit of theocracy often expresses itself as a kind of technology for social change and control which rests upon mistakenly mechanistic models of human society. These models involve spatial metaphors of externality and temporal metaphors of sequentiality, so Hegel goes out of his way to disown any interpretation which suggests that, when society is not going as it should, religion can be brought in from outside or after the fact to improve things, as if it were an antibiotic which, when properly administered, would cure the diseases of the body politic. Far less is it a rudder whose control directly steers the ship of state. Yet it is almost always in such terms that the new theocracy thinks, viewing religion as a means to political ends.

These models, however, are incompatible with the organic character of Hegel's social ontology. On his view there is no distinction between dependent and independent variables. Within the organic whole, rather, there is reciprocity and interdependence. There is no such thing as unilateral, unidirectional change. Through the life of any people a prevailing spirit already runs (its *Volksgeist*), expressing itself in the various dimensions (*Mächte, Momente, Sphären, Seiten, Produkten, Formen, Gestalgungen*) of that life.* There is thus already a unity of spirit permeating the religious and political aspects of a people's life together.

Sometimes Hegel expresses the same basic organicism in a slightly different way. The state in the narrowly political sense, which Hegel also calls the external state, and the actual (*wirkliche*) state is animated (*beseelt*) by the spirit of a people. The relation is that of body to soul. In this frame of mind Hegel tends to identify religion with the *Volksgeist* rather than treating it as one expression thereof, along with others such as the political. Then he speaks of the relation of religion to the state as that of *Wesen* to *Dasein*, of *das Innere* to *das Aüßere*, of *Wissen* to *Wirklichkeit*,

---

* In speaking of the powers, moments, spheres, sides, products, forms, and shapes of the spirit of a people Hegel is obviously not concerned for a fixed, technical vocabulary.

and of *Substantialität* to *Entwicklung* and *Verwirklichung*.*

Whether the picture is of a single *Volksgeist* particularizing itself in a variety of manifestations or of a political body animated by a religious soul, the result is the same. Nostalgia for a past form of theocracy is doubly inappropriate. As the union of church and state it is to be avoided as an impingement on both religious and political freedom, and as the union of religion and state it is always already a reality, but not of the sort which lends itself to the projects of social engineering which are so characteristic of the new theocracy. The different moments of a people's life stand "*in der engsten Verbindung*," "*in innigsten Zusammenhang*," "*in unzertrennlicher Einheit*" with each other and must be seen "*als notwendig übergehend*" into one another.† Under such circumstances, as Edmund Burke insisted, social change can only be holistic, and thus both slow and all but impossible to manage. The notion of engineering comes from the attempt to assert human control over inorganic nature, and the concept of management comes from the project of directing social entities which are constructed so as to be controllable through mechanistic devices analogous to steering wheels, throttles, thermostats, and so forth. Perhaps the very idea of social engineering and of managing a society only makes sense when a society is already dead or dying. Or perhaps, beyond that, the project in question, which has its secular as well as its theocratic versions, has the power to kill a society, to turn it from a living organism into a dead machine, a body without a soul.

Hegel's organic social ontology has a corollary, mostly unnoticed by him, but worthy of mention for its bearing on the project of the new theocracy. In noting the organic inseparability of religion and state as a categoreal feature, an existential, so to speak, of social *Dasein*, Hegel regularly emphasizes that a free state and a slavish religion cannot coexist. (Hegel is not reluctant to identify such religions, which include nature religion, the religions of India, Judaism, Islam, and Roman Catholicism. We shall have

---

* The movement is from essence to existence, from inner to outer, from knowledge to actuality, and from substantiality to unfolding and realization.

† These phrases are virtually synonymous. Since the moments are in closest association, in innermost connection, and in inseparable unity, they must be seen as necessarily passing over into one another.

to return to this point.) For the moment we need but notice that for Hegel, who uses Protestant language to express a general point, it is foolish to try to have a revolution without a reformation.

Suppose, *mirabile dictu*, that a political order based on reason and freedom were established in the midst of a religion based on spiritual bondage. We only kid ourselves, Hegel says, if we think those responsible for embodying such a political order will do according to its letter or spirit rather than according to the spirit of their religion. The latter will rather serve as a kind of inertial force to render the fine principles of the political order empty, abstract, and superficial.

Hegel here speaks as an historical idealist, taking note of the effect of absolute spirit on objective spirit. But his holism requires him (more than he notices) to be just as much an historical materialist, taking seriously the impact of objective spirit on absolute spirit. Thus it is also foolish to try to have a religious reformation (revival, in the language of the new theocracy) without a political and economic revolution.

Suppose, *mirabile dictu*, that a religious transformation were to occur in the midst of a political life opposed to it. Do we not kid ourselves if we think the powers of political and economic life will immediately realign themselves rather than serving as inertial forces to keep the new religious principles at the level of rhetoric rather than operational reality? Suppose, for example, that we became convinced as a nation of the religiously based pro-life position on abortion. Can we expect this conviction to be anything but a formal profession in a society whose political order is based on the principle that the task of government is to provide us with personal affluence and otherwise to stay out of our lives? Even if laws were passed to eliminate or severely restrict abortion, would they be effective? Our experience with prohibition suggests that Hegelian theory is right in answering these questions in the negative. From the Hegelian perspective it would appear that the new theocracy, lacking a holistic ontology and methodology, has given insufficient attention to what society as a whole would have to be like for its fondest dreams to be fulfilled anywhere but on paper.

We turn now to the Hegelian critique of the old secularism's secularism. This will constitute, incidentally, a third critique of the new theocracy, along with the epistemological and ontological critique just mentioned. We have noted that the new theocracy is only selectively critical of the primacy given to pre-ethical goods by the old secularism. Wherever it remains uncritical of this tendency, Hegel's critique of its sworn enemy turns against it as well, the price it pays for its inconsistency.

Not surprisingly, Hegel is opposed to all views which treat the relation between religion and the state as an external one, religion being primarily a private matter. On one such view it is the passive or active enemy of the state, passively undermining it by teaching attitudes of superior indifference to its merely worldly enterprise or actively undermining it by inculcating hostility toward the state as an oppressor of the faithful. Neither Hegel nor the old secularism have any enthusiasm for this view.

Not quite as external is the view that religion provides a legitimating function for the state by making obedience to the state a religious obligation. Both Hegel and the old secularism appreciate this view, but in different versions. The old secularism's version leaves its secularism unchallenged while providing the halo of sanctity which religious legitimation suggests. This is the official religion of the old secularism, which it seeks to encourage both in the civil religion which hovers around the fringes of political life and in the churchly religion which hovers around the fringes of everyday life in general. It will seem paradoxical that the old secularism should have an official religion only if we fail to notice that this kind of religion provides only support and never challenge to its projects.

Hegel's appreciation of this view is limited to contexts where religion has a bearing on the content of the state's life. The bonds of social life need to be sacred bonds and not the bonds of calculating self-interest. But only projects which have an ethico-religious substance beyond calculating self-interest are worthy of such legitimation. The state which deserves the support of religion cannot be the liberal state which defines itself in terms of the right of individual and nation to the pursuit of happiness, defined in terms of pre-ethical goods, limited only by the right of other individuals and nations to the same secular self-interest. The problem with the liberal theory and practice of the state is not just that it misunderstands freedom, thinking of the state as a limitation of freedom for the sake of security, while it has not yet even achieved the true notion of freedom. Beyond that it buys the claim, sometimes made by religion, that religion has a rightful monopoly on spiritual values, leaving political and economic life to be the amoral technology of pursuing happiness, amoral because both the ends and the means of achieving them are immune from ethical evaluation. All questions are technological. None are moral.

In Hegel's eyes this dualism of sacred and secular, which fixes a great gulf between the realm of private piety and churchly worship where ethico-religious values are to be taken seriously and the realm of everyday public life from which they have been, so to speak, excommunicated, rests on a total misunderstanding of both religion and the state. Religion is the knowledge of what is highest and absolute, namely God. But it is a *Wissen* to be seen *als notwendig übergehend* into *Wirklichkeit*. It is a *Wesen* seeking *Dasein* in the whole life of a people, an Aristotelian soul whose τέλος (*telos*) is to animate the body politic, not a Platonic soul seeking separation from all that is worldly. "*Das Wahre ... ist der ungeheure Überschritt des Innern in das Äussere, der Einbildung der Vernunft in die Realität ....* (The genuine truth ... is the prodigious transfer of the inner into the outer, the building of reason into the real world ....)"[5]

Correspondingly, the state is to be not the instrumentalism of the secular life but its *Aufhebung*. The universal principle of truth which is known in religion is to permeate all the particular realms of national life, lest they be, in separation from the truth, barren, cursed like the fig tree without figs, appearance without reality.

This critique of the secularity of the old secularism is also the critique of its idolatry. The *Aufhebung* of secular life in the Hegelian state, whose foundation is religion, is the systematic de-absolutizing of pre-ethical goods and their subordination to and incorporation into a life determined by ethico-religious values. Hegelianism is not a puritanical asceticism which turns against sensual pleasure, wealth, and status as something intrinsically evil. Nor is it an abstract and rigid universalism which denies any legitimate role to the particularity of individual and nation. But it is the prophetic protest against the idolatry which absolutizes any of these by isolating it from the ethical context in which alone it can be its true self.

You will forgive me, nay, thank me, if I restrict myself to but one of the five idolatries of the old secularism for purposes of illustration. Individualism suggests itself as by far the most frequently denounced form of idolatry, and nationalism suggests itself for just the opposite reason. That there are in Hegel's mature (Berlin) thought the elements, not very aggressively developed, to be sure, of a critique of nationalism is a point that ought not to be overlooked in elaborating his views of religion and the state. But I shall choose the sexual form of sensualism as my example, because it makes the point so lucidly and so simply.

Hegel talks a good deal about sex while developing the theme of marriage in the *Philosophy of Right* (§§158–169). But his comments are at first puzzling. Sometimes he seems to suggest a negative relation between sex and marriage, according to which marriage pulls sex down from its haughty claim, puts it in its place, and reduces it to but a moment in something else. But at other times the relation is positive, with marriage elevating sex from the realm of nature to that of spirit.

The dialectical union of these oppositional motifs is found in the formula which summarizes Hegel's position. Sex is the external embodiment of the ethical bond (*das äusserliche Dasein der sittlichen Verbindung*). If we emphasize the *externality* of the embodiment, we have the Hegelian basis for putting sex in its place. It is the *Dasein*, not the *Wesen*, the body and not the soul. Cut off from that which gives it human, spiritual meaning, the ethical bond of marriage, it is, at best, mere nature. Dogs also copulate. But it is worse than that, for when that which is spirit by nature chooses to remain at the level of mere nature, we no longer have mere nature but spirit corrupted. This corruption stems from the idolatry of treating sex as *die Sache selbst* (the thing itself) instead of as the embodiment or manifestation of something else.

If we shift the emphasis, however, to focus on sex as the *embodiment*, however external, of the ethical bond, we have the basis for Hegel's positive view of the elevation of sex to spiritual significance. We can even speak of a sacramental view of sex, for if a sacrament is an outward and visible sign of an inward and invisible grace, sex, for Hegel, is an outward and tangible expression of an inward and spiritual covenant. This is the *Aufhebung* of sex as a pre-ethical good, physical and emotional pleasure, into an ethical good, personal love and commitment in marriage. The sensual moment, pleasure, is not abolished but transformed. By being reduced to a moment it is elevated to authentically human significance. By giving up its claim to be divine it becomes something sacred.

There is something profoundly religious about this idea of finding life through death, of self-realization through self-sacrifice. It is foreign to the old secularism, which never dreams of that sanctifying of economic life which occurs in the *Aufhebung* of *homo œconomicus* by which the production and distribution of goods and services become, not an end in themselves, *die Sache selbst,* but the external embodiment of the ethical bond of a people committed to the other peoples of the earth in that same spirit. It is the perennial attraction of communism (grounded in its Hegelian heritage) that, unlike the old secularism, it is capable of dreaming of such an economic life, just as it is the perennial tragedy of communism that it remains unable to fulfill that dream.

Hegel's vision of *Sittlichkeit* as the ethico-religious *Aufhebung* of pre-ethical goods into their truly human form is powerful and beautiful. His critique of the old secularism and the new theocracy is strong enough to shake our confidence in whichever one may have seemed attractive to us previously or perhaps to help us understand why neither has seemed viable to us. But the question remains whether his vision can lead us beyond his critique, whether he can point the way beyond dissatisfaction with the old secularism and the new theocracy to a viable new experience of religion and the state.

The problem, which needs to be mentioned in closing, is Hegel's insistence that political freedom is not compatible with just any religion whatever. He mentions a number of non-Christian religions as being inadequate foundations for a state in accord with the Idea. But most frequently the Roman Catholic version of the Christian religion is used to illustrate this point. Hegel is as resolutely Protestant as he is Christian, not only in his metaphysics but just as centrally in his politics. Of course this does not mean he wants a theocracy with Protestant clergy running the state. But he is firmly convinced that the spirit of Protestantism needs to permeate national life. This spirit Hegel defines as the transcendence of the authoritarian and other-worldly aspects he finds in Roman Catholicism. It is worth noting that many who call themselves Protestant participate in a religious life which Hegel sees as Catholic, while many who call themselves Catholic exhibit what Hegel thinks of as the Protestant spirit. But this is of little help. For the religion which he finds to be the only acceptable basis of a rational state, even if it does not correspond to external denominational boundaries, is a particular, historically specific form of the religious life, present in some religious communities but absent from others. This is fully in keeping with Hegel's repudiation of the Enlightenment's view of reason as pure and unsituated and with his corresponding insistence on sticking to what is historically concrete. But how is it compatible with the earlier critique of epistemological sectarianism? Does not the Protestantism of Hegel's politics free it from secularity at the cost of sectarianism?

Perhaps it does. Perhaps, in spite of all his efforts to the contrary, Hegel remains within the hermeneutical circle of his own historical particularity in a way incompatible with his own requirements for rationality and freedom. But Hegel himself surely does not think so, though he can hardly have failed to notice how Protestant, and thus apparently sectarian at least, he remains. If he is able to avoid epistemological sectarianism it can only be through the transformation of religious truth into its philosophical form. He is fully aware of this, which accounts for the already mentioned frequency with which he speaks of philosophy as the worldly wisdom which gives the state its religious foundation. This means that the whole project summarized by the notion of translating *Vorstellung* into *Begriff* is every bit as much a political issue as it is a metaphysical and epistemological issue. It also means that we will not have gotten to the heart of the issue so long as discussion is restricted to the relation of images and pictures to so-called pure thought. For at issue is not simply the question of which cognitive faculty is involved in apprehending the highest truth, but also whether this apprehension is privately owned or not. I have little doubt that placing the question of the relation of religion to philosophy in the context of the question of the relation of religion to the state will significantly change the discussion of the former issue. But, happily, that can await another day.

Notes

1. These formulas, either in just these words or in equivalent phrases, are basic to the four most extensive discussions by the mature Hegel on the relation of religion and the state. Two of these can be identified by paragraph numbers which are standard to German and English editions: *Encyclopedia* (*Philosophy of Mind*), §552 and *Philosophy of Right*, §270. The other two come from lectures given in 1830 and 1831 respectively: *Die Vernunft in der Geschichte*, 5te *Aufl.*, *hrsg.* Johannes Hoffmeister (Hamburg:

Felix Meiner, 1955), S. 110ff; *Lectures on the Philosophy of World History: Introduction*, trans. H. B. Nisbet (Cambridge: Cambridge University Press, 1975), pp. 93ff; *Vorlesung über die Philosophie der Religion, Teil I*, hrsg. Walter Jaeschke (Hamburg: Felix Meiner, 1983, S. 339ff; *Lectures on the Philosophy of Religion*, Volume I, ed. Peter C. Hodgson (Berkeley: University of California Press, 1984), pp. 451ff.

2. Aristotle, *Nicomachean Ethics*, 1095b 15ff.

3. "Financing Apartheid—Citibank in South Africa," an ICCR Brief published by the Interfaith Center on Corporate Responsibility, p. 3A.

4. The Tübingen essay is translated in the Appendix for H. S. Harris, *Hegel's Development: Toward the Sunlight* 1770–1801 (Oxford: Clarendon Press, 1972). The other two essays are translated in *On Christianity: Early Theological Writings*, trans. T. M. Knox and Richard Kroner (New York: Harper, 1961). The German texts are in G. W. F. Hegel, *Werke in zwanzig Bänden*, Band I, *Frühe Schriften* (Frankfurt: Suhrkamp, 1971).

5. *Hegel's Philosophy of Right*, trans. T. M. Knox (Oxford: Clarendon Press, 1942), p. 167 (§270Z).

Art as "Aesthetic" and as "Religious" in Hegel's
Philosophy of Absolute Spirit

William Desmond

1. Art, Religion, and Absolute Spirit

In Hegel's philosophy of Absolute Spirit, as is well known, art finds a place, along with religion and philosophy. The ascription of a certain absoluteness to art entailed by this place is perhaps the central problem of Hegel's aesthetics. Any effort to fully understand Hegel's philosophy of Absolute Spirit cannot neglect this issue. Yet the precise status of art in Hegel has always proved problematic. Very broadly, there are perhaps two chief reasons why the precise place of art in Hegel's philosophy of Absolute Spirit has always been controversial. One is the implication that philosophy is "higher" than art, as also is religion: philosophy is the ultimate activity which, it seems, supersedes art and places it in a subordinate position. The second is Hegel's proclamation of the so-called "death" of art; art, Hegel implies, is a thing of the past, particularly given the scientific culture of our age. We should be wary, however, about thinking that these two views, stated thus, adequately represent Hegel: that he was intent, on the one hand, to philosophically reduce art, and, on the other hand, to supersede or leave it behind. The inescapable obstacle to these two possibilities is Hegel's continuing insistence on the absolute character of art. This absoluteness does not square with the intention of reductionism or supersession. For how can something with an absolute character be either reduced or superseded?

The effect of this question is not only to make us re-examine the reductive view but also to return us to the complexity in Hegel's position. How, in effect, are we to understand Hegel's insistence on art's absolute

170

character? We must grant to Hegel this insistence, but its precise nature remains unclarified and requires further elucidation. Can art preserve its absolute character if religion and philosophy are also said to be absolute? How are we to place art relative to the absoluteness of these other two? The approach suggested here is that we look at the connection of art with religion. All too frequently Hegel's commentators initially tend to separate art, religion, and philosophy too strongly. Subsequently Hegel's commentators tend to explore the relations of different pairs of these three activities. These pairings tend to confer a certain predominance on philosophy. Philosophy is coupled with religion and their relations and tensions detailed. Philosophy is coupled with art, whether in a manner which emphasizes their kinship,[1] or in one that more strongly stresses their antagonism. But the pairing of art and religion does not figure strongly. Yet it should, not only for its overall importance in Hegel's thought but also for aesthetical reflection in general. Our attempt to rectify this omission here will throw light, we hope, on art's absoluteness.

To focus on this pairing has the added advantage of inevitably extending us to the full Hegelian triad: philosophical reflection simply cannot be left out of the picture. An understanding of art and religion will facilitate, I believe, a more discriminating view of the interplay of all three activities belonging to Absolute Spirit. I hope to make good this promise below where I suggest that the relation of art and religion has important implications for the overall interpretation of Hegel's thought, particularly on the recurring, thorny issue of Left and Right readings. For this issue has reverberations not only in contemporary politics and religion, but also in contemporary aesthetics. Indeed, as we shall see, aesthetics itself reverberates in the politics of such diverse thinkers as, say, Sartre, Marcuse, and Camus, all of them heirs to some aspects of the "Left-Hegelian" heritage.

A helpful way to elucidate art's absoluteness is through this question: is art in Hegel an exclusively aesthetic or a religious phenomenon? What is meant by art as exclusively "aesthetic" and as "religious" will be clarified as our discussion develops.[2] Our brief answer for now is that art points beyond exclusively aesthetic considerations to a further religious significance. Moreover, this "pointing beyond" and the transition it generates, I will argue, are rooted in the character of art itself as reflected in Hegel's view. Properly understood, there need be nothing artificial in agreeing with Hegel that the significance of art is religious. This need imply no superimposition of a falsifying religious meaning, nor any theological violence to the art work, nor any diminution of the need to consider art on its own terms. Precisely to treat art on its own terms reveals the further thrust of *Geist* towards the religious, indeed the implicit presence of the religious dimension in art itself. To explicate this claim we might proceed thus. First, we need to ask what marks art as an exclusive "aesthetic" phenomenon. Next, we need to examine art as "religious" and its contrast with the "aesthetic" conception. This we must do in two stages: first, historically in terms of Hegel's conception of Symbolical, Classical, and Romantic types of art; second, in terms of the systematic, philosophical issue of whether "creativity" is to be understood in an entirely humanized manner. Finally, this comparison of the "aesthetic" and the "religious" will allow us to make some suggestions of the kind mentioned above concerning the overall reading of Hegel, and particularly the continuing importance of art in the Left-Hegelian reading.

2. Art as Aesthetic

What, then, might be involved in art considered as an "aesthetic" phenomenon? Historically the point might be made by recalling how, proceeding from the Renaissance, art sought to liberate itself from the constraints of religious subservience and increasingly to assert its own autonomy with respect to ecclesiastical control. Especially in the nineteenth century, art came to be seen as an exclusively aesthetic sphere. That is, it came to be seen as a self-contained expression of the human spirit, generated by powers of its own, particularly the imagination, distinguished by certain characteristics that set it apart from other areas of human significance, like history and science.[3] These are very broad considerations, I realize, but the nineteenth century movement of *l'art pour l'art* is indicative in its own exaggerated way of just this strong will to make art entirely self-contained. Of course, this did not prevent the poet, say, from conceiving of himself as a new kind of secular priest, an aesthetic *vates* worshipping, ministering at the shrine of beauty.[4] For the essential point consisted in art's assertion of its own independence, even sometimes to the point of the artist setting himself apart from the common run of men by his special, "poetic" garb.

Why might the artist thus assert himself with such strong distinctiveness? A key element here is that to understand art as an autonomous aesthetic activity is to judge as essential to it the idea of human expressiveness.[5] What does the art work as expressive reveal? Most basically, it seems to reveal the fact that it originates in the creativity of the artist, and that, on being completed, it presents itself for the aesthetic contemplation of its audience. As an aesthetic phenomenon, the art work is something made by man, albeit individuals of special genius, and something made for man's appreciation. Man is to be seen not just as one thing of nature lost in muteness among its other silent things. As Hegel himself implies, man is not just substance; he is also and more importantly to be seen as subject.[6] As such, man can give articulation to his own reality. In the aesthetic realm he struggles with the initially amorphous character of his own sensuous being.[7] In his aesthetic production he tries to imaginatively articulate himself and his sense of being. Hence the aesthetic object reveals that man is not just a simple imitator, or a passive mirror of a given external nature. It rather reveals the expressive powers of man whereby his creative potentiality is actively realized. Man as aesthetic does not just mirror external nature; he also externalizes his own nature, and particularly its plastic, originative, imaginative powers. In the aesthetic products he brings into being, he realizes, he recognizes, and he confirms his own creative powers.[8]

When we speak here of art as an "aesthetic" phenomenon in this sense, what is most noteworthy is a tendency to *humanize* art in its entirety. Man becomes the beginning, middle, and end of art. He becomes the beginning because, *qua* artist, he is an originating source; the middle, because in the art work he gives expressive form to himself, and thus mediates with his own initially inarticulate reality. He becomes the end because the aesthetic products he brings into being are for the essential purpose of man's own self-contemplation. Art emerges from and goes out of man, passes through him and returns to man once again, now with the gain of aesthetic articulation. In becoming conscious of the aesthetic object as the expressive outcome of his own work, the art work itself as the product of his own activity, the artist becomes conscious of himself, aesthetically self-conscious, in and through the work he has created.[9] Indeed, such a view is very persuasive in making art a form of man's self-knowledge, albeit a self-knowledge embodied in and mediated through the variety of sensuous objects comprising the aesthetic realm. Moreover, man's own nature seems so rich in latent resources that the task of giving it creative expression allows of an open-ended future. Thus art as "aesthetic" seems to offer a fertile understanding in terms of man itself, and in this to assure art's future through its appeal to the hitherto unrealized, unexpressed, as yet unimagined wealth of man's being. If we recall the question of art's absoluteness, then the burden, indeed, glory of this absoluteness would here rest completely on the shoulders of man. A version of this view might be, for instance, Nietzsche's glorification of the artist-creator as the supreme human type, bearing also in mind his doctrine of man as the unfinished animal, that is, a being with an opening onto infinite promise.

How does the above general view relate to Hegel? Undoubtedly we must admit that Hegel subscribes in significant measure to this understanding. His insistence that art be treated as a genuine spiritual realm in its own right makes him a forerunner, even an adherent of this view. This may be confirmed not only from the general orientation of his large systematic works, but also by the details of different discussions in the *Lectures on Aesthetics*. Thus Hegel insists that art reveals the plastic powers of human imagination, that art shapes an articulated image of humanity itself, that art provides man with a sensuous self-knowledge answering to his deepest needs and highest aspirations. Likewise, his aesthetics places a strong accent on the creative, expressive powers of man, in contrast to the merely imitative.[10] All of this is clearly granted by Hegel. The fundamental question, however, is whether we can restrict our considerations to man's creative power. Or rather, since Hegel does not deny the artist's creative powers, the questions is better put: how are we to interpret the full significance of such powers? Is art to be subsumed under an entirely humanistic aesthetic? Must we make a model of Feuerbach's anthropological reduction of the religious realm, only now applying this model to the aesthetic realm in the form of the question: is the creative power of the artist also to be completely anthropolgized?[11] Or, granting the real truth of the humanistic aesthetic, must we rather understand its meaning in the light of a further consideration, an added complexity? Art as aesthetic phenomenon reveals art as the dialectical self-mediation of man in imaginative form. The question is whether humanistic self-mediation is adequate to the artist's creative power, whether this points to a more complex mediation where the dialectic is not just between man and his own self. In that Hegel holds to a transition from art to religion in his philosophy of Absolute Spirit, I think we must answer this question in the affirmative. We must grant, Hegel seems to imply, an absolute dimension to man, but the meaning of this absolute dimension directs us further than man. We must grant the essential truth of art as "aesthetic," but a philosophical examination of this truth, Hegel seems to say, points us further to art as a religious phenomenon. Let us now look at this second approach to the matter.

3. Art as Religious: The Symbolical, Classical, and Romantic Types of Art

In treating here of art as "religious" we need to bear in mind the following preliminary points. First, our focus is not on religion in any sectarian sense, and so also not on art as subordinated to some ecclesiastical yoke. Nor is our focus on a special category of art called "religious art" as opposed to secular, profane art, that is, art dealing with subjects generally sanctioned as "religious." So also we are not concerned with art used as a means for a religious purpose or end, as it might be used for religious propaganda or in some forms of liturgical art. With Hegel art is not to be used merely instrumentally; its activity is an end in itself, a value of intrinsic worth. Granting this, the issue is whether the intrinsic worth of this activity calls forth a religious interpretation. Nor is the question here one of art and religion as two irreducible cultural categories, essentially distinct yet capable of different combinations.[12] The question rather concerns the metaphysical meaning of art's creative expressiveness. A creative articulacy runs through all forms of expression as a continuous power: this same power, which Hegel calls *Geist*, articulates itself in a plurality of different forms. Consequently, we do wrong to excessively sediment these forms and separate them irrevocably. The issue is not whether the artistic form can be reduced to a religious form, or perhaps both to a third form, for instance, philosophy,[13] but whether this creative articulacy expressed in art and in other forms can be completely characterized in aesthetic terms, whether the religious form brings out something essential that the exclusively aesthetical form does not fully manifest. In Hegel what unites the three highest activities, art, religion, and philosophy, is not one particular form, but the very power of *Geist* itself, for it runs through all three. Our attention on art as "religious" is not, therefore, on one form alongside other forms, but on *the forming power itself* which indeed is conspicuous in the creative expressiveness of art but which, because it can never be set apart simply as art's privileged possession, calls for a more than aesthetic interpretation, even in the sphere of art itself.

If we now consider Hegel's view more closely, we need to notice an historical consideration and a systematic, metaphysical point, as is so often the case with Hegel. The historical consideration has to do with the fact that even down to Hegel's own era we tend to discover a conspicuous intertwining of art and the religious.[14] Thus it is not irrelevant to recall that in the final movement to Absolute Knowing in his *Phenomenology of Spirit* Hegel's interest is not in art as "aesthetic" but in *Kunstreligion*, the religion of art. Here Hegel's discussion is complex, but in the main he plots a somewhat tortuous emergence of increasingly self-conscious artistry, expressing itself through inanimate nature, through plant and animal life, to the highest self-conscious literature of a people—from the abstract, through the living, to the spiritual work of art. The important point here is that this emergence is essentially religious. Normally we think inspiration, rapture, dreams, the unconscious to be more amenable to religious interpretation in terms of the "pathos" of the artist who receives the divine *afflatus* of the Muse.[15] Hegel is not unmindful of this, but he also affirms that a more complex, full religious significance develops with the development of self-consciousness. Religious significance does not drop from sight with the development of self-consciousness, as if the divine could only emerge in the darkness of night. Rather, this significance is progressively appropriated by man, inwardized, and interiorized, revealing most fully the true nature of the human and divine and their essential relatedness. Again, Hegel's discussion of *Kunstreligion* shows how little art is "aesthetic" in the sense of a specialized, self-sufficient activity. Instead of this compartmentalized *l'art pour l'art*, art here permeates the entire life of a people, in its ethical, political, and religious manifestations. *Kunstreligion* reveals the world of a people, and so as art is a certain articulation of the whole.[16]

An equally significant intertwining of religion and art is to be found in Hegel's schema for elucidating the historical development of art, namely, in terms of Symbolical, Classical, and Romantic art. Given our present intentions we might briefly note how the religious enters into all three types. Thus, when Symbolical art is characterized as permeated by an opaque sense of the indefinite and the sublime, the religious note of reverence before mystery, of awe before the infinite, is unmistakably present. Hegel's own examples of Symbolical art are through and through the carriers of forms of religious consciousness, for instance, the Pyramids and the Sphinx. Though for Hegel Egypt is the "land of symbol" and the Sphinx is the "symbol of symbols," the religious note is equally present when he connects Symbolical art with the pantheism of the Orient, with Arabic mysticism, and with the sublime poetry of the Israelites in the Old Testament.[17]

Similarly, with Classical art, especially in the art of ancient Greece, once again we are not in the presence of an "aesthetic" object, in the sense above defined. Certainly we find here Hegel's special interest in the human figure, but the vital religious note is not lacking here either. We discover the perfection of classical art in the statues of the Greek gods, but this aesthetic perfection springs from the consummate balance with which they make present the gods in physical form. They reveal an immediate sensuous unity between the human and the divine in which all disproportion and discord between the two is banished. We might note also that Hegel implies the defect of Classical art is just its tendency to limit the expression of spirit, *Geist*, to the human spirit and figure. As with the perfection of Classical art, so also with its limitation do we come across a clearly religious import.[18]

Finally, in the third kind of art, Romantic art, the religious note is perhaps the most insistent of all. There might seem some irony in this for, historically speaking, Romantic art makes its most pervasive appearance at the threshold of that humanistically oriented modernity that defines art as an "aesthetic" phenomenon. Yet, right at this threshold certain considerations imply that it is this form of art, in contrast to the Symbolical and the Classical, that is marked by the most explicit and complex religious import. Why so? In Romantic art we come across what can be called an *inwardizing* in man himself of the sense of the infinite. Hegel explicitly calls our attention to this in his *Aesthetics*.[19] The infinite is not just "out-there," as it tends to be in Symbolical art. Nor is it completely proportioned to the human figure as physical, as it tends to be in the aesthetic perfection of Classical art. Deep down within himself man is a kind of world. *Grande profundum est ipse homo,* St. Augustine had exclaimed in his own religious exploration.[20] A similar thought is not uncharacteristic of many nineteenth century Romantics, nor of Hegel's own exploration of the self, particularly in the *Phenomenology*.[21] Subsequently, to Hegel this "inwardized infinite" will tend to be construed in a progressively more exclusive humanistic manner; indeed, such a humanizing of the infinite tends to go hand in hand with "creativity" theories of art, an essential ingredient to art as an "aesthetic" phenomenon, as we saw. But in Hegel himself this inwardizing of the infinite entails the struggle to bring to light, within the interior recesses of man himself, the ultimately religious significance of experience. Not unexpectedly for Hegel, Romantic art only becomes possible *after* the human spirit has been percolated historically through the Christian religion. For in this religion man himself, particularly in the depths of his inward subjectivity, becomes the most rich disclosure of the meaning of divinity, namely, of God as spirit or *Geist*.[22] It is this disclosure of *Geist* in its true form that Romantic art struggles to effect; and, we must add, with the increasing realization that the sensuous embodiment essential to the aesthetic side of art may not always be completely adequate to this task. Unmistakably, with Romantic art, we are witness to a transition beyond art, or better, witness to art pointing beyond itself to a significance which calls for a fuller religious form. Hegel explicitly indicates this when he speaks of Romantic art as "the self-transcendence of art but within its own sphere and in the form of art itself."[23] In this complex utterance we see laid bare the constituents of Hegel's view: that art is its own sphere; that nevertheless within its own sphere the transcendence of the "merely aesthetic" is already at work; but also that this transcending is not the simple negation or supersession of art but is rather tied up with its highest attainment and fulfillment. Art itself, as it were, sacrifices its own exclusively "aesthetic" form to open out upon a fuller religious configuration.

4. Art as Religious: Creativity and *Geist*

These historical considerations concerning Symbolical, Classical, and Romantic art bring us directly to the philosophical point with regard to art's metaphysical meaning. The last citation from Hegel concerning Romantic art particularly requires more systematic elucidation. For Romantic art allows us to affirm man's creativity, but how do we reconcile this with the purported religious import of the same art? To respond to this question we are pointed to the necessity in Hegel, I suggest, of conceiving man's creativity in other than exclusively humanistic terms. In Hegelian terms, man's creativity must be seen to participate in and disclose a "creativity," an "expressiveness" that is more than man as a finite individual:[24] the power of *Geist* understood in an absolute sense. Seen thus, the crucial point is not to reduce art to religion but rather to elevate art as "aesthetic." This we can see more explicitly if we contrast art construed as "aesthetic" with art as "religious." Art as "aesthetic" insists on man's creative powers; art as "religious" concurs, but goes further—these powers themselves point to a more fundamental creative expressiveness, that of Absolute Spirit. Art here has metaphysical significance because the powers it expresses are not private or subjective in the pejorative sense. Nor are they simply man's possessions. They are rooted in the nature of actuality itself and of a piece with its most fundamental essence. For art as "religious" cannot be completely characterized as man's sensuous self-knowledge. Nor is the outcome of the artistic act solely a human product, a human artefact. The artist struggles with his material and gives it form. His material is not only external matter but also his own self. But in his struggle with his external and internal matter, he is really wrestling with a power that is not simply external nor internal, neither just the external things of nature, nor his own finite self. For Hegel this power is *Geist*. It too becomes an ingredient in art's self-knowledge and in the embodied product of creation. Art as "religious" attempts to effect for man the imaginative articulation of this power. It is the struggle for this conjunction that confers the added complexity on art as "religious."

This complexity, moreover, makes more intelligible Hegel's insistence on the absolute character of art. For on this complex view, art is absolute in the mode of its activity: man's creative powers are grounded in and reveal the absolute power of *Geist*. Art is absolute also in the actuality with which it deals the actuality of *Geist* which it seeks to present in its imaginative articulations. Indeed, all great art might be seen as attempting to realize this double aim: to reveal the dignity and glory of man in his original and creative powers, and to strain to display the bond between these powers and what is absolute. Great art, as it were, strains both inwards and upwards towards a limit which it is difficult not to call religious. If the play on words will be allowed, great art both gives us images of the divine in man, and thus in man gives us images of the divine.

The point might be further developed in this way. The Romantic and modern emphasis on "creativity" and "expressiveness" points to an aesthetic norm immanent within art itself. This immanence sometimes tends to be counterposed to the *transcendence* characteristic of the more classical, imitation theory of art. Imitation involves the relation of an image (the imitation) to a transcendent original (the model or paradigm external to the image). Thus it might seem that this imitation theory is more consistent with art as "religious" in this sense: the transcendent original seems to guarantee the difference between man's creativity and something further, and also seems to justify the reference of artistic activity to some reality other than man. A chief difficulty with imitation, however, is its tendency to produce dualism, which may lend itself to a diminution and subordination, even a denial of art's immanent creative powers. Hegel rejects such a diminution, yet how is he to justify art as "religious" without falling back on imitation or something like it, and thus falling into the unacceptable dualistic consequences that seem necessarily to follow?[25]

A way out of this impasse, I suggest, is to conceive the contrast of "creativity" and "imitation" less starkly, not so strongly as a pair of opposites. For Hegel does not completely repudiate imitation, but might be seen as attempting to incorporate it within art in a non-dualistic way. That is, ancient Classical imitation, as it were, refers the art image to an external god, and so tends to appear as antithetical to modern, Romantic creativity. Hegel's view represents an attempted synthesis of the justified emphasis of both these possible positions. But the Hegelian "imitation" does not chiefly refer outside to an external god; art, we might put it, is rather a kind of "interiorized imitation" where the god of its reference is most properly discovered *within* the self as an originating source of creative power. After all, imitation is in fact a relation of appropriation, and so as a mode of representation always involves some inwardizing movement of spirit. The norm of this "interiorized imitation" is an immanent one, and so joins up with the notion of "creativity." It is a most interesting fact that the more accomplished an imitation becomes the more it begins to present itself as a creation in its own right. At a certain point of accomplishment they begin to shade into each other. At this point imitation and creation cease to be just opposites.

All of this can be rendered more explicit by reference to the analogous problem of religious representation in Hegel.[26] For Hegel the most adequate religious representations do not try to fix the divine immovably in sensuous externality. Rather, they point to spirit in the medium of sense, representing the divine as "indwelling." Thus again their representing, "imitating" intention is an interiorizing movement, not an exteriorized one. For their intent is to represent *Geist*, and this cannot be effected without this inward turn. Man discovers himself most fully in this turn, not just as representing an external divinity, but as creatively taking part in the process of *Geist* itself. Maritain puts a similar point well when he says that the artist does not just copy creation but continues creation.[27] On the present view we do not have to jettison "creativity," as perhaps Classical $\mu\acute{\iota}\mu\eta\sigma\iota\varsigma$ (*mimesis*) may suggest. Nor need we inflate man's creativity into the fullness of the Absolute itself, as some extreme Romantics have been tempted to do. It is not a question of either this mere diminution of man nor yet of his simple divinization. It is possible to affirm man's creativity while yet seeing this in the context of a "creativity" more ultimate than man.

Of course, "Classical" and "Romantic" are notoriously ambiguous categories and are not always used with any proper precision.[28] But it is helpful, I believe, to think of Hegel's view of art as religious as somehow bringing these two together. For apart from the triadic categorization touched on in the last section, the Classical and Romantic, in Hegel's rendition of the concepts, might be seen to emphasize key elements in the religious and the aesthetic conception of art. Thus the Classical (here drawing on Hegel's usage) focuses on representations of the divine in human statues of the gods, while the Romantic imaginatively explores the enigmatic recesses of the self. When I suggest that for Hegel art might be seen as religious, I mean to imply that ultimately art points beyond any simple antithesis of these two possibilities. There is no question here of returning to Classical representation or $\mu\acute{\iota}\mu\eta\sigma\iota\varsigma$. Rather, we must move beyond the exclusively aesthetic rendering of the Romantic self—the sense of divinity must be incorporated as an immanent norm. This is perhaps just the religious significance of Romantic art previously noted: the inwardizing in man himself of the sense of the infinite. This revelation of an immanent norm is precisely what is at stake in the "interiorized imitation" that comes to expression in human creativity.

Let us now sum up the contrast of the "aesthetic" and "religious" interpretations of creativity thus. In the "aesthetic" interpretation man is involved in an imaginative conversation with himself. This conversation is complex and rich, and indeed its internal intricacy can be conceived dialectically: man is *both* sides of the conversation, the speaker and the spoken. Man can be his own listening interlocutor. The discords, clashes, and contradictions within man generate this conversation, just as the conversation sometimes yields to man's own agreement with himself, unity with himself, peace with himself. Yet for all this, the dialectic of this conversation makes it ultimately a humanistic monologue. In the contrasting "religious" interpretation of creativity, a further complexity is inherent in the dialectic which makes the conversation into a different dialogue. In this dialogue, of course, man comes to hear himself, but always within the context of a conversation with what is more ultimate than the finite individual, something that cannot be completely "anthropologized." Perhaps this also throws some light on why, for Hegel, art must make way for religion in an even fuller way. As lending itself to an exclusive "aesthetic" interpretation, art tends not to always bring out the full dialectical interplay of the human and the divine. Moreover, tensions between the two may not be entirely resolved on artistic grounds alone. That is, man's finite creative power may not be fully known for what it is in the context of the infinite power of the divine. Outside of this context, we always risk an inadequate conception of human power. In religious terms, God is at work in the artist,[29] but the artist, as finite individual, may fail to see the significance of this. His failure may take the form of asserting, "this work is mine and mine alone," as modern, individualistic doctrines of originality tend to imply. Or it may take the opposite form; the artist then says, "this work is not mine at all but the outcome of some completely other agency, some foreign force which invades me with inspiration." One view may elevate self-activity to an unsurpassed degree; the other may stress the receptivity of the self to a point approaching sheer passivity.[30] With Hegel, I think, neither alternative ought to be asserted exclusively or as they stand in their one-sidedness.

The creative power of art reveals a complex conjunction of self-activity and receptivity to what is ultimate, or what religious representation depicts as the union of the human and the divine. Hegel would insist on avoiding a humanism making man foreign to the power of the divine, and also any alienating religion which makes the divine power completely foreign to man, as, say, in the estranged form of worship of the unhappy consciousness. Both these views reduce to competing dualisms which, though they seem to face in opposing directions, are actually complementary.

Perhaps something of the point might be suggested in the following way. What is chiefly at issue is how we are to understand the riddle of *Geist* itself which, it seems, cannot be simply reduced to either God or man, nor to the competing theological and humanistic dualisms. Rather, *both* man and God are *Geist* which is, as it were, the energy that dynamically articulates their distinct reality and their inseparable continuity. As articulated in man, as creative in man, *Geist* is not reducible to more normal humanistic terms. It is more than the finite individual. This perhaps is part of the point of Hegel's way of exploiting the more than finite connotations of the religious representation of "God." At the same time, since the riddle turns on the enigma of *Geist*, we ought not get bogged down in the representation of "God" in a manner which simply "reifies" or "objectifies" *Geist* as an infinite being over against man. The competing theological and humanistic interpretations sometimes do bog down in complementary dualisms, so that it is forgotten that the reality of *Geist* and what this means are at stake. We might even see both "man" and "God" as two "representations," that is, concrete articulations of *Geist*, which itself is not reducible to one or the other in a dualistically exclusive way. Though again, the language of religious representation, in its acknowledgement of both the infinite and the finite, is ultimately more adequate to the absoluteness of *Geist* than is the humanistic interpretation.

5. The Aesthetic and the Religious: On Right- and Left-Hegelian Readings

These last remarks provide us with a context to discern some relevance in our present theme for the overall interpretation of Hegel. A number of possibilities present themselves here, but our discussion of art as aesthetic and religious throws some suggestive light on that perennial issue of right and left readings of Hegel. Very broadly, these left and right readings are thought to epitomize respectively a humanistically oriented and religiously inclined view of Hegel, corresponding, again very broadly, to the two possible interpretations of art developed above. The complementary dualisms in relation to art mentioned above can be seen to clarify many of the differences thought to separate left and right readings.[31] Let us first ask how these two possibilities link us with the Right-Hegelian reading.

Those who are sympathetic to the defense of the religious dimension of Hegel are sometimes classified as the "right," even though this classification is not always discriminating enough with respect to the *differences* between possible religious interpretations, ranging along the spectrum from the orthodox to the heterodox. Frequently, however, the religious reading of Hegel is thought to emphasize God to the point of attenuation of finite man, precisely as finite.[32] Man risks becoming absorbed in God. Indeed, some claim that this absorption of the finite so proceeds that traditional theism yields way to pantheism. The issue of pantheism, of course, is complex in Hegel, and much discussed. There are many instances where the implication of his thinking does seem to attenuate the difference of the finite and the infinite, yet also it is to be recognized that it is no part of Hegel's deepest intentions to eliminate this difference. The interpretation developed above of art as religious, I suggest, strengthens rather than weakens the view that Hegel does *not* seek to commit us to the eradication of this difference. For the artist, on his own terms and as a finite individual, is a real center of creative power. He is not, as it were, the mere passive puppet of a domineering divine power. Yet within the realization of his power, his participation in the divine power is disclosed. While the difference remains, it now ceases to be a mere dualistic opposition between Absolute *Geist* as infinite and the creative expression of *Geist* in finite man. Hegel's own remarks on pantheism in the *Encyclopædia* indicate his refusal to destroy that difference. This refusal, we may add, is quite compatible with criticizing the relation of finite and infinite conceived as one of dualistic opposition.[33]

There is some irony here in the fact that art as "aesthetic" and "religious" reveals a real point of contact between Hegel and the individual taken to be one of his most trenchant religious critics, namely Kierkegaard. Kierkegaard saw himself as religiously set against Hegel precisely on this supposed attenuation of finiteness within the Hegelian system. The irony here centers on their common attitude to the merely "aesthetic": despite its indispensable role in human existence, both deeply agree on the insufficiency of the exclusively "aesthetical" to meet man's fullest demands for absoluteness. Kierkegaard, it is true, understands this demand as most fully realized in religion, while Hegel ultimately gives the palm to philosophy. Yet both, regardless of their differences, seem to concur on this essential: if it is not ultimately to atrophy and perhaps deform its own inherent seriousness, the "aesthetic" must open to the "religious"—in Kierkegaard's case in terms of the different stages of life's way, in terms of his disclosure of the inner tensions of the purely aesthetical and the necessity for it to yield to the ethical and the religious; in Hegel's case in the self-transcending of art as "aesthetical" with the emergence through it of *Geist* in its religious and philosophical forms.[34]

These very brief indications must suffice with regard to what we might call Right-Hegelian aesthetics. Reflection on Hegel's view of art, taking seriously art's claim to absoluteness, does illuminate the possibility of, as it were, dialectically balancing the artist, as a finite creator, with Absolute *Geist*, as infinite creative power, without causing to vanish the difference of the two. In the Left-Hegelian aesthetic, by contrast, this difference tends to vanish in a contrary way. For here it is man himself who tends to become the creative power, the absolute creative power. The Promethean proclivities of Left-Hegelian humanisms are well known. This Promethean proclivity finds its expression here in the reinterpretation and transformation of any religious reading of "creativity." In this regard, it is the Left-Hegelian view that bears more directly on the fate of art as an aesthetic and religious phenomenon after Hegel. After Hegel art tends to lose much of its religious implication, and the aesthetic conception, insofar as it puts the emphasis on man's expressiveness and originality, comes to dominate. On this we need but cite Marx, the most powerful and influential of the Left-Hegelians.[35] It may be incidental that the youthful Marx was stirred to write some poetry. Yet Marx's more mature emphasis upon the productive powers of man, on his ability to make himself in and through his productions, can be seen as but a more proletarianized version of the aesthetical conception. *Homo æstheticus* becomes *homo faber* who, in turn, is inseparable from *homo œconomicus*. Throughout we find the humanistic emphasis upon man's self-activity, now, however, materialized and made sensuously actual through the historical process of production. Indeed, Marx speaks of man's ability to produce according to the "laws of Beauty," and links this with what makes man's productive powers specifically human. The discovery of the manuscripts of the early Marx, the "humanistic" Marx, served to reawaken some of the aesthetical dimensions inherent in the Marxist vision. Nor is the aesthetical entirely absent in the "mature" Marx. In *Grundrisse*, for instance, the true realm of freedom is said to lie beyond simple material production. Marx cites the case of the composer to illuminate what is involved in genuinely free activity; this is more than mere amusement, involving as it does the serious discipline and intense exertion of self-realization. The aesthetical is inseparable from the full active realization of the human and in its own way epitomizes man's self-realization.[36]

Undoubtedly the line of this Left-Hegelian heritage extends deeply into our time, and, what is more, in its specifically aesthetical form. Here the work of Lukács might be mentioned. We might also recall the importance of art for many of the Frankfurt school, for instance, the importance of music for Adorno, and Benjamin's view of "the author as producer." Perhaps Marcuse provides the most striking example of a Left-Hegelian effort to reassert the essentially liberating power of the aesthetic: free society requires free senses and imagination; aesthetical freedom and political liberty are inextricably linked.[37] Even among the French Existentialists, notably Sartre, we find the aesthetic conception coupled with aspects of the "humanistic" Marx. Literature particularly is revealed not only as the reproduction of man's drama in society; it displays, indeed participates in, the self-production of historical man.[38] Examples might be multiplied instancing the extent of the aesthetic influence of the Left-Hegelian heritage.[39] The crucial point concerns the shift of the center of absoluteness to man himself. This is bound up with the entire modern philosophic problem of subjectivity: whether the creativity of the self is completely independent and self-sufficient, or only intelligible in relation to something more ultimate. Obviously art as "religious" points to this second possibility, though, as we have seen, it is the first possibility that has been most prominent since the historical disintegration of the Hegelian system. As Taylor rightly points out, the self has been loosened from its anchor in cosmic *Geist* and made absolutely creative on its own account.[40]

This development is related to the fact that in the nineteenth century art as "aesthetic" itself sometimes tried to assume a kind of religious character. Art as "aesthetic" made its own claims to absoluteness, as in the "aesthetic" man of the nineteenth century for whom art is all, or the whole. The question is whether this represents an adequate response in relation to art's claim to absoluteness. When Hegel grants art a place in Absolute Spirit I do not think that this was any anticipated endorsement of the exclusively aesthetical in this nineteenth century sense. Hegel, I suggest, would concur with the position implied by Heidegger *vis-à-vis* Wagner's effort to turn art into a kind of religion:[41] rather than art's completion, this may be a sign of decline, in that the effort to make the artist the sole creative absolute represents an attenuation of the sense of the absolute. We require a sense of the absolute stronger than the merely aesthetical can supply. The aesthetic man of the nineteenth century might seem to signify a reaching out of art to the totality of life, but often there is a paradoxical reversal in this. The "aesthetical" man, motivated by artistic "purity," is rather tempted by the "ivory tower" and so towards isolation from that totality. Against the mediocrity, crassness, and philistinism of life, the "aesthetic" man exaggerates this separation to the point of wearing a special "artist's" uniform, almost, one suspects, in imitation, perhaps parody, of the priest's special garb. Art is turned into a totality itself demarcated from other cultural fields. This is only partly an index of the supposed poverty of common life; more importantly, it is a sign of the separation, alienation, and estrangement of the artist, and a struggle against the waning powers of art to affect the whole of life, that waning of art's power which in Hegelian terms would be discussed under the heading of the "death of art."

When Hegel touches on the so-called "death of art" it is his alertness to this waning power of art in the contemporary era that we must keep in mind. If there is a "death of art" it lies partly in the inappropriate centering of the absolute completely in man, or as we can put it, the loss of art as "religious" event. That art becomes separated from the totality of life and sets itself up a totality is very significant here in being tied with the loss of the "religious" dimension of the "aesthetic." For it is this dimension which might support art's claim to absoluteness, and so give it some power over the whole, the totality of life. The "aestheticising" of art seems to reveal the highest glorification of art; yet this "aestheticising" reveals art no longer immersed in but removed from the sense of life's wholeness. The "aesthetic" glorification of art might be thus seen as an attempt to stem the internal hemorrhaging of art which results when its intimacy with a religious sense of the totality goes. Art itself erected into a kind of religion might be seen as an effort to reassert the old, true powers of art. But cut off from the wholeness of life (a separation perhaps justifiable in reaction to the spiritual poverty of aspects of nineteenth century life),[42] any genuine religious inspiration becomes increasingly difficult, and both art and religion begin to wither together. Art as "aesthetic" loses its ground in the religious opening to powers of being more ultimate than finite man. If Nietzsche is correct, the self of modern subjectivism finally runs itself aground on the rocks of contemporary nihilism.

Of course, the Left-Hegelian, recognizing the ultimate bankruptcy of sheer "aestheticism," particularly in its nineteenth century form, does attempt to further radicalize the substitution of the "aesthetic" for the "religious" of the sort just described. Here we come across the reverberation in contemporary politics of some themes of Hegelian aesthetics, as mentioned at the opening of this paper. Put simply, the Left-Hegelian ushers the artist out of the ivory tower and onto the barricades, out of the holy temple of contemplative art and into the raw struggle of the practical world of action. The image of the creative artist shifts from the solitary, secular "priest" to that of the socially engaged engineer, or a member of the elite avant-garde of revolutionary praxis. Revolution itself becomes a new religion with a concept of creativity originally borrowed from aesthetics but now called upon to perform its work in the real, material world. Before the aesthetic was content to dream up imaginative worlds in the art work; now the revolutionary in the artist insists that the dream be realized in fact, that through action it may be translated from ideal image into material reality. This move mirrors in art Marx's own effort to shift philosophy itself from contemplative thought to revolutionary praxis, where the point is not to interpret the world rationally, as Hegel did, but to change it actively, as Marx hoped to do. The point becomes not just the aesthetic creation of works of art but the political creation of a new society as itself a kind of work of art. Not surprisingly, there exists a widespread sympathy among twentieth century artists for revolution and revolutionary figures in politics. This sympathy, we now see, has its roots in a left interpretation of Hegelian aesthetics, where it is not just a question of the "aesthetic" versus the "religious" conception of art, but also of the "revolutionary" versus a "religious" interpretation. Or better, the "aesthetic" conception has been radicalized in its vision of creative originality into an inspirer, an expression and sustainer of revolutionary politics.[43]

Let us now conclude by attempting to gather together the overall direction of our discussion, and by placing these last reflections more firmly in the perspective of Hegel's philosophy of Absolute Spirit. As I hope to have made clear, if the argument presented here concerning art as an aesthetic and religious phenomenon in Hegel holds good, then neither the right nor left alternative is adequate. Art cannot be completely humanized in a manner which makes irrelevant the question of the contribution of something more than man. Nor can what is more than man be so emphasized in art that the real creative contribution of the human individual is neglected. A sheerly aesthetical view might put man in the center, but into man the Hegelian absolute would vanish. A sheerly religious view might put the absolute at the center but into its power the creative contribution of man would be absorbed, and so man as artist would vanish. By contrast with both these alternatives, Hegel's view of art as religious incorporates the aesthetic, but art does not vanish into religion, nor is religion reduced. Rather, we find a complex balance of aesthetic and religious considerations such as we have tried to adumbrate. The aesthetic points beyond itself to the religious, but the creative contribution of man is not jeopardized thereby, while the bond between art and the religious safeguards art's own participation in what is ultimate.

When Hegel affirms art's absoluteness within the realm of Absolute Spirit, it is just such a complex balance that is in question. Because of its complexity and indeed its internal tensions, this "balance" is easily upset. We saw this in the Left-Hegelian stress on the "aesthetic" rather than the "religious": here just as the "aesthetical" and "religious" tend to be assimilated in a certain fashion rather than balanced, so also do the "political" and "religious" become assimilated rather than balanced. It is true, of course, that just as art and religion were deeply intertwined for Hegel, so also were religion and politics.[44] But here a distinction essential to the Hegelian balance vanished in the Left-Hegelian appropriation. In this latter. putting the point in Hegel's own terms. Absolute Spirit tends to be collapsed into objective spirit: or rather. objective spirit, in the shape of the "political." is elevated into the absolute and comes to possess something of the ultimacy and centrality previously possessed by art and religion. In Hegel art and religion may be deeply rooted in the political but they are marked by a dimension not entirely reducible thereto, as we must grant if we acknowledge some truth in his distinction between objective and Absolute Spirit.[45]

Notes

1. On this, see William Desmond, "Art, Philosophy and Concreteness in Hegel," *The Owl of Minerva*, forthcoming.

2. I use the phrase "exclusively aesthetic" here because, as will be clear in the body of the argument, there is no intent to deny the aesthetic dimension of art. The question is whether, granting this dimension, it is susceptible of a religious interpretation. For terminological convenience I will speak below of the aesthetic conception as contrasted with the religious conception, once again bearing in mind that the issue is not one of repudiating the aesthetic but of whether the religious completes the aesthetic—a possibility rendered problematic by the exclusively aesthetical conception. On the difficulty of the religious conception see Charles Karelis's remark that this conception "may seem fantastic" in his interpretive essay to *Hegel's Introduction to Aesthetics*, trans. T. M. Knox (Oxford: Clarendon Press, 1979), p. *xxviii*.

3. On this, for example, see A. Boyce Gibson, *Muse and Thinker* (Harmondsworth: Penguin, 1972), Chapter II; see also Eric Gill, *Art* (London: The Bodley Head, 1934), Chapters II and III, where he discusses the lack of rigid division of labor prior to the fifteenth century, and the fact that art was not a strongly separated, specialized activity, set apart from day to day life, including its religious dimension.

4. See below, section 4, for discussion of this attempt to make art into a religion in the nineteenth century. The concept of the poet as *vates* was, of course, present in Hegel's friend Hölderlin, who in many ways epitomized the tension of the religious and the poetic, prefigured their split that was to become more problematical with the subsequent increasing secularization of life, and responded to the hemorrhaging of the religious spirit within the

poetic impulse. See Johannes Hoffmeister, *Hölderlin und Hegel* (Tubingen: I. C. B. Mohr, 1931); Dieter Henrich, "Hegel und Hölderlin," in *Hegel im Kontext* (Frankfurt: Suhrkamp Verlag, 1971), pp. 9–40; also H. S. Harris, *Hegel's Development: Towards the Sunlight* (New York: Oxford University Press, 1972).

5. On post-Kantian subjectivism, intimately bound up with expressivist currents in aesthetics, see, for example, Hans-Georg Gadamer, *Truth and Method*, translation edited by Garret Barden and John Cummings (New York: Seabury Press, 1975), pp. 39ff. The pervasive presence of the expressivist ideal and its importance for all the areas of human meaning is well treated in Charles Taylor, *Hegel* (London and New York: Cambridge University Press, 1975), *passim*, but especially Chapters I and XX.

6. G. W. F. Hegel, *Phänomenologie des Geistes*, ed. J. Hoffmeister (Hamburg: Felix Meiner, 1952), p. 20; *Phenomenology of Spirit*, trans. A. V. Miller (New York: Oxford University Press, 1977), p. 10.

7. Hegel, of course, was thoroughly conversant with this aspect of art, especially as emphasized by Schiller. In a letter to Schelling Hegel calls Schiller's *Aesthetic Education* a "masterpiece." *Briefe von und an Hegel*, ed. J. Hoffmeister and R. Flechsig (Hamburg: Felix Meiner Verlag, 1952–1960), Vol. I, p. 24.

8. For fuller discussion of this, see William Desmond, "Hegel, Art and Imitation," *Clio* 7, 2 (1978): 303–313.

9. For perhaps the most important instance of this aesthetic of expression, see R. G. Collingwood, *The Principles of Art* (Oxford: Clarendon Press, 1938).

10. See "Hegel, Art and Imitation."

11. There is a clear analogy here between the cases of art and religion. On the strictly religious version of the issue see Walter Jaeschke, "Speculative and Anthropological Criticism of Religion: A Theological Orientation to Hegel and Feuerbach," *Journal of the American Academy of Religion*, XLVIII, no. 3, pp. 345–364. The defense of Hegel's movement from the anthropological to the speculative interpretation of religion here mirrors the shift from art as aesthetic to art as religious in the present paper. On the religious issue *per se* see my "Hegel and the Problem of Religious Representation," *Philosophical Studies* (Ireland), XXX (Spring 1984): 9–22.

12. This is the strategy of Paul Weiss in *Religion and Art* (Milwaukee, Wis.: Milwaukee University Press, 1963). The argument of the present paper is closer to, for example, Paul Tillich's approach to the religious meaning of modern art when he says: "It is not an exaggeration to ascribe more of the quality of sacredness to a still-life by Cezanne or a tree by Van Gogh than to a picture of Jesus by Uhde." *The Religious Situation*, trans. H. R. Neibuhr

(New York: Meridian Books, 1956), p. 89.

13. This tends to be the common interpretation of how philosophy relates to art and religion in Hegel. That is, the emphasis falls on the *difference* in the form of *Geist*, not on the continuity of *Geist* itself as the active content working variously in all three forms.

14. It is true that their separation was already in process since the Renaissance, as already noted. Indeed, we might note how the eighteenth century emphasis on "taste" as a special aesthetic capacity (taken up philosophically in Kant's *Critique of Judgement*) reflects this separation, even to the extent of aesthetics itself becoming a distinct science with Baumgarten. A good deal of this emphasis is retained in Hegel's *Lectures on Aesthetics*, but he always retained key elements of the older outlook. This is not surprising given his early desire, with Hölderlin, to bring about a "new mythology of reason," a desire impossible without the sacral power of art. "Earliest System Programme of German Idealism," *Werke* (Frankfurt: Suhrkamp Verlag, 1969–1971), *Band* I, p. 235; trans. in H. S. Harris, *op. cit.*, p. 511; for discussion of this controversial text see Harris, pp. 249–255. It is not by the way that in the twentieth century Heidegger's interlocutor (in his dialogue of thinker and poet) is so often Hölderlin, given that this dialogue has much to do with the kinship of poetry and the holy in an age which experiences the eclipse of divinity.

15. On the divine *afflatus*, see G. W. F. Hegel, *Enzyklopädie der Philosophischen Wissenschaften*, *Werke*, *Band* X, §560; on the "pathos" of the artist as coming from the gods, see, for instance, *Vorlesungen über die Ästhetik, II*, in *Werke*, *Band* XIV, p. 52; *Aesthetics*, trans. by T. M. Knox (Oxford: Clarendon Press, 1975), Vol. I, p. 458.

16. See particularly *Das Geistige Kunstwerk*, *Phänomenologie des Geistes*, pp. 506ff; *Phenomenology*, pp. 439ff.

17. *Vorlesungen über die Ästhetik, I*, pp. 456ff, 466ff; *Aesthetics*, Vol. I, pp. 354ff, 362ff.

18. On the religious limitations of the anthropomorphic art of classical Greece, see *Vorlesungen über die Ästhetik, II*, pp. 23–24; *Aesthetics*, Vol. I, pp. 435–6.

19. On *Erinnerung* see *Phänomenologie*, pp. 563–564; *Phenomenology*, p. 492; *Vorlesungen über die Ästhetik, II*, pp. 128ff; *Aesthetics*, Vol. I, pp. 518ff.

20. Mention of Augustine is not irrelevant to romantic art in that for Augustine it is not the external world of things but the inward self that is the proper, most rich way to God. Not surprisingly, Augustine has been spoken of as an important ancestor of existentialism, which in turn has been called a late product of the romantic spirit. On this see William Desmond,

"Augustine's *Confessions*: On Desire, Conversion and Reflection," *Irish Theological Quarterly* 47, 1 (1980): 224–233.

21. On this see Mark Taylor, *Journeys to Selfhood: Hegel and Kierkegaard* (Berkeley: University of California Press, 1980), *passim*.

22. *Vorlesungen über die Ästhetik, II*, pp. 132–133; *Aesthetics*, Vol. I, pp. 521–22.

23. *Vorlesungen über die Ästhetik, I*, p. 113; *Aesthetics*, Vol. I, p. 80.

24. As one indication of this we might perhaps think of how the poet's words come to say *more*, suggest *more* than he self-consciously intends; how the power of language, λόγος (*logos*), takes on an inexhaustible life of its own, never entirely within his possession.

25. On imitation and dualism see "Hegel, Art and Imitation"; also Karelis, pp. *xxix–xxxii*.

26. On this inward turn with Romantic art see Eric Heller, *The Artist's Journey into the Interior* (New York: Random House, 1959), particularly Chapter V on Hegel. On this interiorizing movement within religious representation see "Hegel and the Problem of Religious Representation."

27. Jacques Maritain, *Art and Scholasticism and the Frontiers of Poetry*, trans. J. W. Evans (Notre Dame, Ind.: Notre Dame University Press, 1974), p. 60.

28. See Jacques Barzun, *Classic, Romantic and Modern* (Garden City, N.Y.: Doubleday, 1961), Chapter X.

29. On the god and the artist see *Enzyklopädie*, §560.

30. The idea of "inspiration" (as in Plato's divine madness, or Nietzsche's Dionysian intoxication) is extremely important, of course, for the religious interpretation of art. The question is not one of denying the experience but of whether our interpretation of it entails the complete abnegation of finite selfhood. See, for instance, Owen Barfield, *Poetic Diction* (London: Faber & Faber, 1928), pp. 109, 169–170, 189–190; also G. Van der Leeuw, *Sacred and Profane Beauty: The Holy in Art*, trans. D. E. Green (New York: Holt, Rinehart & Winston, 1963), pp. 148–151. On this contrast of passivity and self-activity, we might think of the contrast between some medieval artists who did not sign their work and some contemporary artists, whose signature on a table napkin is sold. We do not buy pictures of apples and pears, say, but a Cezanne, a Matisse—we buy the artist in his self-expression, the artist's *name*.

31. On Left- and Right-Hegelians see K. Lowith, *From Hegel to Nietzsche*, trans. D. E. Green (New York: Doubleday & Co., 1967), especially Chapter 11; Lawrence S. Stepelevich, ed., *The Young Hegelians: An Anthology* (New York and Cambridge: Cambridge University Press, 1983);

David McClellan, *The Young Hegelians and Karl Marx* (London: Macmillan, 1969).

32. It is not only religious critics, like Kierkegaard, who tend to fault Hegel on his purported attenuation of finiteness. Twentieth century philosophy, in the main, sees itself as un-Hegelian on this issue, whether in continental thought, with its emphasis on finiteness, particularly with Heidegger and developments from his thoughts, or in the Anglo-American analytic tradition, with its antisystematic stress, its rejection of idealism, and its often modest conception of the capacity of philosophy.

33. *Enzyklopädie*, §573. For a recent defense of Hegel against the charge of pantheism, see Quentin Lauer, *Hegel's Concept of God* (Albany: State University of New York Press, 1982), pp. 274ff; also pp. 250ff. The unity of the divine and the human can be viewed, of course, from very different angles ranging from the mystical to the reductionistic. In the *Aesthetics* Hegel speaks of Christianity and its art-form, romantic art, as completing the *anthropological* principle, the revelation of God in human form. This completion need not imply a humanistic reduction, or anthropological reduction of God, but rather the revelation of the full religious significance of the anthropological, the human. On the religious completion of the anthropological by Christianity in the *Aesthetics* see note 17 above. Lowith, *op. cit.*, pp. 36–39, does not do proper justice to this in relation to art in Hegel, though he is superbly sensitive to Hegel's ambiguous complexity in relation to religion.

34. Kierkegaard sometimes speaks of Hegelianism as an aesthetic system, implying here a certain limitation. There is a revealing contrast here between Kierkegaard and Hegel. For Kierkegaard the aesthetical, when viewed from the absolute seriousness of religion, is not ultimately serious: it is a kind of game, a playing with life's possibilities, not an ultimate coming to terms with actuality. For Hegel, given the relation of art and religion, there is a deeper seriousness to the aesthetical, even on its own terms: it is a coming to terms with the actual, with all the seriousness, pathos and depth of its concern with the absolute.

35. Max Stirner's essay "Art and Religion" (Stepelevich, *op. cit.*, pp. 327–334), is a revealingly clear example of the "aesthetic" as opposed to the "religious" conception of art. See also Lowith, *op. cit.*, pp. 294ff, on Ruge and the "politicization of aesthetic education."

36. On this see, for instance, Piotr Hoffman, *The Anatomy of Idealism: Passivity and Activity in Kant, Hegel and Marx* (The Hague: Nijhoff, 1982), pp. 98–99, 104–105; also my review of this, *Philosophical Studies* (Ireland), Vol. XXX, forthcoming. See also Istvan Meszaros, *Marx's Theory of Alienation* (London: Merlin Press, 1970), Chapter VIII. Meszaros well

emphasized the intertwining of humanistic, aesthetic, and economic strands (e.g., p. 190). Henri Lefebvre, in *Dialectical Materialism*, trans. John Sturrock (London: Jonathan Cape, 1968), grants the importance of Hegel's aesthetics for the problem of fragmentation of modern man (p. 47), but levels the standard charge of conceptual reductionism (p. 48). Labor takes on a "creative" or "poetic meaning" (p. 129) in the production of "the total man" for Lefebvre (see pp. 148–167, especially pp. 164–165). For a recent concise discussion see Terry Eagleton, *Marxism and Literary Criticism* (Berkeley and Los Angeles: University of California Press, 1976).

37. See A. Arato and E. Beghardt, eds., *The Essential Frankfurt School Reader* (New York: Urizen Books, 1978), Part 11, "Esthetic Theory and Cultural Criticism," especially Benjamin's "The Author as Producer," pp. 254–269; and Adorno's "On the Fetish Character in Music and the Regression in Listening," pp. 270–299. Marcuse has developed the importance of the aesthetic in *Eros and Civilization* (Boston: Beacon Press, 1955), Chapter 9; *One Dimensional Man* (Boston: Beacon Press, 1964), pp. 238ff; *An Essay on Liberation* (Boston: Beacon Press, 1969), *passim*, particularly Chapter 2. George Lichtheim's *Lukács* (London: Collins, 1970) is excellent on what he calls "Lukács' attempt to fuse Hegelian aesthetics with Marxian sociology" (p. 123).

38. J.-P. Sartre, *What is Literature?*, trans. B. Frechtman (New York: Philosophical Library, 1949). Some recent studies emphasizing aesthetics and politics include R. Aronson, *Jean-Paul Sartre—Philosophy in the World* (London: New Left Books, 1980); Pietro Chiodi, in *Sartre and Marxism*, trans. K. Soper (Atlantic Highlands, N.J.: Humanities Press, 1976), brings out the Hegelianism in Marxism and Existentialism, even when these oppose Hegel (pp. 124– 144); Dominick La Capra, in *A Preface to Sartre* (Ithaca: Cornell University Press, 1978), gives a "deconstructive" view of Sartre and literature. See the interview with Sartre, "The Purpose of Writing," in *Between Existentialism and Marxism*, trans. John Mathews (New York: Pantheon Books, 1974), pp. 9–32.

39. Camus also places the artist, conceived of as a creator, at the center of a world which has discarded both Hegel's Absolute and any nostalgia for such an Absolute. Like Nietzsche's Dionysian man, the artist becomes a guardian against nihilism, a rebel struggling for man's meaning against an absurd world. Even a dash of Marxist proletarianism is introduced into this aesthetical ideal, for, as Hochberg puts it (in "Albert Camus and the Ethics of Absurdity," *Ethics* 75, 2 [January 1965]: 87–102), since we must have plumbers as well as painters, Camus' solution lies in turning the plumber into an artist. Hochberg recognizes the Hegelian element in Camus, though it is Hegelianism without the Absolute. Though Camus seems to find something absolute in art, and though this seems akin to Hegel, the precise nature of

this absoluteness is not Hegelian, for it is one which rejects the relation of art and religion; indeed, it defines art in its opposition to religion, not in their dialectical kinship.

40. Charles Taylor, *op. cit.*, p. 546. The entirety of Chapter XX, "Hegel Today," is directly relevant here, though Taylor is perhaps too acquiescent in post-Hegelian expressivism, reading this in too post-Hegelian a fashion.

41. Martin Heidegger, *Nietzsche, Volume I: The Will to Power as Art*, David F. Krell, trans. (New York: Harper & Row, 1979), pp. 88–90.

42. On the spiritual malaise of the eighteenth and nineteenth centuries in relation to Hegel and Kierkegaard see Mark Taylor, *Journeys to Selfhood*, Chapter 2.

43. On the pervasiveness of this among contemporary movements in art and literature in France, see Herbert Lottman, *The Left Bank* (Boston: Houghton Mifflin, 1982).

44. Harris, *op. cit.*, treats extensively of the intertwining of religion and politics in the young Hegel. Charles Yerkes' *Hegel's Christology* (Albany: State University of New York Press, 1982), is also illuminating. See my review of Yerkes in *Bulletin of the Hegel Society of Great Britain*, forthcoming.

45. I have argued against collapsing this distinction and for the importance of art in relation to the "end" of history in "Hegel, Art and History," in *History and System: Hegel's Philosophy of History*, Robert L. Perkins, ed. (Albany: State University of New York Press, 1984).

Commentary on "Art as 'Aesthetic' and as 'Religious' in Hegel's Philosophy of Absolute Spirit

Donald Phillip Verene

It is a pleasure to comment on Professor Desmond's chapter, first, because I think he is right, and second, because of the clarity and style with which he presents his views. Professor Desmond's chapter could serve as a model of how to discuss Hegel. It is free of jargon and of the scholastic repetition of Hegel's terminology and manner of expression that is so often the basis of professional interpretation of Hegel. Professor Desmond sets out to say something importantly and clearly without clouding the issue by casting it in anglicized German. I suspect that his model in this approach, besides his general good sense, is more Collingwood than Hegel himself, although Hegel writes much more clearly than most of his commentators.

Professor Desmond's chapter attempts to make sense of one of the most difficult parts of Hegel's philosophy of spirit—the status of art in absolute spirit. He attempts to explain how art can be its own unique form of absolute spirit and yet how it is implicitly religion. The key to his account of art is his insistence on understanding art as a power of *Geist* rather than a comparison of the form of art with the form of religion. This allows him to avoid the dead end of simply repeating from Hegel that art is something immediate and religion goes beyond this immediacy of form. Art and religion are one because *Geist* is a power that forms itself as art but is at the same time something more than art. Thus *Geist* as a form is art, but as the power behind this formation *Geist* is something more—religion—and further, philosophy.

Given this approach and its dynamics, I was disappointed that Professor Desmond did not say more about philosophy as the third form of

Geist. It is unfair to ask him to do everything in a single chapter, and I can imagine how he might move from religion to philosophy, following the lines of his analysis, but I would like to know more. How does religion become philosophy? How is absolute spirit all three of these forms at once? Is philosophy both art and religion? Is philosophy as a third element not in some way a factor in understanding how art is implicitly religion? Is philosophy as a power of *Geist* not in some way actively behind the scene of the transition between art and religion? About this Professor Desmond has said very little.

In the middle of his chapter, Professor Desmond suggests that Hegel's treatment of *Kunstreligion,* his treatment of art and religion together in the *Phänomenologie des Geistes,* is important for the understanding of his conception of art and religion in absolute spirit. I much agree with this. I think Hegel's views during this early period of the *Phenomenology* are most suggestive for how to read his later system. To what Professor Desmond has said I wish to add something of Hegel's from this early period, not from the *Phenomenology* but from the lecture material of this time on which Rosenkranz reports, the actual texts of which have only been discovered in the last ten years. I mean in particular the fragment called *"Über Mythologie, Volksgeist und Kunst,"* the manuscript of which can be seen in the Staatsbibliothek Preußischer Kulturbesitz in West Berlin.[1]

In the central passage of this interesting fragment Hegel says:

> Mnemosyne, or the absolute Muse, art, assumes the aspect of presenting the externally perceivable, seeable, and hearable forms of spirit. This Muse is the generally expressed consciousness of a people. The work of art of mythology propagates itself in living tradition. As peoples grow in the liberation of their consciousness, so the mythological work of art continuously grows and clarifies and matures. This work of art is a general possession, the work of everyone. Each generation hands it down embellished to the one that follows; each[2] works further toward the liberation of absolute consciousness.
>
> Those who are called geniuses have acquired some special skill or other whereby they make the general forms of a people their work, just as others do other things. What such geniuses produce is not their invention, but the invention of a whole people, or the *finding* that a

people has found its essence.[3] What belongs to the artist as such is his formal activity, his particular skill in this kind of presentation and he is brought up to this in the general skill. He is like someone who finds himself among workers who are building a stone arch, the scaffolding of which is invisibly present as an idea. Each puts on a stone. The artist does the same. It happens to him by chance to be the last; in that he places the last stone, the arch carries itself. By placing the last stone, the artist sees that the whole is one arch; he declares this to be so and thereupon is taken to be the inventor. Or, as in the case of workers who are digging for a spring, he to whom it falls to take up the last layer of earth has the same work as the others. And to him the spring bursts forth.

It is the same with a revolution in a state. We can think of a people as buried under the earth, above which there is a lake. Each intends to be working only for himself and the preservation of the whole by removing a piece of stone from above and employing it in the general subterranean construction. The tension in the air, the general elements begin to change; it produces a desire for water. Uneasy, the people do not know what it is they are lacking and to help they dig even higher in the belief of improving their subterranean condition. The crust becomes transparent. One catches sight of it and calls: "Water!" Tears the last layer away and the lake rushes in and drowns them all by giving them drink. So is the work of art the work of all. There is always one who brings it to its final completion by being the last one to work on it and he is the darling of Mnemosyne.

When in our time the living world does not form the work of art within it, the artist must place his imagination in a past world; he must dream a world, but the character of dreaming, of not being alive, of the past, is plainly stamped on his work.[4]

This raises many interesting issues about art as a form of consciousness, especially about the nature of the artist as creator and his relation to memory, in addition to what Professor Desmond has brought out concerning $\mu\iota\mu\eta\sigma\iota\varsigma$ (*mimesis*). But in terms of the problem of the relation of art and religion it raises a particular possibility: the role of mythology. Myth is at the basis of both art and religion. What is Hegel's view of myth? If religious representation comes from art as a receptivity to what is ultimate or divine by absolute spirit as it works in art, is the ground of this activity already there in art in its connection with myth? Is the awareness of the divine first in art, in its connection with myth? And is this original presence of myth in the aesthetic in some way the basis for the transformation of art to religion in absolute spirit? These are at once speculative and interpretive questions that cause us to connect Hegel's views in the *Phenomenology* and earlier pieces with those of his later system.

Notes

1. See Eva Ziesche, "*Unbekannte Manuskripte aus der Jenaer und Nürnberger Zeit im Berliner Hegel-Nachlass,*" *Zeitschrift für philosophische Forschung* 29 (1979): 430–44.

2. In Rosenkranz's quotation of this passage in *Hegels Leben* (Berlin, 1844) there appears *oder*. The original manuscript reads *jeder*.

3. There is a word play here on *Finden* as contained in *Erfinden*.

4. "*Über Mythologie, Volksgeist und Kunst,*" my translation. See Chapter 3 of my book, *Hegel's Recollection: A Study of Images in the Phenomenology of Spirit* (Albany: State University of New York Press, 1985).

Speculation and Theonomy at the
Close of Hegel's System

Martin J. De Nys

Hegel devotes the closing pages of his *Encyclopædia* to an "exposition of the reciprocal relations of philosophy and religion."[1] His remarks in those pages comprise for the most part an "exoteric discussion"[2] dealing with charges made against philosophy from the religious standpoint regarding atheism and pantheism. The discussion is exoteric because of the nature of the charges, and because "the close of philosophy is not the place ...to waste a word on what a 'notion' means,"[3] even if "the esoteric study of God and identity, as of cognitions and notions, is philosophy itself."[4]

In fact, Hegel approaches a speculative and in that sense "esoteric" discussion of the relation of philosophy and religion in his discussion of revealed religion in the penultimate chapter of the *Encyclopædia*. There he presents "three syllogisms" which, "constituting the one syllogism of the absolute self-mediation of spirit, are the revelation of that spirit whose life is set out as a cycle of concrete shapes in pictorial thought."[5] I want to discuss this speculative appropriation of religious self-understanding in two ways. I want first to examine it with reference to Hegel's treatment of Christian consciousness in the 1807 *Phenomenology*. There, Hegel analyzes the nature of the representations which belong to the absolute religion, and of the thinking which deals with those representations. Consideration of that analysis will help in understanding what Hegel achieves as he moves towards the conclusion of the system.[6] I also want to discuss briefly Hegel's systematic views about "the reciprocal relations of philosophy and religion" with reference to a claim about those relations made by a twentieth century philosophical theologian, Paul Tillich. Hegel's sketch of a systematic retrieve* of religious self-understanding, discussed with reference to his phenomenology of Christian consciousness, offers a resolution to a difficulty in Tillich. This indicates the fruitfulness of a retrieve of Hegel for current philosophical theology.

1. It is essential to the absolute religion, Hegel insists, "that it be *revealed*, and, what is more, that it be revealed by God."[7] In religion, finite spirit encounters its relatedness with absolute Being. Because the relatedness in question is spiritual, it must consummate itself in knowing. Because absolute Being or God is a term in the religious relationship, it must make itself known in that relationship. Philosophy can detect inconsistencies in the concept of a religion that claims to be absolute and that fails to recognize the necessities of revelation and knowing.[8] The consciousness of the absolute religion, from its side, is also aware of these inconsistencies and does not fail to recognize these necessities. Its starting point and center is a representation of the divine as that which, from out of its otherness from the human, unites itself with and reveals itself in human selfhood.[9] The incarnational center of Christian consciousness constitutes it as a form of religious consciousness to which, as Hegel points out in the *Phenomenology*, revelation and knowing radically belong.[10] This same representation inaugurates in a radical way in Christian consciousness the unity of consciousness and self-consciousness which is, for Hegel, characteristic of religious consciousness.[11]

This is not the place to present even an outline of Hegel's account of the religious representation.[12] Suffice it to say that religious representations proceed from images but also include within themselves the analyses and reflections of that consciousness which seeks to know its object through them. That consciousness, in turn, is in its dealings with representations a form of thinking, representational thinking. The representation which centers and inaugurates Christian consciousness in particular

---

* "Retrieve," the standard translation of *Wiederholung*, is used in the Heideggerian sense to refer to the activity of thinking through what is given in a tradition for the sake of discovering the possibilities which it offers to thinking.—*Ed.*

is, Hegel states in the *Phenomenology*, an "immediacy" which "is equally pure mediation or thought, and it must therefore exhibit itself in its own sphere as such."[13] This occurs as the "negativity"[14] which belongs to the inaugurating representation of Christian consciousness is articulated by the consciousness which deals with that representation. That articulation occurs in two phases.

In the first place, the representation from which Christian consciousness proceeds implicitly contains within itself a cycle of interrelated but also distinct representations. These need to be expressed and distinguished. Thus, Christian consciousness recognizes the God whom the Incarnation reveals as possessed of an inner, self-related, absolute life, a trinitarian life.[15] Through this absolute life, God is further represented as one who "*creates* a world,"[16] which world is both the other of its divine principle, and radically dependent thereupon because created. But finite, self-determining persons, parts of the created world because it reflects its divine source, assert their autonomy by denying dependence on the divine in favor of otherness from the divine. This is a "withdrawal into self-centeredness,"[17] a denial of creatureliness which ruptures the relation of the human with the divine; it is a "fall" from that relation which constitutes the finite self as "evil."[18] The rupture, though, is to be healed and evil overcome. This occurs as the divine unites itself with that which has alienated itself from the divine, such that "...actuality has ceased to be something alien and external ..."[19] to the divine, even with respect of death, the extreme consequence of that alienation.

A cycle of representations has now been built out of the original Christian representation, through which cycle the consciousness of the absolute religion now poses before itself its knowledge of the divine, of itself, and of the relation between them. The development of this cycle is the first unfolding of the mediations which belong to the original Christian representation. Two features belong to the contents of this cycle. First, those contents form an interconnected whole, in which each discrete representation contributes to the intelligibility of the other and to the whole. Second, each of these contents nonetheless is discrete, independent of and different from the others. They belong to a whole and are also "externally connected with each other."[20] Since each is an other of the others, the relations among them are negative relations.

This negativity explicitly needs to belong to Christian representations. It also needs to be surpassed. Christian consciousness has expressed through a multiplicity of representations its vision of the divine, of itself, and of the relation of the divine with itself. That consciousness now needs to surpass the externality of the connections among those representations. This surpassing occurs within Christian consciousness as a form of representational thinking, from the standpoint of its own experience, as Christian consciousness appropriates the revelation inaugurated in the Incarnation and articulated through its own mediations.

The Incarnation reveals the unity of the divine and human natures. Finite consciousness, in the face of this revelation, recognizes the "fallen" character of its own self-centeredness, its own self-asserted independence from the divine. It withdraws into itself again in self-recognition. But this "withdrawal consists, therefore, in *convincing itself* that natural existence is evil."[21] Self-centered consciousness, Hegel says, recognizes in "...the propitiation of the absolute Being ..."[22] its own self-centeredness, and the evil which belongs to it because of the same. This consciousness further recognizes divine Being as that which unites itself with its other, and which remains self-identical in its union with its other, for the sake of overcoming the alienation of that which is other than itself from itself.[23] This consciousness, therefore, recognizes its own existence to be an existence which "...preserves itself in its otherness."[24] It knows its otherness from the divine to be an other-directed otherness. It knows that its own self-identity is achieved in its union of itself with that which is other than itself, and that the activity of self-recognition which brings about this union, and which fulfills the identity of consciousness and self-consciousness which for Hegel belongs in principle to religious consciousness, is at once its own activity and the activity of a divine indwelling within itself.

These remarks suggest that negativity now belongs in a new way to the representational structure of the consciousness of the absolute religion. Before, a cycle of diverse representations was articulated in that consciousness, which representations were negatively interrelated in a sense already specified. Now the negativity of those interrelations has been surpassed in a second negativity which overcomes the externality which belonged to the connections among the representations of Christian consciousness in their first articulation. Christian consciousness now represents that which is of concern to it—infinite Divine Being and finite human existence—as each identical with itself in its union with its other. It is important to note that these developments have occurred within a consciousness whose activity is determined *as representational thinking*. Christian consciousness, as Hegel observes its experience in the *Phenomenology*, has articulated and then overcome the externality of its representations just in its dealings with those representations themselves. It has realized the negativity belonging to its representations, in a first way and then in a second way for which the first prepares, for the sake of actualizing its own religious self-understanding, and *has not passed beyond* that self-understanding in those realizations. At the close of its experience, the self-understanding of Christian consciousness remains religious. It has become a recognition of that divine self-othering which permits the divine and the human each to be self-identical in its union with what is other than itself.

2. In the *Encyclopædia* Hegel notes that the absolute religion, insofar as it depicts the realities which concern it through representations, give to those realities

> a separate being, making them presuppositions towards each other, and phenomena which succeed each other; their relationship it makes a series of events according to finite reflective categories. But on the other hand, such a form of finite representationalism is also overcome and superseded in the faith which realizes one spirit and in the devotion of worship.[26]

The speculative treatment of religious self-understanding begins by identifying the achievements of that understanding and proceeds from a recognition of its limitations.[27] Religious consciousness, when it seizes upon its absolute form, articulates its understanding by representing the elements which belong to that understanding as "a series of events" related "according to finite categories," and then on its own terms overcomes the finitude of those relations in "faith ... and in the devotion of worship." This occurs through the two ways in which negativity comes to belong to the contents of Christian consciousness, as discussed above. On its own terms, Christian consciousness learns to represent the divine and the human as other, and to understand the otherness of each term through the self-identity it enjoys in its union with its other. This Christian consciousness can do while dealing with representations.[28] It cannot, however, think the categories which radically determine these achievements. Categories are operative in the processes of Christian consciousness. But that consciousness cannot think those categories, and it cannot think the realities which concern it explicitly through those categories, just because it is a form of representational thinking. Christian consciousness can know the self-identity of human existence and its divine other in terms of the "union of union and non-union" of each with its other, but it cannot think self-identity, union, or otherness categorially, and it cannot explicitly think the negativity which is essential to the definition of these categories. But just because those categories are operative in, albeit not thematically present to, representational thinking, that thinking points beyond itself to another thinking which surpasses representations in speculation, by seizing upon and thematizing the categories which belong to representational thought and by thinking through those categories the realities which concern religious consciousness.

This speculative thinking repeats in its own processes the division of representations "... into special spheres or media ..." and progressively discovers "... the different functions of the notion ..." in each of them.[29] Thus this thinking first comprehends God in the "eternal sphere" as the process of "begetting himself as his *son*, with whom, though different, he still remains in original identity—just as, again, this differentiation of him from the universal essence eternally supersedes itself,"[30] a comprehension which knows divine reality as absolute "Spirit."[31] Speculative thinking proceeds "under the 'moment' of *particularity*, or judgement," to comprehend absolute, spiritual being as that which "divides itself to become two separate worlds,"[32] in which domain finite spirit "... completes its independence till it becomes wickedness ...."[33] But further, speculative thinking, "under the 'moment' of *individuality* ...," comprehends absolute spiritual being as that which is "actualized out of its abstraction into an individual self-consciousness,"[34] an individuality which signifies the "universal unity of universal and individual essentiality," and which realizes "the Idea of the spirit, eternal, but alive and present in the world."[35]

The speculative retrieve of the self-understanding of the absolute religion which systematic philosophy effects thinks the elements that belong to that self-understanding notionally. In doing so, speculative thought re-enacts the self-understanding of the absolute religion in categorial terms. As such, it is

> the revelation of that spirit whose life is set out as a cycle of concrete shapes in pictorial thought. From this its separation into parts, with a temporal and external sequence, the unfolding of the mediation contracts itself in the result—where the spirit closes in unity with itself—not merely to the simplicity of faith and devotional feeling, but even to thought.[36]

Speculative thinking systematically re-thinks in categorial terms the self-identity which divine being and human existence enjoy in the union which each possesses with the other, which union simultaneously preserves the otherness of each from its other. This speculative thinking surpasses representational thinking in making explicit the categories operative in the latter, and in thinking that which is of concern to the latter in a way which makes explicit use of those categories. For this reason, speculative thinking surpasses that thinking which expresses its consciousness of the infinite and the interrelatedness of the finite and the infinite by placing before itself rationally ordered images of the infinite. Speculative thinking thinks the concerns of religious self-understanding not through rationally ordered images, but through the categories which radically determine the rational ordering of those images, thereby comprehending the being of finite existence and infinite reality in terms of the concrete interrelatedness which each enjoys with the other.

More specifically, speculative thinking comprehends the first and then the second sort of negativity which the consciousness of absolute religion realizes unthematically in its dealings with representations. The thinking which retrieves and categorially re-enacts the content of the absolute religion explicitly comprehends self-identity in terms of self-othering, just as it also comprehends otherness as the domain of the self-identical presence of that which is other. In explicitly categorial terms, speculative thought thinks the self-mediation of Absolute Spirit in its union with finite spirit, thus exhibiting the manner in which "the Being of Beings ... through this mediation brings about its own indwelling in self-consciousness, and is the actual presence of the essential and self subsisting spirit who is all in all."[37] Speculative thinking surpasses the representational thinking of absolute religious consciousness. It deals with the contents of the latter in terms of a negativity which representational thinking cannot achieve on its own terms. But this new negativity is a categorial thematization of that sense of negativity which representational thinking does bring about in its own processes but cannot thematize on its own terms. For this reason the speculative and systematic re-enactment of absolute, religious self-understanding comprehends the intelligibility of the latter in a way in which the latter cannot comprehend itself. In just these terms speculative thinking surpasses the self-understanding of religious consciousness. But one may also say that speculative thinking is the self-surpassing of religious self-understanding. Representational thinking points beyond itself to speculative thought for the sake of a radical, ontological articulation of its own intelligibility. The speculative transfiguration of absolute religious self-understanding, adumbrated by Hegel in the penultimate section of the *Encyclopædia*, gives radical articulation to that intelligibility, and as such is its own systematic re-enactment.

Revealed religion, Hegel writes in the *Encyclopædia*, "includes in its forefront the propositions: God is God only so far as he knows himself: his self-knowledge is, further, a self-consciousness in man and man's knowledge *of* God, which proceeds to man's self-knowledge in God."[38] The content of the revealed religion implies the truth of these propositions. The systematic and philosophical retrieve of that content exposes the categories through which the intelligibility of that truth is most fundamentally shown. Philosophy comprehends divine being as absolutely self-related and self-knowing; as self-related in its human other; as the ground, through this self-relatedness, of human knowledge of the divine; and as the ground of the self-knowledge which finite spirit enjoys through its appreciation of its union with its divine other. And philosophy comprehends the identity-in-difference of the moments ingredient in this conceptualization of the interrelatedness of the divine and the human. For this reason, philosophy, as it re-enacts the elements that belong to representational thinking, not only "keeps them together to make a totality, but even unifies them in the simple spiritual vision, and then raises them to self-conscious thought."[39] The systematic, philosophical retrieve of religious self-understanding is an act which radicalizes the unity of consciousness with self-consciousness which, as noted above, is according to Hegel characteristic of the intentionality of religious consciousness. In this retrieve thinking attends to and knows systematically the radical constituents of religious self-understanding, thus articulating in a radical way the self-consciousness which finite spirit enjoys in that understanding, through its vision of its own relatedness to the divine. Systematic philosophy is, at its close, the thought of religious consciousness in both senses of the genitive. It elevates religious consciousness to a categorical transfiguration, and it is simultaneously the self-elevation of that same consciousness into its own categorial reinstatement.

3. In his *Systematic Theology*, Paul Tillich holds that theology deals with the content of religion through concepts which are ontological and through a rational process that is theonomous. Ontological concepts refer to "those structures of being which we encounter in every meeting with reality."[40] Theology necessarily employs such concepts because "theology, when dealing with our ultimate concern, presupposes in every sentence the structure of being, its categories, laws, and concepts. Theology, therefore, cannot escape the question of being any more easily than philosophy can."[41] Ontological concepts for Tillich include categories and what he calls elements of thought. Elements of thought conceptualize the polar characteristics which belong ontologically to things in virtue of their self-relatedness and their interconnectedness with other things.[42] The ontological elements include Individuation-Participation, Dynamics-Form, and Freedom-Destiny.[43] Categories, which for Tillich include space, time, causality, and substance, determine all thought and experience.[44] They conceptualize the finitude of finite things[45] and the ontological ambiguity which belongs to things because of finitude.

The thought of finitude, Tillich holds, drives ontological thinking forward to a recognition of the abysmal, infinitely transcendent "ground" or "power of being"[46] which is present in and sustains all that is finite. Reason can, and when fully actualized does, acknowledge this ground as its own "depth,"[47] as that which is manifest and expressed in every rational expression while at the same time escaping the possibility of conceptual comprehension because of its infinite character. Religion names that which reason acknowledges as its own depth with the symbol "God."[48] Religion's consciousness of God, of ultimate "being-itself," proceeds through finite images of the infinite which are therefore symbols. Reason, when it is both theological and philosophical, interprets religious symbols while simultaneously attempting to think their content on its own terms. In this latter task, reason thinks the relation of finite to ultimate being and the nature of the power of being through the categories and elements of thought. But rational applications of the categories and elements of thought to that which is ultimate are of necessity themselves symbolic. Categories conceptualize finite relations among finite things. Rational applications of the ontological elements of thought necessarily include unresolved tensions among the polar constituents of those elements, which tensions belong to finite beings because they are finite and cannot be attributed to that which is ultimate and divine.[49]

"Theonomous reason" is Tillich's term for that reason which acknowledges the ultimacy given in its own recognition of its own depth, strives to think that ultimacy through the means available to it, and relates its various particular projects to this acknowledgement and these strivings.[50] It is distinct from "autonomous reason," which determines its processes according to its own rules but which prescinds from its own recognition of that which is ultimately given in all its particular acts. It is also distinct from "heteronomous reason," whose processes are determined by a given, extra-rational starting point.[51] Philosophical theology requires a rationality which is "theonomous," neither "autonomous" nor "heteronomous." The warrants for a concept of reason as theonomous, Tillich holds, are not only theological but independently philosophical as well. Theonomous reason both occurs in continuity with and surpasses common religious self-understanding. It interprets the traditional symbols which belong to that self-understanding for the sake of expressing their meaning, and also thinks that to which those symbols refer in its own, properly rational terms, even if those terms are also symbolic when applied to ultimate "being-itself."

Hegel's speculative and systematic appropriation of religious self-understanding overcomes this anomaly. As he moves towards the close of the system, Hegel appropriates religious self-understanding by retrieving categorially the examination which religious consciousness makes of its own contents, the examination which Hegel exhibits from its own standpoint in the penultimate chapter of the *Phenomenology of Spirit*. In this retrieval, Hegel re-enacts the contents of the absolute religion by comprehending and making explicit the notional determinacies present and effective in, but unavailable in thematic terms to, representational thinking. In doing so, he in one stroke reinstates the content of religious self-understanding in speculative thought and comprehends that content in terms which are speculative, i.e., fully rational. His argument, on my analysis, exhibits the incompleteness of a philosophical appropriation in which reason only grasps that which is also ever beyond its grasp. His argument simultaneously accomplishes a philosophical appropriation of religion, in which reason fully achieves theonomy by comprehending that which it recognizes, in its retrieve of religion, as ultimate and absolute.

Hegel, then, radically challenges those positions in philosophical theology which hold that a rational hermeneutic of the religious symbol must itself remain symbolic. Hegel claims to show that a rational interpretation of religious discourse, which is symbolic, both preserves the religious content of that discourse and comprehends that content in rational, speculative terms. The anomaly which belongs to Tillich's concept of theonomous reason, and the manner in which Hegel overcomes that anomaly, recommend consideration of Hegel's claims to those who pursue hermeneutics in current philosophical theology.

Notes

1. G. W. F. Hegel, *Enzyklopädie der philosophischen Wissenschaften im Grundrisse* (1830), hrsg. F. Nicolin und O. Pöggeler (Hamburg: Felix Meiner, 1969), §573; *Hegel's Philosophy of Mind*, trans. by William Wallace and A. V. Miller (Oxford: The Clarendon Press, 1971), p. 302. Hereafter, references will cite *Enz.* by paragraph, followed by a citation of the Wallace translation.

2. *Enz.*, §573; p. 305.

3. *Enz.*, §573; p. 311.

4. *Enz.*, §573; p. 313.

5. *Enz.*, §571; p. 301.

6. Albert Chapelle, in his *Hegel et la religion*, vol. 3 ([Paris: Editions Universitaires, 1969], pp. 60–111), discusses Hegel's treatment of religion in the *Phenomenology* and its relation to Hegel's discussion of the absolute religion in the *Encyclopædia*. Another interpretation of Hegel's treatment of Christianity in the *Phenomenology*, different from Chapelle's and from the remarks which will follow herein, is offered by Merold Westphal in *History and Truth in Hegel's Phenomenology* ([Atlantic Highlands, N.J.: Humanities

remarks which will follow herein, is offered by Merold Westphal in *History and Truth in Hegel's Phenomenology* ([Atlantic Highlands, N.J.: Humanities Press, 1979], pp. 187–210).

7. *Enz.*, §564; p. 297.

8. Quentin Lauer, in his *Hegel's Concept of God* ([Albany: State University of New York Press, 1982], pp. 42–43) emphasizes Hegel's views regarding these inconsistencies.

9. See Hegel, *Phänomenologie des Geistes*, hrsg. J. Hoffmeister (Hamburg: Felix Meiner, 1952), p. 527; *Hegel's Phenomenology of Spirit*, trans. A. V. Miller (Oxford: The Clarendon Press, 1977), p. 458. Hereafter, references will cite *Phän.* by page, followed by a citation of the Miller translation.

10. See Johannes Heinrichs, *Die Logik der 'Phänomenologie des Geistes'* (Bonn: Bouvier Verlag Herbert Grundmann, 1974), pp. 442–443.

11. See *Phän.*, p. 475; p. 412. See also Quentin Lauer, *A Reading of Hegel's Phenomenology of Spirit* (New York: Fordham University Press, 1976), pp. 232–233.

12. Discussions of Hegel's account of the religious representations are found in Emil Fackenheim, *The Religious Dimension in Hegel's Thought* (Bloomington: Indiana University Press, 1967), pp. 154–155; Quentin Lauer, *Hegel's Concept of God*, pp. 34–36; Paul Ricoeur, "The Status of '*Vorstellung*' in Hegel's Philosophy of Religion," in *Meaning, Truth, and God*, ed. Leroy Rouner (Notre Dame, Ind.: University of Notre Dame Press, 1982), pp. 70–88; and James Yerkes, *The Christology of Hegel* (Missoula, Mont.: Scholars Press, 1978), pp. 89–117.

13. *Phän.*, p. 530; p. 461.

14. *Ibid.*

15. *Phän.*, p. 534; p. 465.

16. *Phän.*, p. 536; p. 466.

17. *Phän.*, p. 537; p. 468.

18. *Ibid.*

19. *Phän.*, p. 540; p. 471.

20. *Phän.*, p. 533; p. 463.

21. *Phän.*, p. 543; p. 474.

22. *Ibid.*

23. See *Phän.*, p. 545; p. 475.

24. *Ibid.*

25. Merold Westphal, in his *History and Truth in Hegel's Phenomenology* (pp. 203–204), claims that, for Hegel's *Phenomenology*, Christian representational thinking brings about externality among its contents which

that my reading of the relevant chapter of the *Phenomenology* suggests evidence for an interpretation which differs from both of these claims.

26. *Enz.*, §565; p. 299.

27. Heinrichs, in *Die Logik der 'Phänomenologie des Geistes'"* (pp. 452–460), points this out from the standpoint of the *Phenomenology*.

28. Michael Theunissen, *Hegels Lehre vom Absoluten Geist als theologisch-politischer Traktat* (Berlin: Walter de Gruyter, 1970), p. 307: "*Der Begriff aber ist nichts anderes als Einheit von Vorstellung und Andacht.*"

29. *Enz.*, §566; p. 299.

30. *Enz.*, §567; p. 299.

31. *Ibid.*

32. *Enz.*, §596; p. 300.

33. *Ibid.*

34. *Enz.*, §569; p. 300.

35. *Ibid.*

36. *Enz.*, §57l; p. 301.

37. *Enz.*, §570; p. 301.

38. *Enz.*, §564; p. 298.

39. *Enz.*, §572; p. 302.

40. Paul Tillich, *Systematic Theology*, volume I (Chicago: University of Chicago Press, 1951), p. 20.

41. *Ibid.*, p. 21.

42. See *ibid.*, pp. 164–165.

43. See *ibid.*, pp. 174–186, for Tillich's discussion of the ontological elements of thought.

44. *Ibid.*, p. 192: "The mind is not able to experience reality except through the categorical forms."

45. See *ibid.*, pp. 82, 192–193.

46. *Ibid.*, pp. 79–237.

47. *Ibid.*, p. 79.

48. Paul Tillich, *Dynamics of Faith* (New York: Harper & Row, 1957), p. 46: "God is a symbol for God."

49. Tillich, *Systematic Theology*, vol. I, p. 243: "While the symbolic power of the categories appears in the relation of God to creatures, the elements give symbolic expression to the nature of the divine life itself. The polar character of the ontological elements is rooted in the divine life, but the divine life is not subject to this polarity. Within the divine life, every ontological element includes its polar element completely, without tension and without threat of dissolution, for God is being-itself."

50. *Ibid.*, pp. 85–86.

51. *Ibid.*, pp. 83–85.

49. Tillich, *Systematic Theology*, vol. I, p. 243: "While the symbolic power of the categories appears in the relation of God to creatures, the elements give symbolic expression to the nature of the divine life itself. The polar character of the ontological elements is rooted in the divine life, but the divine life is not subject to this polarity. Within the divine life, every ontological element includes its polar element completely, without tension and without threat of dissolution, for God is being-itself."

50. *Ibid.*, pp. 85–86.

51. *Ibid.*, pp. 83–85.

52. See Merold Westphal, "Hegel, Tillich, and the Secular," *Journal of Religion* 52 (July 1972): 232. Westphal points out that Tillich means to understand theonomous reason as that reason which "...preserves autonomy ...while dispensing entirely with heteronomy."

Commentary on "Speculation and Theonomy at the Close of Hegel's System"

Louis Dupré

Professor DeNys' paper consists of two distinct parts. In the first part he attempts to show that revealed religion itself overcomes its representational character. In the second he compares Paul Tillich's philosophical theology to Hegel's transformation of theology into speculative thought. Since my disagreements with either position are minor, I propose to take Martin DeNys' conclusions somewhat further and show how they open up problems with which he has not dealt in the paper. Because of time limitations I shall deal only with his first thesis. It is stated succinctly in the conclusion of part 2:

> The systematic, philosophical retrieve of religious self-understanding is an act which radicalizes the unity of consciousness with self-consciousness which, as noted above, is according to Hegel characteristic of the intentionality of religious consciousness. In this retrieve thinking attends to and knows *systematically* the radical constituents of religious self-understanding, thus articulating in a radical way the self-consciousness which finite spirit enjoys in that understanding, through its vision of its own relatedness to the divine. Systematic philosophy is, at its close, the thought of religious consciousness in both senses of the genitive. It elevates religious consciousness to a categorical transfiguration, and it is simultaneously the self-elevation of that same consciousness into its own categorical re-instatement.

According to this passage, speculative thought recapitulates the internal development of Christian doctrine. Revealed religion initiates what philosophy completes; moreover, it invites and perhaps demands this completion. But, of course, it surpasses religious thought by fully *thinking* its content.

I am not convinced that Professor DeNys' description of representational thinking as expressing the consciousness of the infinite and its relatedness to the finite through "rationally ordered images" (p. 191) is wholly accurate. Hegel does not equate representations with images. In religion, certainly in the revealed religion, whatever images remain are already transformed into symbols and allegories of a transcendent content. In fact, religious doctrine includes highly abstract concepts. Hegel himself insists on the non-empirical quality of the central concepts of revealed religion. "When we say: the world has been created, we refer to an activity which substantially differs from any empirical." He then goes on to explain in what the real difference with speculative thought consists: "Even the expression 'activity from which the world proceeded', although abstract, is still representational and notional, insofar as the two sides are not connected in the form of necessity: the connection which in itself is entirely unique and incomprehensible is expressed and signified in an analogy with natural life and events."[1] To be sure, the image is never far, but, wherever present, it becomes overdetermined by its transcendent content to the point of losing its original character. Indeed, the religious representation is basically iconoclastic with respect to its image material. Here is a crucial text:

> Religion has a polemical aspect insofar as its content cannot be perceived immediately in the sensuous intuition or in the image, but only mediately by abstraction, this is, by elevating the imaginary and the sensible to a universal level. This elevation implies a rejection of the image. At first only the form would seem to be rejected, but in fact the content itself is affected insofar as the religious meaning is connected with the image and the image, the beautiful, precisely implies that the universal, the thought, the notion cannot be separated from the image ....[2]

In some religions the image has remained powerful. But precisely that aesthetic quality constitutes their limitation and, in the case of classical Greek religion, caused its decline.

I do not want to belabor this point, however, and, instead, prefer to move on to the more central issue: what is it that revealed religion surpasses? Professor DeNys speaks of a double negativity that belongs to the Christian consciousness. The first is the "negative" relation between the whole and its parts, and between the various contents with respect to one another. (Is negativity the proper term here?) The second consists in the movement whereby the Christian consciousness surpasses the externality of the connection and its representations. This takes place objectively in the Incarnation mystery and subjectively in its assimilation in faith and in worship (p. 190). Not the representational character as such but the mere juxtaposition of various representations is overcome in this highly articulated unity in opposition. But is not precisely this juxtaposition the main characteristic of representational thinking? What is left for speculative thought? DeNys answers: it makes explicit the categories operative in Christian representational thinking. The answer is obviously correct. But does it tell the whole story? Does Hegel not at the same time perform a profound transformation of these categories? Can one continue to claim in good faith that Hegel's philosophy merely "thinks" what Christian faith "represents"? Are we really dealing with the same content?

Let us consider the crucial idea of God. How would it relate to the Christian representation? The weight will obviously fall upon Absolute Spirit. Even if we continue to regard the idea of God as a speculative idea in its own right, not absorbed in Absolute Spirit—there are solid grounds for doing so since Hegel repeatedly made the existence of God the subject of his lectures—the idea will clearly have to fit in the philosophy of spirit. I do not see how it could be anything but the transcendent moment of a process that also includes the development of the finite. I am by no means convinced that such a view might not be defensible, indeed that, as Whitehead and Hartshorne have argued about a related conception, it might not be the only coherent philosophical view. But it certainly leaves us with a number of questions concerning the relation between idea and representation which are not answered by a simple reference to the "thinking" of the *necessity* of what the Christian faith represents. The *religious* potential of such an all-comprehensive Spirit and of any moment thereof (including the transcendent moment) is no longer obvious. Whatever transcendence Spirit as the total process contains with regard to any of its finite movements refuses to limit its self-revelation to any particular privileged community. Spirit is by its very nature *universal*, and its transcendence cannot be exhaustively expressed in historical institutions or messages. Clearly, then, the consciousness of Spirit can no longer be restricted by the limits of an ecclesiastical community. The consciousness of Spirit emerges "when *the subject itself* becomes Spirit and thereby a citizen of the kingdom of God."[3] Such a spiritualization of consciousness cannot be definitively contained in Church or doctrine. The question then is: how can the idea of Spirit transcend its original doctrinal limits without losing its religious significance altogether? That it must transcend them is unquestionable. Spirit defined as unself-conscious openness overcomes any opposition between a particular, allegedly "spiritual" community and the human community at large. Failure to recognize the narrowness of its own spiritual vision made the "religion of the heart" such an easy prey of the secular mentality. Advanced religions have always begun by relegating the worldly consciousness outside the sacred realm proper. At best they have adopted a neutral (Judaism) or a dominial (medieval Christianity), at worst a hostile (substantial sections of Islam) attitude toward it. As a result, the modern worldview, with its claim of universality and its refusal to become subordinate to any *particular* board of authority, had to gain its autonomy at the expense of any religious justification.

Nevertheless, Hegel refused to equate the all-comprehensiveness of Spirit with the secular self-consciousness of the modern age. He stubbornly insisted that the culture of self-consciousness needs itself a legitimation—which can only come from a continued transcendence. While conceiving the legitimation of that culture by Spirit to be as universal and comprehensive as modern consciousness itself rather than being the expression of an infinite, historically revealed Being, he still maintained the need for the *critical* distance of a permanent transcendence. Hegel justified the modern age, but also condemned it precisely for the loss of the transcendent perspective which only a religion provides. In the pessimistic conclusion of the *Lectures on the Philosophy of Religion* of 1821 he assigns to philosophy the task of preserving the transcendent message through the dark age of modern secularism, but cautions that this can be no more than a "partial solution."[4] Was he fully aware of the discrepancy between the speculative philosophy which he proclaimed to be based upon the Christian revelation and that revelation itself?

The purpose of my remarks has not been to deny the ultimate compatability of one with the other, but to suggest that Hegel's philosophy does more than simply "thinking what the revealed religion represents"— and that this creates problems unmentioned by him or by Professor DeNys.

Notes

1. G. W. F. Hegel, *Vorlesungen über die Philosophie der Religion* (Hamburg: Felix Meiner, 1925), vol. I, p. 113.

2. *Ibid.*, p. 285.

3. *Op. cit.*, vol. IV, p. 194.

4. *Ibid.*, p. 231.

INDEX

This index covers the text of the chapters, citing only some material in the footnotes. Because of the interconnectedness of Hegel's philosophy, all indices involving him pose difficulties: for instance, every mention of the master-slave relation could be listed also under spirit, community, dialectic, freedom, and other headings; but then the index would become long and unwieldy. This index intends and attempts to refer to all important mentions of a topic and, for some headings (such as dialectic, *Sittlichkeit*, and spirit), to pages where the topic is discussed but not named. Authors of books about Hegel are not indexed unless the text engages extensively and explicitly their arguments. Citations to an individual's name include references to the individual's philosophy: e.g., Kantianism or Kantian idealism is indexed under Kant.